THE ART OF
DIRECTING

John W. Kirk & Ralph A. Bellas
Illinois State University

Wadsworth Publishing Company
Belmont, California
A Division of Wadsworth, Inc.

Theatre Editor: *Kristine Clerkin*
Production Editor: *Leland Moss*
Designer: *Andrew H. Ogus*
Copy Editor: *Jonas Weisel*
Technical Illustrator: *Susan Nelson Tuynman*
Cover: *Andrew H. Ogus*
Signing Representative: *Katie Konradt*

Printed in the United States of America

1 2 3 4 5 6 7 8 9 10–89 88 87 86 85

ISBN 0-534-03891-3

Library of Congress Cataloging in Publication Data
Kirk, John W.
  The art of directing.

  Bibliography: p.
  Includes index.
  1. Theater—Production and direction. I. Bellas,
Ralph A. II. Title.
PN2053.K54 1985   792′.0233   84-7529
ISBN 0-534-03891-3

to Kenneth Burke
fellow seeker in the quest to make
"The way things are and
the way we say things are, one"

Contents

Preface *xi*
Introduction: What is a Play Director? *xv*
Background Readings *xvi*

THE NATURE OF DRAMA 1

WHAT IS ACTION? 2
Action in the Universe 2
The Difference between Action and Motion 4

THE PRIMACY OF ACTION IN THE DRAMATIC FORM 5
Conflict: The Essence of Dramatic Action 5
The Necessity of Conflict *5*
The Source of Conflict *8*
The Effects of Conflict *10*
Action, Motive, and Structure 10
Climax as the Moment of Resolution 12
Time: The Fourth Dimension of Action 12
Distinguishing between Action and Plot 13
Action-Centered Character 14
Action in the New Drama 15

Exercises *17*
Notes *18*

2

ANALYSIS: DISCOVERING THE PLAY'S STRUCTURE   19

THE CASE FOR ANALYSIS   21

STRUCTURAL ELEMENTS   24
Primary Structural Elements   24
Root Conflict   24
Root Action   25
Climax   29
Secondary Structural Elements   30
Inciting Incident   30
Crisis   31
Catastrophe   32
Interdependence of Structural Elements   33

CYCLES OF ACTION   34

POINT OF CLASH   35

CHARACTER ANALYSIS   36
Motive Happening   36
Motive Distinguished from Purpose   38

ANALYSIS AT WORK   39
Discovering the Root Conflict   40
Root Conflict in Hello Out There   *41*
Discovering the Root Action   45
Root Action in Hello Out There   *46*
Discovering the Climax   47
Climax in Hello Out There   *48*
Discovering the Inciting Incident   49
Inciting Incident in Hello Out There   *50*
Discovering the Crisis   51
Crisis in Hello Out There   *51*
Discovering the Catastrophe   52
Catastrophe in Hello Out There   *52*
Discovering Character   52
Character in Hello Out There   *53*

Avoiding Word-Bound Analyses   56
Kenneth Burke's Pentad and Analysis   58

Exercises   61
Notes   62
Play Analysis Form   63

ACTION IN TIME AND SPACE   64

DEVELOPING A PRODUCTION DESIGN   65

A VISUAL AESTHETICS FOR THE THEATRE   68
Basic Dimensions of a Visual Aesthetics   69
Conflict, Contrast, and Perception   74

POINT, LINE, AND PLANE   77
Point   77
Line   78
Plane   80

THE FOURTH DIMENSION: THE FLOW THEORY   85
Imbalance: Creating the Demand for Flow   87
Movement: Managing the Physical and
Psychic Dimensions of Flow   88

BLOCKING: DESIGNING MOVEMENT TO SUPPORT ACTION   92
Developing a Floor Plan   92
Blocking and Conflict   96
Blocking and Arena Staging   99
Blocking and the Actor   102

Exercises   104
Notes   106

4

WORKING WITH ACTORS IN THE SEARCH FOR CHARACTER   108

WHERE IS CHARACTER FOUND?   110
Character Defined   111
Living Is the Battle Against Dying   *112*
The Void, Absence, and Premotive   *113*
Character and Action   116
Finding the Power Source in the Space Between   *117*
Actor-Puppet vs. Actor–Human Being   *120*
Burke's Pentad and Action-Centered Character Study   120
Definition of Pentadic Character Analysis Terms   *121*
Purpose of Pentadic Analysis: To Clarify Motive   *123*
Example of Pentadic Analysis   *123*

REHEARSALS: THE QUEST FOR MOTIVE   125
The Director's Role in Character Study   125
Action Rehearsals   126
Improvisation as a Device for Character Study   130

THE DIRECTOR AS ADVISOR TO THE CREATIVE ACTOR   132
A Creative Atmosphere   133
Communication   134

PREPARING FOR PERFORMANCE   135
Preparing Roles in Breadth and Depth   135
Ensemble: Playing in Context   138
"Root, Not Result"   138
Preblocking and the Actor   139

Exercises   *141*
Notes   *142*

5

THE DIRECTOR AND THE PRODUCTION   144

GETTING READY   144
Readings   145
Analysis   146
Style   148
Script Revision   149
The New Script   151

DESIGN CONCEPT   153
The Director and the Designer   154
Steps in the Design Process   155

PROMPT BOOK   157
The Assistant Director or Stage Manager
and the Prompt Book   158
Prompt Book Format   160

PREBLOCKING   167

TRYOUTS AND CASTING TECHNIQUES   169
Preparing for Auditions   169
Information Cards   169
Character Description Handouts   169
Conducting Auditions   170
"Pre-Audition" Auditioning   170
Taking Notes   170
Directing During Auditions   171
Releasing "Totems"   171
Augmenting Auditions   172
Individual Interview   172
The Best Audition: Performance   173
Callback Session   173
Casting Dangers   173

REHEARSAL   175
Purpose of Rehearsal   176
Number of Rehearsals   176
Cycles of Action   177
Schedule Design   177
Types of Rehearsals   181
Pattern   181
Action   182
Continuity   182
Technical   183
Dress   185
Rehearsal "Performances"   186

PERFORMANCE   187

POSTPERFORMANCE EVALUATION   188

Exercises   190
Notes   191

A FINAL WORD   192

Hello Out There   195

Suggested Readings   213

Biographical Notes   219

Glossary   225

Index   233

Preface

SOME YEARS AGO a critic made the following observation about drama theory and the modern theatre: "What has been apparent for some time is the need for a revision of accepted theatrical concepts. Today we are hard put to say what a play is. Stage practice has outrun the conventional sources of theory."[1] He goes on to note: "What the young artist finds today is an assortment of theoretical sources: . . . works that have little practical application even were he disposed to turn to them; and polemical works which require a total acceptance and which in fact may not be satisfactory for him."[2] Indeed, in the theatre today we see an almost desperate need for a serious study of the theory of drama and for the application of sound theory to practices. The theory must be comprehensive and infused with a philosophy that will guide directors in staging any play.

This book intends to meet that need. It proposes to lay the foundations for successful directing by examining the nature of drama and by determining "how a play happens" before an audience in the theatre.

We regard directors as artists, similar in many respects to play-

wrights. As playwrights give structure and thereby meaning to experience, so directors strive to understand this structure. They use
analysis, synthesis, intuition—whatever means necessary to achieve
understanding. At all times they rely on their knowledge of the nature
of the dramatic event. Their major responsibility to the people collaborating in the production of a play is to aid their understanding and
efficiency by making stage practices relevant to theory.

The book has five chapters, which should be studied in sequence.
Chapter 1 develops a theory of the nature of the dramatic form. The
theory derives in part from the work of Aristotle, Kenneth Burke, John
Howard Lawson, Constantin Stanislavsky, and Paul Klee. Chapter 2
introduces a system of play analysis based on the theoretical foundation developed in Chapter 1. Chapter 3 examines the director's challenge to design a production that reveals dramatic action in time and
space. Chapter 4 deals with the director's efforts to help actors in their
search for character. Chapter 5 focuses on various phases of the production process, from getting ready to postperformance evaluation.

The Art of Directing is intended primarily for prospective directors. It can help them build an aesthetic foundation for directing. It
can also be useful to actors who want to meet the challenge of acting
creatively and to design students whose work requires close collaboration with directors. Experienced theatre practitioners should find provocative ideas here that can contribute to the continuing development
of their craft. Finally, we hope that anyone interested in the study and
appreciation of drama will find the book informative and stimulating.

Although we are ultimately responsible for what appears in this
book, our work reflects the criticisms and suggestions of a number of
people. For their helpful reviews we would like to thank: Stephen M.
Archer and Richard Klepac of the University of Missouri–Columbia;
Maranne Mitchell, Texas A&M University; Anthony Schmitt, Wayne
State University; William J. Bruehl, State University of New York at
Stony Brook; Lynette McClean, San Diego State University; Sally O.
Norton, California State University at Los Angeles; and Yvonne Shafer,
Ohio State University.

For his advice and support, we thank Alvin Goldfarb. We also thank Calvin Pritner and Margaret Kirk for their close critical reading of the manuscript. To Leland Moss for his perceptive and knowledgeable editorial assistance, and to Kristine Clerkin for her enthusiastic support, our deep appreciation.

NOTES

1. Bernard Beckerman, "Dramatic Theory and Stage Practice," in *Papers in Dramatic Theory and Criticism*, ed. David M. Knauf (Iowa City: University of Iowa Press, 1969), pp. 30–31.

2. Beckerman, p. 33.

Introduction: What Is a Play Director?

PLAY DIRECTING has had a long and rather mysterious history. Sophocles' directives on how his plays should be produced and Shakespeare's comments on play directing in *A Midsummer Night's Dream* and *Hamlet* indicate that they recognized the need for a director. Undoubtedly, others did also. Little of who directors were in ancient times or what they actually did, however, has been recorded. In fact, what directors are supposed to do today remains something of a mystery.

This much we know: Directors are sculptors who sculpt in tidal sand; they are artists who sketch with vanishing ink. They create something that lives for a brief time for an audience and then dies. Or if it survives at all, it does so in fragments in the memory of the spectators. When the production is reborn before another audience, it is in essence a different event.

Short-lived though the director's creation is, it is fashioned from marvelously complex elements. These elements must all be brought to bear on the basic challenge for the director: to present human beings in an action before an audience. This major concern with action in drama sets it apart from most other arts. But we often have difficulty in keeping action clearly before us. Our attention is diverted by politics, poetry, music, and other such elements in a play. We must school ourselves to maintain a sharp focus on action. We propose here a theory based on the primacy of action, a theory that will lead to effective ways for a director to stage the theatrical event.

This theory is not intended to shackle creativity. It recognizes that every play and every director require, in some measure, a different approach. Yet the director's art should be based on universal principles that transcend the individual production and should provide an aesthetic core for one's work.

BACKGROUND READINGS

To clarify and illustrate many of the ideas in *The Art of Directing*, we refer mainly to four plays: Sophocles' *Oedipus Rex*, William Shakespeare's *Hamlet*, William Saroyan's *Hello Out There*, and Arthur Miller's *Death of a Salesman*. Anyone not familiar with these plays ought to read them.

For the ambitious we recommend these additional plays: Anton Chekhov's *The Seagull*, John Millington Synge's *Riders to the Sea*, Thornton Wilder's *Our Town*, Samuel Beckett's *Waiting for Godot*, Tennessee Williams's *A Streetcar Named Desire*, and William Inge's *Bus Stop*.

We suggest you keep a note card for each of the plays you read and organize your information under these headings: (1) title, (2) list of major characters, (3) brief synopsis of plot, (4) list of "good" scenes, and (5) your opinion of the play.

Having read the plays, you will find the textual references more meaningful and will have a better basis for critical interaction. The cards will serve as a handy recall index of key information about the plays.

CHAPTER

1

The Nature
of Drama

WE BEGIN with a premise that seems too obvious for words: A director must understand the play before he can direct it successfully.* Unfortunately, some directors go through an entire rehearsal period without being able to account for all the elements of a play. They may be ignorant of their ignorance. If a director does not commit himself to a serious analysis of the play or if he does not ask the right questions to unlock meaning, he may never identify important elements of form. And if he discovers mistakes in late rehearsals, he may not be able to do anything about them.

The key to understanding a play is to discover the principles of its form, its very nature—how it happens. Children explore the nature of an object by looking, feeling, smelling, tasting, and otherwise examining it. They use their senses as tools. Directors, too, need tools to ex-

---

*   In the interest of a straightforward style, we use *he* and
    she in alternate chapters when referring to a director
    or an actor.

plore the nature of drama. Their most important tools are the principles that underlie all drama, principles interrelated by a theory of dramatic action.

WHAT IS ACTION?

Critical commentary on drama had its origin in Aristotle's *Poetics*. One term, paramount to Aristotle, is fundamental to an understanding of drama. That term—**action**—is often misunderstood and misused. In *The Idea of a Theatre* Francis Fergusson argues that a common definition of dramatic action is not possible because the action ("the thing done") differs in every play. The actions of *Hamlet* and Samuel Beckett's *Waiting for Godot*, for example, have so little in common that no definition can account for both.[1] Fergusson says that since we are unable to isolate characteristics of action that apply in all instances, we must confine ourselves to defining action "analogically" (by analogy, that is, by finding partial likenesses and comparing them). Thus, he states that by studying the specific action in *Hamlet*, we can get some idea of the nature of action in other plays. *Hamlet* functions, therefore, as an analogy for a concept of dramatic action.

But if we are to evolve a comprehensive theory upon which to base a methodology of directing, we must formulate a definition of dramatic action that transcends a single play. That is the basic problem: Directors must have something that will inform their work and provide them with a plan of attack for *all* plays.

Action in the Universe

The vast question of how to describe the universe seems, at first, unrelated to the theatre; but two aspects are pertinent to understanding the nature of action in drama.

Modern thinkers are fond of pointing out that everything in the universe is a process. This perception emphasizes the fourth dimension: time. We tend to think of objects as motionless, having an immutable character, because their rate of change is so slow that we cannot easily perceive the change. Certain kinds of glass, for instance, seem unchanging, but in reality are "rivers" slowly flowing toward the center of gravity. Visitors to very old houses have found that the windows have flowed down over the sills. The passage of many years has revealed movement that is normally imperceptible in a limited time perspective. All objects are in fact "dances of atoms," forever changing in aspect; the universe itself is not a "thing" but an act constantly in process. Rather than being static or mechanistic, the universe is dynamic and organic.

The idea of the universe as an act is given another perspective by some physicists, who suggest that the universe is slowly running down, gradually losing heat energy. This principle of disintegration, commonly called *entropy*, inexorably breaks down form. According to this theory, formal arrangements of molecules fight against disintegration. All life exists as an integrated form, an island of resistance against the great entropic flow.

An obvious example of entropy is the ultimate disintegration of the human body. Or perhaps you remember the slow but inevitable destruction of the doll or baseball glove you cherished as a child. Examining closely a table or the chair where you sit, you might notice the breaking down of form: The once sharp corners are being rounded by the continual encounter with the entropic force.

What is the relevance of these ideas to the theatre? We know, of course, that a play as a work of art has order, a structure. A close study of the structure reveals the action. Action in a play is similar to action in the universe. It is a process that is partially defined by the fourth dimension, time. And just as the conflict between entropy and order in time creates the action in the universe, so the conflict of competing forces in time creates the action in drama.

> ## "Conflict is the essence
> ## of dramatic action."

The Difference between
Action and Motion

Another way of clarifying action is to look at what it is not. Kenneth Burke, a twentieth-century American literary critic and philosopher, noted a distinction between action and motion: *Action is purposeful activity; motion is activity without purpose.*[2] A leaf snapping off and drifting to the ground represents motion. The activity is not the result of purposeful effort by anyone. A child jumping from the branch of a tree is action, since such an event would require a decision on the child's part.

If the child should resolve to climb higher and then slip, falling from the tree, the incident would be considered motion. It is an accident, not the result of a decision. (Of course, a critic could see the fall as the direct result of the decision to climb the tree. Or a mother who had told the child not to climb the tree in the first place might regard the incident as action, because the child's deliberate act of disobedience led to certain consequences.)

Action without movement is possible. A decision not to move when told that a rattlesnake is coiled under your chair is an act that has no accompanying movement. Mental "action" may or may not be accompanied by physical movement.

An event, therefore, may contain both motion and action. The purposeful part is action. The purposeless part is motion. A play director may object to the amount of motion in a performance if an actor engages in purposeless activity—activity that does not illuminate motives.

THE PRIMACY OF ACTION IN THE DRAMATIC FORM

Of the central significance of action in tragedy, Aristotle wrote:

Tragedy is essentially an imitation not of persons but of action and life, of happiness and misery. All human happiness or misery takes the form of action; the end for which we live is a certain kind of activity, not a quality. . . . So that it is the action in it . . . that is the end and purpose of tragedy; and the end is everywhere the chief thing.[3]

What Aristotle says of action in tragedy applies also to other forms of drama. In analyzing drama of any kind, we are seeking to discover the nature of the act or, to put it in other terms, the process of the form.

Conflict: The Essence of Dramatic Action

The Necessity of Conflict

Ferdinand Brunetière, a nineteenth-century French critic, wrote in "The First Law of the Theatre" that the essential element of drama is **conflict**. Without conflict, he says, there is no drama.[4] Many others, of course, have made the same observation; we, too, declare that conflict is the essence of dramatic action.

Picture, if you will, a small, sleepy western town. A man is sitting on a chair whittling. The street is empty, and a dog lies twitching its tail to chase away flies. If this were the opening of a television show, you might be eagerly expectant, sensing that something must happen to disturb this peaceful scene and render it dramatic. A man whittling and a dog twitching are not the "stuff" of which drama is made.

Consider another simple illustration: a pleasant ordinary conversation between two acquaintances who meet on the street. They greet each other, they discuss the weather, they fill each other in on recent events in their lives. If you are watching this scene as the opening of a play, you know that they are leading up to something. If it does not come, you are disappointed, even angry at the waste of your time.

In each case, what we expect to come is conflict. Very little of a good play passes before the introduction of a conflict. If there is any extended delay in revealing conflict, the play is said to drag. We become bored and puzzled. Although contemporary playwrights, such as Beckett, Harold Pinter, and Sam Shepard, treat it in special ways, conflict is always present in their plays. One reason some audiences reject these playwrights is the failure of spectators, as well as performers, to perceive the conflict.

Conflict is not unique to drama, but it is essential. What we call "dramatic" is our perception of the clash of forces. For whatever reason—perhaps explained by a stage in our primitive past—human beings are drawn to conflict. Conflict arouses our interest and engages our participation in an event. Without conflict, life would be lifeless.

That conflict generates dramatic interest is illustrated by the phenomenal success of professional football on television. This success is due to the suitability of the television screen for showing the clash of elemental forces in the game. Football is raw, primitive conflict. It is tremendously dramatic.

Conflict in the theatre may not be created on this scale, but it is developed on a moment-by-moment basis. To be engaged in the conflict of a performance is vital to effective acting. Rehearsal for actors is the process of finding the point of connection or the **point of clash** in the conflict at every moment. When each actor focuses on the precise frustration that engenders his character's need to act, he will find the power source for his acting.

Conflict in the theatre can take many forms. Sometimes conflict lurks powerfully or menacingly beneath a scene. Sometimes it explodes into physical confrontation. Its form depends on the nature of the play. A brash shouting match in a scene that demands subtlety is a misuse of conflict, and the audience rejects it. The dramatic impact of the play suffers.

A play may seem to have very little conflict or, rather, it may be produced as though it has little conflict. But if it is a good play and a good production, it has conflict. In any case, as the audience's perception of conflict diminishes, its interest in the play lags. Productions that do not reveal conflict are bad art, and they are doomed to fail.

A student once suggested that *Waiting for Godot* is a play without conflict since the characters are incapable of doing anything. Yet in a successful production of the play they must do something. They must struggle. Vladimir and Estragon desperately want confirmation that they are living. Godot's coming or not coming is essential to this confirmation. That they continue to wait—albeit with increasing hopelessness—seals their doom. At the end they cannot muster the courage to abandon the "here and now" by leaving their "safe" place and to search for Godot. The audience must be able to confirm their inability to act and yet to admire their continuing struggle even as their awareness of its futility grows. Vladimir and Estragon have accomplished nothing, but they have been engaged in a desperate conflict. That struggle is what makes the play compelling drama. If the struggle is not emphasized by the director, the play becomes talky and dull.

Conflict is as essential to comedy as to serious drama, but in comedy it is expressed in a different mode. In comedy, focus is more on the way something is done than on why it is done. In Nikolai Gogol's *The Inspector General* a simple man is mistaken for the Inspector General, and the discrepancy between the way townspeople view the situation and the way the man does creates the conflict—the irony and absurdity that expose the pretensions of small-town bureaucracy. In tragedy, conflict is of heroic dimension and has an ennobling effect. In the tragic character, motive is so powerful that even the possibility of death does not deter him. The comic character, on the other hand, is belittled by conflict, appearing presumptuous and ridiculous. The character readily compromises for the sake of comfort or well-being; he will save his skin before he will save the maiden in distress.

The Source of Conflict

The fundamental cause of conflict is the presence of mutually inhibiting or opposing motives. A person wants something that frustrates the wants of another person. Searching out these motives is one of the first steps in determining the dramatic resources of a play.

We begin to understand the sources of the trouble in *Hamlet* by searching for the motives of Claudius and Hamlet and by noting how opposite they are. Claudius has the throne. He has Gertrude. He has supplanted Hamlet's father in every way except one. He must have the acceptance, if not the love, of the son. Hamlet, on the other hand, is troubled that his mother has been diminished in his view by her quick marriage to Claudius, and that the normal succession of royal power from father to son has been subverted. He wants his mother for himself (and for his dead father). He equates the acceptance of Claudius with the denial of his father and the debauching of his mother. Many reasons for the clash of forces are already present when the ghost appears. Whether the ghost really exists or is a figment of Hamlet's imagination does not matter. Conflict is inevitable. The ghost serves as a catalytic agent.

But directors have just begun their work when they clarify the root, or basic, conflict in a play. They must continue to look for specific manifestations of the conflict in each moment of the drama. Questions about each moment should be asked. In *Hamlet* (IV,v), for example, why does Ophelia give flowers to members of the court in her mad scene? What does she want to get from or to do to the court? Is she just "mad" and doing meaningless, irrational things? If so, there

> ## "The fundamental cause of conflict is opposing motives."

is no conflict. If there is no conflict, then we should cut it—it is not "dramatic." However, observing the pathetically mad Ophelia is important to the action: It inflames Laertes and gives Claudius a way to destroy Hamlet. But the actress cannot play plot necessities. What about the specific moment? Why does Ophelia talk about flowers? What is her point of clash?

Pursuing these questions leads to at least one possible conclusion: Ophelia is giving flowers not to the court, but to Hamlet. She is reliving in her imagination a scene with Hamlet—a love scene in a field, which ends with her strewing him with flowers just before he touches her in a way that makes her suddenly think of her father. At that moment, Ophelia betrayed her father (Polonius) by loving Hamlet. Later, when Hamlet murdered her father, Ophelia felt responsible. Her guilt triggered her madness. Meaning is revealed by finding the specific point of clash at each moment in the scene.

Sometimes a scene is written so that there appears to be no point of clash. But there must always be a clash if the scene belongs in the play. One of the most poignant scenes in the theatre occurs in Act III of Thornton Wilder's *Our Town*. In this scene Emily is given the privilege of coming back from the grave to relive her twelfth birthday. What makes the scene dramatic is not nostalgia, though that is an important quality, but the conflict of mutually inhibiting motives.

Emily is immediately struck by the fact that her mother is not aware of the passage of time. Because she is so immersed in living, Mrs. Webb cannot fully appreciate the wonder and beauty of it. But Emily cannot get through to make her aware of the present from the perspective of the future. The wall between the living and the dead cannot be pierced. Intent on the everyday task of preparing breakfast, Mrs. Webb does not respond to Emily's entreaties. Each activity of Mrs. Webb causes a point of clash that evokes a specific response from Emily. In this interpretation the frustration of motives creates the dramatic power of the scene.

Inherent in the conflict caused by mutually inhibiting motives is the necessity for change. Because there is frustration occasioned by unfulfilled wants, there is a tremendous impetus to change. Any conflict implies imbalance, an untenable situation demanding change, thus

creating the power source of the play. Something must happen to resolve the imbalance, and we are in suspense until we find out what.

In the opening scene of *Oedipus Rex*, for example, Oedipus is
confronted with an untenable situation. The whole land suffers under
a curse: All the newborn children are dying, and there is a terrible
drought. The chorus laments the people's plight and demands release
from the burden—demands change. Oedipus vows to lift the curse,
and the action is under way, powered by the need for change and
Oedipus' commitment to bring it about.

The Effects of Conflict

Conflict, then, is an essential component of dramatic action, and
performers must constantly respond to it. Conflict also evokes empathic response from the audience. Muscles actually contract and expand with the action on stage. Breathing becomes labored or easy.
Pulse rate fluctuates. People move in their seats during intense confrontations. Often they respond vocally. A powerful theatrical performance elicits sensory, emotional, and psychic responses.

Contemporary critics suggest that by participating vicariously in
the transgressions of the protagonist, members of an audience rid
themselves of the frustrations imposed by the repressions of society
and life in general. They can "sin" through the protagonist and then
let the character suffer the consequences. The protagonist is often a
"cultural" hero because he is suffering or dying for the sins of society,
that is, of the audience. The hero in this sense is everybody's scapegoat.

As the action of a play develops, it may arouse guilt, fear, pity,
sympathy, and other emotions, and part of the pleasure of an audience
is in having these emotions purged by the play's end. The empathic
responses in melodrama and comedy are similar to, though less intense
than, those in tragedy.

Action, Motive, and Structure

The central motive, or ordering principle, of any play is that play's
struggle to resolve its root conflict. The process of identifying this con-

flict and determining the way it is resolved constitutes the dramatic action. When actors seek the specific point of clash in each scene, they find the action; all the conflicting wants of the various characters become meaningful in terms of the central motive.

In *The Philosophy of Literary Form* Kenneth Burke contends that motive is identical with meaning and structure.[5] Who we are is determined by what we want. This idea should be easy for theatre people to grasp. We readily accept the dictum that understanding a character means discovering the character's basic motive. In broader terms Constantin Stanislavsky, the influential Russian theatre director and teacher, talked about discovering the "super-objective" of a play.

Discovering the structure of anything is discovering not simply what is there but how the parts are related. If we truly know the structure of something, we know the principle by which one part is related to another. If we do not know the relational aspects, the thing examined remains a mystery. It is incomprehensible because the ordering principle of its structure is not known.

You can probably recall seeing greatly enlarged photographs of parts of familiar things and being challenged to identify them. That the mysterious images were usually hard to identify illustrates what happens when the ordering principle of the structure of something is not made apparent. Until we supply the rest of the pattern—until we can visualize how the part photographed is related to the whole—the true meaning of the picture escapes us.

Consider the prospect of trying to put together a jigsaw puzzle without the picture of the subject to guide us. The task is enormously complicated by our ignorance of the relationship of the various shapes and colors. Once we learn these from studying the picture, some of the mystery is gone, and we gain an understanding of the structure that helps us complete the puzzle.

In both cases we understood structure only when we perceived how the parts were related to one another. In the pattern of any form, each part serves a purpose in relationship to the whole. When the motive or the purpose of each part is discerned, the structure becomes meaningful. The search for structure, then, is the search for motive.

> ## "The resolving of the conflict
> ## is a process in time."

So, too, in drama. The director concentrates his analytical efforts on discovering the central motive of a play. Insofar as he succeeds, he also discovers the play's structure and meaning. With this knowledge, he prepares himself for the directing task.

Climax as the Moment of Resolution

The most significant moment in the structure of a play occurs when the conflict, which has been creating the tension and driving the action forward, reaches resolution. At that moment the play becomes totally meaningful. After that moment, the action is finished because there is no more conflict. Additional events may comment on or illuminate the climax, but they are not part of the root action of the play. The word *climax* has been used to designate different structural points in various schemes of play analysis. For instance, Gustav Freytag, a German playwright and critic of the nineteenth century, used it to name the peripety, or turning point, in a play. We use the term to describe what happens at the culminating moment of action when the root conflict is resolved.

Time: The Fourth Dimension of Action

Because action is a process that proceeds from the incident that incites the conflict to the climax, *time* is a dimension of action. Characters on stage have the dimensions of depth, width, and height, but a director must also realize that a play is a temporal form. The resolving of the conflict is a process in time that is not completed in any part until it is completed in all parts. The beginning of a play continues until the end. We do not fully appreciate the significance of a beginning until all of its consequences are clear at the end. Thus, as it moves through time, the play also adds dimension to the beginning.

In the same sense, the end of a play is already present in the beginning. Indeed the beginning is a seed that contains the whole play. As the play progresses, we get an unfolding of all that was potentially contained in the seed. The particular nature of the first event in a play is decreed by the demands of the final resolution. The end of a play is the goal of every moment of the play. Thus, as it moves through time, the play also adds dimension to the ending. Once directors understand the temporal interdependence of the parts, they are thinking four-dimensionally and can create special effects and orchestrate the audience's response.

Distinguishing between
Action and Plot

While some theories of dramatic form do not distinguish between action and plot, our definition of action as the power source of the play requires that we make such a distinction. **Plot** is the series of events that reveals action. The events are shaped by the demands of the action. If action is the quest for resolution of the conflict, plot is the physical manifestation of this quest. An action might be accomplished by any number of different sets of events.

English novelist and critic Aldous Huxley claimed that under the influence of peyote he was able to discern instantaneously the essential form of objects.[6] He looked at a particular chair, for example, and perceived its "chairness." Although we cannot ordinarily do that, we do recognize a chair when we see one, whether it is a Renaissance Dante chair or a contemporary chrome kitchen variety. We know that a chair is an object upon which we sit. We discern the essence or basic "motive" of the object while still recognizing the various ways designers express that motive. If, like some primitive tribes, we had no concept

> ## "Character can be defined as an individual locus of motives."

of chair, if we did not know about objects designed for sitting, we might see each example of the object as a separate form with no linking structural motive. Each design would seem like a completely different structure. A native might hang one from a tree or stick another in the ground as two different kinds of ornaments.

Plot is analogous to the physical chair. Action is analogous to "chairness." Action gives the plot meaning, just as chairness (or "to sit") gives all individual chairs their meaning. It is the playwright's problem to decide which plot best accomplishes the motive of the play. He has to decide if the action is best served by a tearful farewell at the bus station or an angry argument in the living room. Plot is therefore more important to the playwright than to the director. The director's job is to discover just how the plot selected by the playwright functions to reveal action.

Action-Centered Character

The primacy of action in drama has significant implications for the actor's search for character. Action is potential energy until converted into kinetic energy by the characters. Without characters, events of the play cannot happen. The potential for action inherent in conflicting motives is translated by characters into flesh and blood acts.

Character can be defined as an individual locus of motives, that is, a centering of wants. The wants are controlled by a single, compelling motive that accounts for everything a character does. This central motive is engendered by the interaction with other characters, which makes up the conflict of the play.

An actor cannot effectively create character by assuming a collection of characteristics (stooped, shaky, loud, silly, and so on) or plunging immediately into his own subconscious through interior monologue. An actor must find the power source of his character outside of himself, at the point of clash where his character's motives collide with the motives of the other characters. From the point of clash—in the **space between** the character and all that he encounters—the actor begins a process that leads him to discover the psychic and emotional resources needed to meet the challenge of the conflict.

An actor cannot find the essence of a character by observing life. A play is not life. Unlike life, a play is a closed system. Events in a play happen, not by the unpredictable game of encounter that characterizes life, but by the necessities of an order determined by the playwright.

Although some controversy exists concerning Constantin Stanislavsky's theories of actor training, there can be no question that the substance of contemporary acting theory comes mainly from his work. Stanislavsky maintained that the search for character is a search for basic motive, or **spine**, as later disciples called it. The term is apt, for everything a character does has its origin in his basic motive, which in turn derives from the motive of the play, from what Stanislavsky referred to as the "super-objective" of the action. Any work on character that does not start with the play's action, therefore, can be detrimental to staging the play.

Action in the New Drama

Action, the conflict of motives, has always provided the soul of storytelling, but the techniques for revealing it have changed over the years. Narration preceded drama as a literary form. A storyteller recounted heroic events. Then dialogue was introduced; two or more persons spoke directly in present time. Eventually the narrators portrayed characters in the story. The technique was narrative, but the elements of drama were now present.

Later, plot began to assume greater importance. Actors no longer merely narrated the story; they illustrated certain events (plot) before their audience. These events (the plot) revealed the story. Later still in the history of drama, dramatists relied very little on narration. They concentrated on plot as a vehicle for presenting action.

Contemporary dramatists are using a new approach that subordinates or eliminates plot as a vehicle for revealing action. Dramas of almost pure action represent a significant stage in the evolution of dramaturgy. Playwrights like Pinter, Beckett, Shepard, and Eugène Ionesco have moved beyond the conventional mode of using plot to convey action. They try to express action directly.

In Pinter's *The Caretaker*, for example, we do not know where the characters have come from or where they are going. We cannot, except in the most rudimentary fashion, piece together plot events to account for their being there. We cannot profitably devise a "life" for them. Indeed, the characters themselves are confused about their past. Nonetheless we have an intense, powerful confrontation and vicariously participate in a clash of wills. Although the characters exist in a kind of limbo, our knowledge of them derives directly from the struggle between them. We are not told a story. We are shown an action.

In Beckett's plays the characters seek to find meaning from each other in a meaningless world. They attempt to interact in a way that will give them some respite from the deep agony of estrangement. They have no past, only a confused sense of having lived. Surrounded by nothingness, frozen in place, they have no future—only a vague promise of something that should come, but will not. The characters are locked inside the phenomenon, having nothing outside the "now" of sufficient strength to pull them out. Actors in this context must seek their characters in the immediate moment, at the point of contact. Nothing else is legitimately available to them.

The new drama demands that we reevaluate our traditional approaches to theatre. The director should place less importance on narrative and plot techniques, such as writing a biography for a character or dwelling on what happens before or after a scene. Concepts in this text, grounded in action and emphasizing the four-dimensional aspect of drama form, are especially relevant to directing the new action-oriented drama.

EXERCISES

1. Given the definition of action developed in Chapter 1, what is the action in the following examples?
    a. A man walks to the sink and fills a glass with water.
    b. A girl puts a pencil into a pencil sharpener.
    c. Everything that Oedipus does in *Oedipus Rex*.
    d. a, b, and c.

2. Is conflict essential to action? Why?

3. Is action essential to conflict? Why?

4. Reread the Ophelia mad scene analysis in this chapter. Do the same kind of analysis for the Hamlet–Rosencrantz and Guildenstern scene (III, ii). Remember to ask specific questions to find what each character wants to get from or to do to the other at each moment.

5. Give three examples of motion. Give three examples of action. Change the motion examples to action. Can you change the action examples to motion?

6. Can you have movement without action? Why? Can you have action without movement? Why?

7. Use the following sentence to prove that motive is structure, or, conversely, that structure is motive: "Oh, George, let's not park here." (*Hint*: Removing words changes structure if it changes motive.)

8. In the fourth dimension, which comes first—the chicken or the egg?

9. Why is a play a closed system? Give an example of an open system.

NOTES

1. Francis Fergusson, *The Idea of a Theatre* (Princeton, N.J.: Princeton University Press, 1949), pp. 243 ff.

2. Kenneth Burke, *A Grammar of Motives* (New York: Prentice-Hall, 1945), p. 136.

3. W. Rhys Roberts and Ingram Bywater, *Aristotle's Rhetoric and Poetics* (New York: Modern Library, 1954), p. 231.

4. Ferdinand Brunetière, "La Loi du Théâtre," in *Les Annales du Théâtre et de la Musique*, 1893 (Paris: Charpentier, 1894), pp. I–XX.

5. Kenneth Burke, *The Philosophy of Literary Form* (New York: Vintage Books, 1957), p. 90.

6. Aldous Huxley, *The Doors of Perception* (New York: Harper & Brothers, 1954).

 CHAPTER

2

Analysis: Discovering the Play's Structure

THE ARTIST is in love with chaos, but she is transfixed by order. She yearns to capture chaos and give it form and meaning. To fail as an artist is to be defeated by chaos. Nonart has in it the seeds of its own destruction. Art survives.

Greek classical writers held that the common principle of art is imitation. The talent of artists depends in large part on their ability *to see* the object of imitation in ways that transcend the ordinary person's abilities. Dramatists imitate action. The director in her turn must discover and see clearly the action that she is to imitate on stage.

We developed a definition of dramatic action in Chapter 1. In this chapter we introduce a system of analysis that will enable the director to discover the action so that she can understand the play's form.

The artist knows that every part of a form makes demands that must be met in every other part. A form has a life of its own, one to be encountered and understood. The poet, the painter, and the playwright who deal honestly with the necessities of form know the agony and frustration of the encounter. But when successful, the artist also

19

"What conflict does the play exist to resolve?"

discovers the joy of creation. She feels the touch of immortality, for if the relationships are true, the form becomes its essence and has an existence that transcends time and place.

The fledgling artist nearly always equates creativity with freedom and interprets freedom to mean the banishing of all restraints on free-wheeling intuition. The mature artist, however, recognizes that form itself imposes restraints greater than any imposed from without. When the talented person acknowledges the discipline imposed by form, she is moving from dilettantism to artistry.

The difference between what the ancients called "poetic" (the work of art) and "rhetoric" (the process of persuasion) is that the poetic carries its own milieu, while rhetoric depends on society for its milieu. The poetic work of art contains its own order and meaning. Poetic is eternal. Rhetoric dies with its age.[1] Lincoln's Gettysburg Address, a poetic work, imaginatively applies the birth image to a nation in artistic terms that are still relevant today. Edward Everett's speech on the same occasion, although it seemed to have a strong effect at the time, is now buried with the people and customs of Civil War America.

The innate order of a work of art holds the key to its deepest understanding and appreciation. The director of a play has the responsibility to find this order. She should be interested first in the play's function as art, as a form with internal demands. Her concern for the play's function as rhetoric—as an argument for or against something—should be secondary, at least in the beginning. The artistic problems must be solved first. If the play has validity as a work of art, the argument will usually take care of itself. If a director realizes early that a play has validity only as rhetoric, not as art, she can avoid frustrating hours searching for internal principles of order that are not there.

THE CASE FOR ANALYSIS

A director's principal method for discovering the intrinsic order of a play is analysis. Instead of analysis, some directors inflict their egos on a play and engage in various forms of autotherapy. Such misplaced egos come between the director and the work of art. But conscientious directors humbly recognize their obligation to know the play intimately. They find in it an order all its own, not one prescribed by preconceptions or by how they might have directed a previous production. Even the author's stated intentions should not turn the director away from a close analysis. The "fallacy of intent" is a well-known pitfall for critic and director. In short, the director must be concerned not with the author's intention but with what has actually been written.

In her analysis a director's first task is to find the controlling motive that keys the action and resolves the conflict. She poses this question: What conflict does the play exist to resolve? When the director finds the conflict, the process by which it is resolved can be uncovered step by step, and the vital moments in the action process can be isolated. Having grasped the play's action, she is ready to prepare her strategy for revealing it in time and space.

All the other elements of a play's structure are keyed to the action. When we discover the basic conflict–resolution process of a play, we can determine the relative importance of all the events. If we do not concentrate first on discovering the action, we may assign to a play meaning that is inappropriate to its structure.

The English playwright and critic Bernard Shaw, among others, was influential in causing us to think of the plays of Ibsen as "social dramas." This idea is still being imposed upon Ibsen's plays, stressing their rhetoric to the detriment of their artistic integrity. One critic, believing *John Gabriel Bjorkmann* to be about the social consequences of Bjorkmann's embezzling funds, wrote that the fourth act is superfluous—a meaningless appendage. But analysis of the play's action reveals that the core of the play concerns Bjorkmann's rejection of love. By marrying for profit, not for love, Bjorkmann has rendered bleak and loveless the lives of himself and those nearest to him. With this interpretation, the fourth act, a reconciliation to love, becomes tenderly and beautifully meaningful. It should have occurred to the critic—especially when dealing with a playwright of such stature— that since Ibsen chose to write a fourth act, he must have had another, broader conflict in mind.

If a director does not discover the controlling motive of the action, she may ask an actor to do things that are at war with the intrinsic demands of the play, thereby inhibiting the actor's performance. A scene designer cannot design properly if the director's conception does not fit the action or is hazy. Conversely, a valid conception, well articulated, can inspire the other people in the production to high achievement. Indeed, the true director-artist must establish a close, harmonious relationship with the form she is struggling to create. In a sense, the form must be translated into the director's vision of the play. Some directors may not be able to articulate their vision to others or they may not wish to do so, but it must exist if they hope to be at all successful.

While a director may be able to create a production without a systematic analysis, the production and inevitably the director suffer. The main purpose of a systematic analysis is to understand the structural relationships and forces in a play. An auxiliary purpose is to facilitate communication about the play among director, actors, designer, and other personnel. During the performance of a play the structural highlights must be illuminated, so that the motive is clearly and powerfully transmitted to the audience.

By the same token, a director must realize that analysis is only the foundation for a successful production. At some point the analysis must evolve into an artistic synthesis that takes into account the contribution of the various people, as well as the demands of the theatre and audience. Analysis provides the informed stimulus for the director's creative instincts.

The initial reaction of many readers to John Millington Synge's masterpiece *Riders to the Sea* is to wonder what all the fuss is about. The story seems to be about an old woman who tries to keep her last son from going to sea to be drowned. She fails, and when his body is brought in, she just gives up. After fighting furiously to save her son, she appears to surrender meekly to the fact of his death. If the instructor mentions that *Riders to the Sea* has been called a one-act tragedy, the students are incredulous. Maurya's "passivity" seems inappropriate to the nature of a tragic character.

Under analysis, however, facets emerge to modify these first impressions. When we notice, for instance, that Maurya's final speeches sound more like victory than defeat, a new interpretation is possible. Maurya is not defeated by the sea. She has discovered her innate human power to transcend adversity. She rises above those about her who are still caught in the trappings of death to an understanding of how to achieve spiritual victory over death. Analysis, we see, provides the framework for encouraging second thoughts, offering the potential for productions that achieve greater complexity and power.

William Saroyan's *Hello Out There* opens with a young man discovered in a jail cell. We learn that he has been unjustly charged and that a mob is on the way to lynch him. A young girl, who works in the jail, is attracted to the young man; she agrees to help him escape and promises to run off to San Francisco with him. She fails to save him. The young man is shot, and at the end of the play, the girl is alone.

Here again first impressions can be misleading. Many people think the play is mainly about the boy. However, as we shall see later in this chapter, analysis reveals that this view does not take into account important elements of the form. While the boy is the catalyst—the mover—the play is more concerned with what happens to the girl.

One production of the play betrayed a faulty analysis the moment the curtain opened. The jail cell was center stage, allowing very little room for developing focus on the girl (who was outside the cell). Be-

> ## "Root action is the process by which the root conflict is resolved."

cause this production emphasized the boy's situation, the end of the play became awkward and confused.

Not all plays will turn about in such dramatic fashion. However, under searching analysis of structural components, most plays will reveal dimensions and complexities that are not apparent in an ordinary reading.

STRUCTURAL ELEMENTS

Analysis is a vitally important tool that enables the director to identify the structural elements of the play's form and to understand the forces at work. But we must bear in mind that analysis is not sufficient in itself. The quality of a director's work depends not only on how well she analyzes a play, but on how well she applies what she learns by analysis to her directing.

We divide the structural elements of a play into two principal groups, primary and secondary. The primary elements—root conflict, root action, and climax—provide the fundamental power sources of the play. The secondary elements—inciting incident, crisis, and catastrophe—identify key moments in the evolution of the action process.[2]

Primary Structural Elements

Root Conflict

The **root conflict** is the single, underlying conflict in a play. It consists of the fundamental competing forces that create the action. The

protagonist is the initiator of the action and is usually the focal figure in the conflict. The **antagonist** is the principal opposing figure or force.

The root conflict of *Oedipus Rex* might be "Oedipus vs. the gods." Oedipus vows to solve the mystery of the curse that plagues the land. He appeals to the gods through the oracle at Delphi and discovers that there is an unknown offender whom he must find and punish. The gods know who it is; Oedipus does not. He proceeds to solve the mystery, even though he is warned by the prophet (a representative of the gods) not to do so. With searing irony he discovers that the offender is himself. He becomes the victim of his own victory.

The protagonist and antagonist are almost always persons in the play. In the example just cited, however, the gods exert such a powerful influence on the action that they best represent the force working against the protagonist. In drama it does not work to have the protagonist opposing himself. Although there is usually an element of inner struggle in the major characters, the nature of drama decrees that the forces motivating the protagonist and antagonist be personified in some way. Otherwise the conflicts lack intensity, and their power to move spectators is lessened.

Sometimes identification of the main forces in a play is easy. They leap out from the script. At other times identifying them is difficult. Several characters may play important roles, and it is hard to see which characters or which forces emerge as dominant. But eventually the root conflict must be identified. If it is not, the production may well lack clarity, focus, and power.

Root Action

Root action is the process by which the root conflict is resolved. A statement of root action tells us not only who the competing agents are or what the competing forces are, but also how the conflict is resolved. The statement must be consistent with root conflict and must tie together all other elements of the play. The root action statement must contain the following elements: protagonist, protagonist's motive, protagonist's act, antagonist, antagonist's motive, antagonist's act, and the resolution.

We can formulate a "grammar" for a root action statement by filling in the blanks in Figure 2.1. One or two sentences capture the key elements of a root action: the major combatants, their motives, their acts in response to those motives, and the resolution.

At the end of *Oedipus Rex*, Oedipus has overcome the obstacles to his understanding and discovers that the guilt of Thebes is on him; whereupon he tears out his eyes and returns to receive the judgment of his people. The root action of the play, then, might be stated as shown in Figure 2.2.

Root action statements should illuminate the conflict between competing agents. Therefore, the motives and the acts of the protagonist and antagonist should be in direct conflict. If they are not, there is a danger that the production will not be properly focused and that the actors will not find the precise point of clash in their performance. As we pursue the motive statements of the protagonist and antagonist, we should ask, "What does the protagonist want to get from or to do to the antagonist?" and "What does the antagonist want to get from or to do to the protagonist?"

FIGURE 2.1   Root action statement

_____/wanting_____/____		
(Protagonist)	(Protagonist's motive)	

_____/but___
                    (Protagonist's act)

_____/wanting_____/____
  (Antagonist)   (Antagonist's motive)

_____/resulting in____
          (Antagonist's act)

_____
          (Resolution)

Applying this test to the root action statement for *Oedipus Rex*, we can perhaps find a way to improve it. Oedipus' motive, "to lift the curse from Thebes," encounters the motive of the gods, "to display their power over the human race." How directly do they clash? To some degree, but not enough. We might try this: "Oedipus' wanting to maintain his status as king by lifting the curse" against "the gods' wanting to display the insignificance of humans by revealing Oedipus' impotence." These motives are more confrontational and provide a stronger power source for the action of the drama.

Now let's examine the acts these motives engender. How directly do they clash? Oedipus' act, "tries to find and punish the guilty one," conflicts with the gods', "attempt through their agents to defeat and discredit Oedipus." While there is clash implied, the statements are not conflicting enough. We need better focus on the clash.

We next try the following: Oedipus "assigns to himself the role of savior of Thebes and proceeds to find and punish the guilty one." Meanwhile, the gods "use their agents to battle him at every step in

FIGURE 2.2   Root action statement for *Oedipus Rex*

OEDIPUS /wanting **TO LIFT THE CURSE FROM THEBES,** /
(Protagonist)   (Protagonist's motive)

TRIES TO FIND AND PUNISH THE GUILTY ONE,   /but
(Protagonist's act)

THE GODS, /wanting **TO DISPLAY THEIR POWER OVER THE HUMAN RACE,**
(Antagonist)   (Antagonist's motive)

                                        OEDIPUS,
ATTEMPT THROUGH THEIR AGENTS TO DEFEAT AND DISCREDIT/resulting in
(Antagonist's act)

OEDIPUS' SUCCEEDING IN HIS QUEST — THOUGH IT COSTS HIM EVERYTHING.
(Resolution)

order to frustrate his quest and thus discredit him." We may still do better in our next draft, but, by focusing the clash, we have improved the root action statement and can formulate this resolution statement: "Oedipus defeats the gods and saves Thebes, but at the cost of everything that gives him status as a man: his throne, his wife, his children, and finally even the control of his own personal destiny."

We are now ready for a restatement of the root action (Figure 2.3), which clearly points toward a stronger production.

Oedipus elevates all humanity in his magnificent victory, but he also reveals the ironic vulnerability of anyone who, having so much, is capable of losing so much. Everyone might not fully accept this root action statement. However, it gives focus and direction to a particular production. A different statement would lead to a different production. The best statement is the one that best accounts for everything in the script.

One production of Molière's *Tartuffe* was based on the following

FIGURE 2.3   Restated root action statement for *Oedipus Rex*

OEDIPUS   /wanting TO MAINTAIN HIS STATUS AS KING BY LIFTING THE CURSE   /
(Protagonist)   (Protagonist's motive)

ASSIGNS TO HIMSELF THE ROLE OF SAVIOR OF THEBES AND PROCEEDS TO FIND AND PUNISH THE GUILTY ONE,   /but
                    (Protagonist's act)

THE GODS   /wanting TO DISPLAY THE INSIGNIFICANCE OF THE HUMAN RACE BY REVEALING OEDIPUS' IMPOTENCE /
(Antagonist)   (Antagonist's motive)

USE THEIR AGENTS TO BATTLE HIM AT EVERY STEP IN ORDER TO FRUSTRATE HIS QUEST AND THUS DISCREDIT HIM,   /resulting in
                    (Antagonist's act)

OEDIPUS' DEFEATING THE GODS AND SAVING THEBES, BUT AT THE COST OF EVERYTHING THAT GIVES HIM STATUS AS A MAN: HIS THRONE, HIS WIFE, HIS CHILDREN, AND FINALLY EVEN THE CONTROL OF HIS OWN PERSONAL DESTINY.
                    (Resolution)

root action statement: "Tartuffe, wanting to possess what is Orgon's, proceeds to take his wealth and tries to take his wife, but the household (family and servants), wanting to prevent the destruction of Orgon, conspires to expose Tartuffe's base motives and strip him of his mask of piety, resulting in Tartuffe's invasion of Orgon's island of piety being shipwrecked on the shoals of flesh." Tartuffe's human weakness, his desire for Orgon's wife, Elmire, was emphasized throughout the production. Tartuffe's phony piety makes him cold and distasteful, but his lust is a humanizing factor that gives him more appeal as a character. The "shipwreck" theme was stressed continually. Acres of Elmire's flesh were exposed as a constant and vexing diversion to Tartuffe's main plan. The tone of this production—a light-hearted sexual romp with serious satirical overtones—was suggested in the root action statement.

A root action statement must indicate the entire conflict–resolution process. Such a statement is a "naming" of the process that gives clarification and emphasis to our understanding of the root action. The root action statement guides our subsequent thinking about the play. But we can never hope to capture all the complexities and nuances of the root action in a single statement.

Climax

When the root conflict is resolved, the **climax** of the play occurs. It is the key moment at which the controlling motive is most fully revealed. We can say that the action of a play is the struggle to reach the climax. At the climax the action ends because the root conflict is over.

The climax is usually the highest dramatic point of a play. Sometimes what appears to be the highest point on first reading gives way to a subtler, more profound moment once the conflict and its moment of resolution are clarified by analysis.

Events may follow the climax, but they are not truly part of the action. They clarify and illuminate the climax. We call these events, if they occur, the **denouement**.

In *Oedipus Rex* the climax is probably the moment when Oedipus

> ## "The action of a play is the struggle to reach the climax."

ends his struggle by blinding himself in an act of ritual sacrifice. With this analysis, a question for the director is, Does the climax occur off-stage when Oedipus actually commits the act, when the messenger describes it, or when Oedipus reappears with the blood streaming down his face? The answer will significantly affect the production. Our reconsidered analysis would probably place the climax at the moment when Oedipus, no longer in control of his destiny, is sent inside while others decide his fate, and his tragic fall from eminence is complete.

Secondary Structural Elements

Inciting Incident

The **inciting incident** is the moment that begins the root conflict. Sometimes exposition, which provides information the audience needs for background or context, precedes the inciting incident. Exposition that does not further the action is called *static*. Exposition that is an integral part of the developing action is called *functional*. Exposition prior to the inciting incident is static because it occurs before the action begins. Most playwrights try to make exposition functional in order to avoid the "dragging" effect. That is, they want the audience to feel a sense of progression, a sense that the action is under way.

The inciting incident should be close to the beginning of the play. It almost never occurs before the play begins, although there may be a temptation to place it in past events that lead up to the action of the play.

A play usually opens with characters whose lives are already well advanced and may contain conflicts that have been going on for years.

The inciting incident, however, applies not to these conflicts but to the particular root conflict that makes this play happen. The play focuses on a specific conflict, which, when resolved, may also resolve a lifetime of conflicts.

In *Oedipus Rex* the inciting incident is Oedipus' opening response to the chorus, when he says, "Speak, for I, you know, would give all aid." By thus identifying with the Suppliants' cause, he commits himself to the struggle. The inciting incident is not the solving of the riddle of the Sphinx or the abandonment of the infant Oedipus. These events form part of the Oedipus myth, but they do not form part of the action of the play.

Crisis

The **crisis** is that event which makes the resolution of the conflict inevitable. In life a conflict between two people may go on for years without resolution. Some life conflicts are never resolved. They just peter out, or one of the participants leaves the scene or dies. In most dramas of the Western world, however, we have a resolution of the conflict. The form is given a completeness.

Although resolution is implicit in the Western drama genre (because we have come to expect it of the aesthetic form), it is made explicit by the crisis. Think of the two major contending forces as travelling on parallel lines. They face each other and take potshots across no-man's-land until the moment of crisis. The crisis turns the two forces toward each other on a collision course. After this moment the conflicting forces become not only mutually antagonistic, but mutually destructive. One, or both, cannot continue indefinitely after the crisis. A showdown is inevitable. The crisis does not reveal the nature of the resolution. It merely says that after this event a climax must come.

In classical tragedy the crisis occurs early, which accounts for the strong sense of inevitability that pervades Greek tragedy. Most directors see Oedipus' vow to discover the cause of the curse as the crisis in the play. By then we have already learned enough about Oedipus' character to feel that he will keep his word. Knowing that a vow was a

> ## "The catastrophe signifies that the resolution, promised by the crisis, will occur now."

very serious commitment to ancient Greeks supports our feeling. One did not break a vow without incurring the wrath of the gods. Indeed, it is said that men on trial in Greek courts were immediately released if they took a vow attesting to their innocence. Thus, we do not expect Oedipus to turn from his decision to pursue the quest to its end. Oedipus is on a collision course with the gods.

Finding the crisis requires a close reading of the script. If Oedipus' vow functions as the crisis in the play, it does so not because the Greeks thought a vow irrevocable but because the internal logic of the action demands that after the vow Oedipus cannot be turned from his course. A climax is inevitable.

Another director might hold that Jocasta stood a good chance of persuading Oedipus to change his mind and stop his search. In a powerful scene Jocasta (his wife-mother) pleads with Oedipus to cease his quest for answers to the mystery. Oedipus rejects her plea, and Jocasta leaves, we learn later, to commit suicide. If Oedipus truly was hesitant, we might argue that the crisis occurs in this scene, which would alter the action dramatically and create a different production. It seems probable, however, that Oedipus was already firmly committed, and Jocasta's futile plea was her poignant, though doomed, effort to avert the tragedy she had foreseen.

Catastrophe

The **catastrophe** is the moment that precipitates the climax. It is the event that signifies that the resolution, promised by the crisis, will occur now.

The catastrophe and the crisis might, as often happens in melodrama, occur at the same time. In a television thriller, the bandits flee from a jewelry store with the loot and would make a clean getaway if they turn left. But they turn right and into the arms of the approaching police. The conflict might not be resolved but for the fortuitous accident of a wrong turn. In this example, the moment of crisis occurs simultaneously with the catastrophe, scant seconds before the climax.

Generally, the crisis and the catastrophe are separate events. The reason is that playwrights build dramatic interest by creating anticipation of the culminating confrontation. Therefore, they place their crisis at some distance from the climax and use another galvanic event, the catastrophe, to bring the action to a resolution. Recalling our image of two parallel lines, we see the catastrophe as the moment that converts the gentle angle of convergence, created by the crisis, to an immediate head-on collision.

In *Oedipus Rex* the catastrophe is probably the testimony of the Shepherd. His testimony finally convinces Oedipus beyond a doubt that he is the guilty one. Following this, Oedipus storms off stage and does not return until he has blinded himself. He has finally confronted the unalterable truth. Nothing is left but the resolution—his self-sacrifice.

Interdependence of Structural Elements

The three primary elements are absolutely dependent on each other. The root conflict must be the confrontation depicted by the root action process. The climax must resolve the root conflict and end the root action. If the analysis suggests a certain root conflict and then it appears that the root action concerns another conflict, something is wrong with the order, that is, the internal relationship of the parts.

The primary and secondary elements are also interdependent. In particularly difficult cases, we can turn to the secondary elements as an aid in the analysis of primary elements. In either case, whether used in conjunction with or after the analysis of the primary elements, the secondary elements will further illuminate the primary elements by identifying key moments in the action.

A system of checks and balances is a valuable feature of the analysis plan. Each element must be reconciled with the others. When this can be done satisfactorily, there is a good chance that the formal structural elements of the play have been properly identified.

A device to help the director reconcile the elements is to pose the **dramatic question**—the question the play exists to answer. The dramatic question is fully answered at the climax.

In *Oedipus Rex* we might begin by asking, "Will Oedipus solve the riddle and lift the curse from Thebes?" Does this question account for the whole play? Is this the question the play exists to answer? What about Oedipus' punishment—the price he pays for his victory? Obviously that is an important part of the play. We must formulate, therefore, a more acceptable dramatic question, one that intensifies the conflict: Is Oedipus willing to face self-destruction in order to persevere in his commitment to his vow?

CYCLES OF ACTION

Analysis leads us into the play, starting with root conflict and proceeding to the other structural elements. A further extension of this process is to identify the subsidiary conflicts that develop the root action. These conflicts are miniature action processes that function in much the same way as the root action. We refer to them as **cycles of action** because they are recurring minor conflicts. They correspond roughly to what are called "action units" or "motivational units" in other systems of analysis. Cycles of action, however, are conflict–resolution processes. They are not *scenes* in the conventional sense; nor are they **French scenes**—a more formal definition, codified by French academicians in the seventeenth century—requiring a scene to begin or end at the entrance or exit of any character, unless those events incite or resolve conflict. A cycle is also distinguished from an actor's beat. A **beat** is the small goal an actor pursues in quest of her main objective, viewing the action from only one side of the conflict. For instance, one actor might have as her beat "to get out of the room." The other actor in the cycle of action might have as her beat "to keep her here until help arrives." The cycle of action is made up of the two or more beats of the opposing actors' meeting each other.

Cycles usually have inciting incidents and end with a climax. Analyzing all secondary elements in a cycle, however, is usually unnecessary —a tedious extension of analysis. Nonetheless, a thorough analysis of a particularly difficult action cycle may be helpful in understanding its relationship to the main action. Each cycle should be titled and its boundaries marked carefully. The title need not be as fully phrased as the root action statement, but it should capture accurately the point or motive of the cycle of action.

Sometimes one cycle of action will overlap another; that is, the inciting incident for one action will come before the climax of the previous action. The new action will begin to build its tension before the previous action has released its tension through resolution of the conflict. These tension–relaxation segments provide a way to understand the rhythms of the play. If a play must be cut, directors will find a knowledge of the action cycles very helpful. Cycles that contribute least to the root action may be cut. Knowing where the cycles begin and end helps directors to orchestrate the production and to anticipate and control the audience's reaction to a play.

POINT OF CLASH

Analysis has led us from the broad outlines of the root conflict to the individual cycles of action. This process continues in rehearsal as the director focuses on the conflict in each specific moment. Each moment is created from a clash of forces. The actors must find this point of clash in each moment if they are to act with profundity and power.

As they perform, many actors focus their attention on sources or keys that are not precisely in the moment. Their focus lingers on something just passed or strays to something about to occur. But a strong performance results when the actor focuses on the precise point of clash in the "space between" her character and all that is acting upon that character. During rehearsal each actor must ask, "What do I want to get from or to do to this person *at this moment?*"

CHARACTER ANALYSIS

Motive Happening

An analysis of character ought to be based on the same principles that apply to the analysis of the play as a whole. Uncovering motive is the key. Motive identifies character. A character acts because she *wants*; what she wants determines what she does. We begin our study of character by examining the character's acts in order to expose the motives beneath them. Character is motive made manifest. Motives are engendered by the conflict. Directors must make certain that each character's wants are grounded in the root action of the play, and they must be prepared to help an actor find the essence of her character.

A character in a play often resembles a character in life. Indeed, in contemporary realistic drama, resemblance to life is an important requisite. But a character in a play is not like a person in life in one important respect: A character's life is already ended. Her resolution or "death" has been determined by the playwright. A person in a play must do what is in the next line or on the next page. The character

> "What do I want to get from or to do to this person *at this moment?*"

lives in the "determined form" of the play and dies when that form is complete. A person in life is faced with the illusion, at least, of infinite possibilities in the next moment, hour, or day. Life is a "free form."

Psychology can be misleading on this point. The actor is often encouraged to "psychoanalyze" her character as if she were a living person. When this is done, the character may be given possibilities that do not exist. The motive, or essence, of a character may be developed independently of her motive in the play. The actor begins to work at cross-purposes with the demands of the play's form.

A "character-centered" analysis may lead to a kind of artistic anarchy. Because an actor's interest tends to be focused mainly on bringing her character "to life," difficult and subtle motives of the play's action are often not isolated and articulated. (Directors, who usually started out as actors, sometimes focus their efforts almost exclusively on character.) Actors often pursue the logic of individual psychological motivation. Sometimes this pursuit will take a course compatible with the demands of the play; sometimes it does not.

The "deception" scene between Laura and Amanda in Tennessee Williams's *The Glass Menagerie* (I, ii), for instance, is difficult because young actors—and directors—often get caught up in the psychology of "poor crippled" Laura. They forget that the scene is not about how to play a girl who is both psychologically and physically disabled, but about the relationship between daughter and mother. Once the actresses begin seeking the motive for their performances in the interaction between daughter and mother, they are letting the action— rather than character-centered introspection—guide them.

A character's motive, then, refers to her function in the play's structure. It accounts for everything the character does in the play. If a character changes her opinion drastically, the basic motive must account for the change. There must be a want deep enough in the character to provide a single motive for both of the conflicting opinions.

After the character's motive has been determined, the actor may then use psychological analysis to help find the proper attitudes and feelings to give the character a realistic human basis for action. If the playwright has written characters appropriate to the play, these will be implicit in the script.

> ## "A character has only one motive in a play, but she may have many purposes."

The actor must, however, never allow psychological analysis to divert her attention from the "point of clash." Character is ultimately found outside the character's psyche. It is found at the point of contact between the character's wants and all that frustrates those wants. Introspection tends to lead an actor away from the "space between" herself and the other actors. The actor must not make decisions about specific moments before she has approached the rehearsal experience with an open mind, ready to discover her character from contact with the other characters.

Psychiatry recognizes the primacy of a basic motive underlying human action. Under analysis a person unfolds her past so that the psychiatrist can help her find the source of her actions. In life, however, the discovery of a basic motive is possible only in the past, the part of the person that has already happened and is therefore determined. What the future holds for a person in life is never certain. But for a character in a play, the future has already been determined.

The motive, or spine, of a character is stated as an infinitive phrase to emphasize that motive is a spur to action. Oedipus' motive might be "to solve the riddle" or "to lift the curse." Here again, different statements lead to different interpretations of character.

Motive Distinguished from Purpose

The basic motive driving a character to act lurks deep in the psyche. But it may manifest itself in various wants that are only obliquely related to the basic motive. These relatively superficial wants we shall call **purposes** to set them apart from the single basic "motive" that remains the same for each character throughout the play. These expedient purposes may be used by a character to mask her true motive, or a character may mistakenly conceive a purpose to be her motive. Indeed one definition of insanity might be based on the dichotomy between purpose and motive. The more a person's purposes work counter to her motive, the more neurotic or psychotic she is. The character controls her purpose, but her motive controls her. The butler may have as his immediate purpose to make the visitor comfortable. But his motive, decreed by the subsequent action, is to murder him.

A character has only one motive in a play, but she may have many purposes. Oedipus' purposes, among others, are "to placate the crowd," "to unravel the mystery of the oracle," and "to get the truth out of Tiresias." His motive may be to retain his status as savior king of the Thebans.

ANALYSIS AT WORK

In the following discussion William Saroyan's *Hello Out There* will be used as a prototype. The full text of the play can be found beginning on page 195.

The first step is to become familiar with the script. It is hard to read through the script several times without becoming impatient to get on with the analysis. For this reason it is useful to break the script into cycles of action before proceeding with the analysis. The time spent in determining where the minor conflicts in the play begin and end will serve to open and clarify the play even before work on the analysis begins.

It is usually helpful to title the cycles of action. Sometimes only a few of the most important or puzzling cycles need to be titled in the preliminary work. The rest may be presented to the cast for them to title during rehearsal. One possible action schedule (in part) appears in Figure 2.4.

In the script the precise beginning and ending of the cycles are marked. Sometimes they overlap, but sometimes there is a brief pause in the flow after the completion of an action and before the start of a new action. We can call these moments "interactions" because they come between actions. They are also listed in the action schedule as

FIGURE 2.4   Action schedule for *Hello Out There*

Action	Characters	Pages	Title
1.	The Young Man	3	"Hello, Out There"
2.	Young Man and Girl	3–5	Lonesome as a Coyote
3.	Young Man and Girl	5–15	Katey and Photo Finish
4.	Young Man and Girl	15–17	Not Alone Anymore

interaction 1, 2, 3, and so forth. The average-length play might have thirty actions in it. One schedule for a production of *Hamlet* listed fifty actions. The action schedule is also important in constructing the rehearsal schedule, which is based on the cycles of action.

Discovering the Root Conflict

By the time we start the analysis, we may already be familiar enough with the script to propose a statement of the root conflict. If two opposing forces seem clearly to emerge, we may postulate a statement of the root conflict and proceed to test it by finding the climax and the root action it implies. If these elements seem to have an internal consistency and seem to give an honest picture of the total structure of the play—that is, if there is nothing of consequence left over—and if our conclusions square with our intuitive sense of order and propriety, we may proceed with the analysis.

If our proposal fails the test, and the testing process does not immediately suggest another postulate, we will leave it and try to find the climax. Perhaps a moment stands out. We try this moment as the climax and determine what conflict it resolves. If the conflict discovered in this way passes the test for root conflict, we may proceed once more.

If both of these approaches do not yield a satisfactory statement of the root conflict, we might try the dramatic question approach. We ask ourselves what question the play exists to answer. Does *Death of a Salesman*, for instance, pose the question "Will Willy Loman get his job back?" No. It seems larger than that; it has something to do with his relations with his son. "Will Willy Loman prove himself to his son?" Closer, perhaps, but still not quite the point. How about "Will Willy Loman vindicate his way of life in the eyes of his son?" Maybe. If we like the last statement, we go back and try to formulate a statement of the root conflict based on answering this question and proceed from there. In this case our dramatic question would lead to the root conflict "Willy vs. Biff."

Another approach to the root conflict—if the other methods fail—is to try to find the conflict through the characters. We check to see if the motives or spines of the characters are easily discernible. Since characters are activators of conflict, this approach might bring the mutually opposing motives sharply into focus. The root conflict would then be obvious. The character approach should be saved until last, and the results should be thoroughly checked by other tests because of the danger of falling into a character-centered analysis. As we have seen, many motives may be possible for certain types of characters, but only a few are relevant to the particular conflict in a given play.

Root Conflict in *Hello Out There*

Having read the script of *Hello Out There*, we know that it concerns a man locked in a prison cell, accused of rape, and befriended by a girl who works in the jail. The Young Man is an interesting character with an unusual but charming outlook on life. We find out that he is not really guilty of rape, but the victim of an unscrupulous woman, who bestowed her favors freely and then demanded payment. When the Young Man refused, she called for help and caused him to be beaten and thrown into jail. Near the end of the play, the husband and his cronies arrive, prepared to take the Young Man from jail and lynch him. The husband, left alone with the prisoner, shoots the Young Man and leaves. The Girl, who had gone to get the Young Man a gun, returns and finds him dying. The lynch mob returns and takes the Young Man's body away in spite of the Girl's protestations. The Girl, left alone, echoes the Young Man's opening words, "Hello—out there!"

One of the first statements of the root conflict might be, "The Young Man vs. Society." He is clearly a rebel, an outsider who is being victimized by the local establishment. But immediately a problem arises: The other side of the conflict, the forces of society, do not appear—in the persons of the husband, the wife, and others in the mob—until nearly the end of the play. And even then their roles are relatively minor.

In fact, the major portion of the play is taken up with the scene between the Girl and the Young Man, where we discover that the Girl is mistreated and laughed at by the locals and exploited by her father. Convinced of her worthlessness, she is more of a prisoner than the Young Man. The Young Man tells her she is beautiful, that he loves her. He tries to convince her to leave her miserable existence and go with him to San Francisco.

Our postulate is getting a little shaky, but let's test it further by finding the climax. It seems probable that the conflict between the Young Man and society would be resolved when the Young Man is killed. Does this moment seem to leap out as the climax of the play, the high point of the action? Is there no more conflict after this? The proponents of this postulate might answer yes to these questions. Others, looking at the play more analytically, might point out that the last moment seems like the high point of the play, when the Girl, after trying to fight off the lynchers, moves downstage and tentatively utters the phrase the Young Man had used, "Hello—out there!" At least it is an important part of the action: You could not cut it and have the same play.

Remembering that no part of the action can appear after the climax, because the climax marks the end of the action, we discover another problem. Placing the climax where the Young Man is killed is inconsistent with our thinking about the action—an indication that something is wrong with our analysis. Others might contend that the title of the play, *Hello Out There*, argues for the importance of that last moment.

At this point the analysis might lead us to an important question: Whom is the play really about? If the Young Man's story is finished and we still find the action going on, it is possible that the root action concerns the Girl more than it does the Young Man. Someone might observe that when Hamlet is dead, Fortinbras is still around to comment on his death and have him carried off for a royal burial, but that does not mean the play is about Fortinbras. The question here, however, is not whether the play is still going on but whether the *action* is still going. In *Hamlet* the conflict has been resolved with the death of the principal characters. Fortinbras's scene is denouement, an event that clarifies and illuminates the climax but that does not contain further conflict. Is the Girl's last speech denouement, or is it a necessary and important part of the action? Does the Young Man's death resolve the conflict or does the Girl's last line?

To help us answer this question, we might move to another approach to the analysis: phrasing the dramatic question. What question does the play exist to answer? Is it "Will the Young Man get out of jail?" That certainly is an important question in the play, but is it the question the play exists to answer? If it is, we can cut the play when the Young Man's dead body is carried out and the play will not be significantly altered. The very fact, however, that the play continues is an argument against that phrasing of the dramatic question. And most people would agree that it would not be the same play without the last moment with the Girl alone on stage.

Let us phrase a dramatic question that centers on the girl: "Will the Girl save the Young Man?" No, that will not do. The same objections apply. That question is settled long before the last moment. How about "Will the Girl's life be changed by her contact with the Young Man?" That is closer to it. Such an event is bound to make an impression on her. Can we be more specific about the nature of the change?

At first it seemed that the problem of the play is getting the Young Man out of prison. But analysis has led us to see that the real problem has to do with the Girl, who is locked in her own prison—the prison of the mind. She has been so trampled by her life that she does not even reach out for the simplest joys of the human condition. The Young Man's purpose changes from saving his own skin to providing some escape for the Girl. But her contact with the Young Man is terminated by his brutal murder. Will this event drive the Girl back into her shell, or will she keep the spark lit by the Young Man and reach out for what is rightfully hers?

"Will the Girl escape from her mental bondage and make a try for freedom?" That is good. It can be improved, perhaps, but we are on the right track.

The answer to the question (the climax of the play and the resolution of the conflict) comes when the Girl, alone and forlorn, makes her first tentative contact with the new world that awaits her. She takes a few steps downstage and calls out to the world, "Hello—out there!"

We started out to find the root conflict and have been led to consider climax and root action as well as character motive. The interdependence of elements is obvious. A close analysis of an element can help us to find the others and can lead us to reject those answers that are not consistent with the whole.

What statement seems to emerge from all of this? Clearly the root conflict involves the Young Man and the Girl. The Young Man tries to get the Girl to do something that she is reluctant to do. At first he has to coax her to come out of the shadows. Then he tries to convince her that she is beautiful and that he loves her. Then he tries to get her to help him escape. Finally, he tries to convince her to go to San Francisco no matter what happens to him. He even gives her his money so that she will have the means of escape.

The Girl gradually succumbs to his charm, accepts what he says, and finally shows her love and commitment by risking her own safety by trying to help him. At the end, when she summons the courage to call out to the world in the Young Man's words, she shows that he has succeeded even though he is gone.

The root conflict may be, "The Young Man vs. the Girl." By giving the Young Man's name first, this statement asserts that the Young Man is the protagonist and the Girl is the antagonist. This choice is not as easy as it might seem on the surface. One test for identifying the protagonist is to determine the initiator of the action. In this play it is clear that the Young Man initiates most of the action. The girl, however, does initiate action to some degree with her decision to remain behind in the empty jail. Another test is to determine who is changed most by the action. This would apply to the Girl more than the Young Man. Usually a play is about the protagonist. The protagonist is the central figure. But a play can be about the antagonist. If most of the tests for determining the protagonist apply to a character who does not have central focus in the play, then we have a play about the antagonist. In this case the values come out very close. It is preferable to name the Girl the antagonist—the responder rather than the initiator. Perhaps subsequent work will alter this decision, but it seems *Hello Out There* is primarily about the antagonist.

One might ask, "How can you say 'the Young Man vs. the Girl' when it seems they are on the same side?" In a social context they do represent similar points of view, but in the dramatic context of the play, they represent the opposite sides of a root action. If drama depends on conflict for its interest, and we find this play dramatically interesting, there must be conflict during the scene between the Girl and the Young Man. We have tried to show how that conflict develops.

As we shall see in Chapter 4, even a love scene—if it is dramatically interesting—depends on conflict. What makes a character act is the absence of something she wants. The other characters represent means by which each character can achieve her wants. The power source of the play resides in this conflict. If there is no resistance to wants, there is no conflict. If one character does not represent a frustration of wants that must be acted upon by the other character, there is no reason for the character's existence in the scene. Love without seduction is of little dramatic interest. Seduction is the overcoming of frustrations to desire. A good love scene is full of conflict.

Discovering the Root Action

Once the root conflict has been determined, it is possible to extend its implications to the root action. Remembering that root action is not a plot summary but a statement about the way the root conflict is resolved, we now try to fashion such a statement. This statement must do more than just blandly report how the conflict is resolved. It must indicate the nature of the resolution process. An earnestly serious statement about a rollicking comedy might belie the form instead of illuminating it. The root action statement should function as the controlling image or metaphor of the director's approach to the production. The statement should then employ imagery that reflects the root conflict discovered by the analysis. It probably will undergo improvement in phrasing as work on the analysis progresses. Sometimes work on root action will even lead to a reformulation of the root conflict statement.

Root Action in *Hello Out There*

A statement of the root action in *Hello Out There* must identify the protagonist, the protagonist's motive, the protagonist's act, the antagonist, the antagonist's motive, the antagonist's act, and the resolution of conflict. When preparing this statement, we must keep in mind the questions "What does the Young Man want to get from or to do to the Girl?" and "What does the Girl want to get from or to do to the Young Man?"

We find from the dialogue that the Young Man is a drifter who has not made much of his life. He is a gambler who is down on his luck. But he is also a free spirit who is full of idealism in spite of the reversals of his life. As he reveals more about himself to the Girl, it becomes apparent that his advice so freely given has not worked well in his case. But the Girl in her naiveté and innocence accepts everything he says.

We note that, although the Young Man's motive at first seemed to be to enlist her help in getting him out of jail, it gradually takes on another dimension. He is smitten with her candor, her unquestioning acceptance of him as he wishes to be. He assures her that with her beside him, his luck will surely change. He may not really believe what he is saying, but she does, and that makes it true for one glorious moment. For this gift, he owes her something. His apparent motive shifts from saving himself to saving her. He sees that in her he is himself perfected. When we reach the end of the play, we know that his motive is deeper than just getting out of jail. That desire is relegated to the level of a purpose.

As he realizes that his minutes are probably numbered—a lynch mob is rumored to be on the way—his interest shifts to her. She must be the vehicle of his salvation—that is, not the saving of his skin, but the saving of his most perfect self. As his interest shifts, the focus of the play shifts to the Girl, struggling to understand, to believe that what he describes is possible for her.

With these thoughts in mind, let's prepare a root action grammar for *Hello Out There* (see Figure 2.5).

Discovering the Climax

If the first efforts at analysis have not proven helpful, it may be necessary to look for the climax as a means of illuminating root action and root conflict. The high dramatic point of the play may be easy to

FIGURE 2.5 Root action statement for *Hello Out There*

THE YOUNG MAN /wanting TO "SAVE", TO PERPETUATE, HIMSELF THROUGH THE GIRL
  (*Protagonist*)   (*Protagonist's motive*)

TRIES TO CONVINCE THE GIRL OF HER VALUE AS A HUMAN BEING AND LOVER SO
SHE WILL SAVE HIM, SPIRITUALLY, IF NOT PHYSICALLY, BY PERPETUATING HIM /but
                  (*Protagonist's act*)

THE GIRL /wanting TO OBSERVE AT A DISTANCE THE YOUNG MAN AND LIFE
  (*Antagonist*)   (*Antagonist's motive*)

TRIES TO RESIST HIS "BLARNEY" AND ITS DANGEROUS CALL FOR
HER TO DEMAND SOMETHING FROM LIFE /resulting in
            (*Antagonist's act*)

HER MAKING A COMMITMENT TO HIM AND TO LIFE, WHICH SURVIVES HIS BRUTAL DEATH.
            (*Resolution*)

see. We can then postulate that this moment is the climax, determine what conflict the event resolves, and call that the root conflict. If the root action that evolves from that satisfies our intuition about the play and does not leave important parts out, we can assume we are on the right track.

If we are satisfied with our first root action statement, we can find the climax immediately by finding the event that resolves the root conflict. But if that event does not seem to be the culminating moment, or if there is obviously conflict continuing after it, the root action and root conflict statements are called into question. Perhaps we need to start over again.

It may be necessary to make several postulates about the climax by trying moments that seem to be high points in the action or that have a sense of finality about them and then applying the tests for climax. When making these postulates, the director should keep in mind that first impressions are often false. However, each false attempt can deepen the impression of the play and lead to other formulas that prove successful.

The climax can also be discovered by using the dramatic question approach. Since it resolves the conflict, the climax is the moment that answers the dramatic question.

Climax in *Hello Out There*

Because elements of the analysis constantly interact with each other, we have now reached a fairly clear idea of how the conflict is resolved. We know that the play is about the Girl and that the real point of the play is made when she utters her last line, showing that she is making the first tentative steps to escape from her prison. It is always comforting when the climax comes neatly on the last line of the play. If it comes earlier, there is a stronger possibility of misinterpreting action. If we think it comes too far before the end of the play, we have almost certainly made a mistake. The best playwrights write very little that is not part of the action.

Now that the basic analysis questions have been answered, the fundamental shape of the action has been determined. It remains to isolate certain key moments in the progression of the action so that we can understand exactly how the action unfolds as it moves toward resolution.

Discovering the Inciting Incident

It is important to place the inciting incident within the confines of the action occurring on stage. Although the roots of the conflict may be in the past, usually some event within the play triggers this particular quest for resolution. For example, Blanche's whole life has been preparing her for what happens in Tennessee Williams's *A Streetcar Named Desire*, but her arrival at the flat of Stella and Stanley launches the culminating episode of her life, which is the play.

Students in a group analysis had difficulty finding the inciting incident in Williams's *The Lady of Larkspur Lotion*. There are three characters—the Lady, a Writer, and Mrs. Wire. The scene is a rooming house in the squalid quarter of New Orleans. Mrs. Wire, the landlady, berates and humiliates the Lady because she has not paid the rent. Suddenly the Writer enters the room and joins the battle. Mrs. Wire finally leaves, yelling back a threat through the closed door, and the two derelicts are left to put their worlds back together.

There are many interesting dimensions to this play, but let's deal with just the problems of inciting incident. It turns out that the best statement of the root conflict has the Lady and the Writer vs. Mrs. Wire. But the Writer enters after the conflict has been going on for some time. You cannot make his entrance the inciting incident. Yet, until he enters, one side of the conflict is not complete. It seems muddled.

One solution is that the Writer has been involved from the start. He says he has been listening through the paper-thin walls. Mrs. Wire's disruptive influence has penetrated to him as if he had been in the room all along. Reaching this conclusion has important implications for the director staging the climax in the play. Students in a group analysis will usually propose that when the Writer shoves Mrs. Wire out of the room, the conflict is over. What remains is denouement. But further discussion reveals important parts of the play are yet to come. When Mrs. Wire shouts through the door after her expulsion, it must be clear that her presence is still possessing the room. It will take more than mere doors and walls to shut her out of their lives. This fact of Mrs. Wire's remaining presence can be reinforced by her earlier effect on the Writer in the next room. Now the climax can be clarified as the Writer and the Lady expel the spiritual presence of Mrs. Wire by rebuilding each other's fantasy world.

Placing the inciting incident at the moment Mrs. Wire knocks on the door of the Lady's room adds power to this interpretation. The knock, loud and intrusive, jars and frightens the Lady within, as well as the Writer next door.

The director who has discovered the key moments in the unfolding of an action can carefully design the moments so that they augment each other. The production begins to have unity—the mark of mature artistry. Analysis, therefore, is not just an exercise for the study. It leads to solutions that affect every moment of the production.

Inciting Incident in *Hello Out There*

By analyzing the primary elements, we have identified the broad outlines of the action in *Hello Out There*. The other significant moments, identified by the secondary elements, will probably now fall into place.

The inciting incident is the opening speech of the play, the Young Man calling out to the world from his lonely cell, "Hello—out there!" The nice juxtaposition of the Girl's echoing his words at the climax creates a sense of fruition, or completeness, which is artistically very satisfying.

Wait a minute! If the play is about the Girl, and the conflict therefore concerns her, how can we say that the conflict begins when she is not even on stage? No matter how nice, it must be consistent with the other parts of the analysis.

That is correct. But she is there, in the shadows listening to the Young Man. The plaintive calls of the Young Man draw her into the episode. One director might say that the inciting incident should properly be when she answers the call, since this is the first overt indication of the conflict, her first reluctant emergence from the shadows. The solution is a matter of interpretation. Both positions may be acceptable, but they would lead to somewhat different productions.

Discovering the Crisis

The crisis, the moment when the conflict is committed to resolution, is usually the last moment to be identified. The main shape of the action has to be determined before the director can examine the changes of direction within the action flow. The director must strive to understand all she can about the development of the action and how every event in the play relates to the root conflict. The crisis is usually more important in tragedy than in many comedies or melodramas because of the stronger sense of irrevocable commitment to resolution.

Crisis in *Hello Out There*

Hello Out There is fundamentally a melodrama; that is, the characters are not as profound as in tragedy. The Girl is not a tragic character because she is not possessed of a powerful will and a strong commitment from the start of the play. We have discovered that, although the Young Man is a catalyst, the play is about the Girl. The dramatic question of the play is, Will the Girl be saved? When does the conflict posed by this question reach a point where resolution is inevitable? Might they not kill the Young Man and cart his body off while the Girl watches dully, perceiving it as just another in a long succession of incomprehensible disasters? Yes. But this does not happen. The Girl breaks out of her shell as the killers pick up the body. She cries out suddenly, fiercely, "Put him down!" She has made her bid. Under the Young Man's influence, she has lashed out against the world's injustice. The result of her act is that she is slapped and pushed to the floor, where she remains until they have carried the body out and she is alone on the stage.

The placement of the crisis is partly a matter of interpretation by an individual director. But it must be consistent with the other decisions about the action. If the play is about the Girl, then the crisis must be a moment in her struggle. The moment she decides to fight, a resolution is inevitable. That the resolution comes swiftly is a characteristic of melodrama. The Girl's cry of defiance is clearly a high point in the play. We shall call it the crisis. The Girl has committed herself irrevocably to the fray. A resolution is inevitable.

Discovering the Catastrophe

Because the catastrophe is the moment precipitating the climax, we must always look for it immediately preceding the climax. Obviously, the discovery of the catastrophe is keyed to the discovery of the climax. Isolating this moment often helps to illuminate the climax.

Catastrophe in *Hello Out There*

Immediately after the Girl's outburst, she is slapped down. This response to her outburst seems to be the event precipitating the climax. She will either be defeated by this and withdraw into her shell, or she will find some way to withstand the attack and continue her emancipation. In either case, the conflict will be resolved. The next event is the climax.

The catastrophe does not necessarily indicate the nature of the resolution, just that a resolution will now come. In this case, one director might decide that the Girl's whispered speech, "Hello—out—there! Hello—out there!" is the last dying gasp of her frustrated hopes. She has lost.

Preferable, from another point of view, is the conclusion that her speech is the first tentative step on her own toward freeing her spirit. The Young Man has not died in vain. We see a frail little Girl alone on the stage, perhaps in a faint pin spotlight, softly and tentatively demanding her just due from a cruel and insensitive world.

Discovering Character

Having completed the structural analysis of the play and having divided it into cycles of action so that she understands the forces and rhythms at work, the director is ready to lay the groundwork for character analysis. One should always keep in mind, however, that work on character is fundamentally the actor's task. The problems of working with actors in the search for character will be discussed at length in Chapter 4. At this point it suffices to say that we ought not try to discover character independently of the action. The characters are part of a closed system created by the playwright, and what they do is decreed by the action. They grow out of the conflict of mutually opposing motives. The director's job is to clarify the conflict in the minds of the actors and to help them see how their characters' motives come from the play's motive.

The motive statement, as we have mentioned before, must account for everything a character does in a play. Subordinate "purposes," which are usually in a play and which may even be contradictory, are subsumed under the general motive statement.

Character in *Hello Out There*

We shall deal with the two major characters in the play, although the complete analysis would involve all the characters. The Young Man is discovered as the play opens. What does he want? We can look at his purposes to determine if any of them are large enough to encompass all the others and serve as a basic motive or spine. Remembering that wants are always listed in infinitive phrases to clarify their relation to acts, we might list the following wants for the Young Man:

- To get out of prison
- To dispel loneliness
- To use the Girl
- To impress the Girl
- To help the Girl
- To save the Girl
- To save himself
- To convince the Girl to think as he does
- To perpetuate himself

These are some suggestions that might come out of a personal or group analysis. They are obviously not definitive, but they can give direction to further discussion. It seems clear that the Young Man's purposes change during the play. He discovers that the young Girl is being exploited by the same kind of people who are his enemies. As the play goes on, he sees in the Girl a kind of pure possibility. She is innocent and honest. She will accept him for what he says he is. He wants to be with her for what it will do for him. Finally, his innate idealism draws him out of himself. He becomes interested more in saving her than helping himself.

What accounts for all these changing wants? For one thing, each of the wants comes out at a specific moment. As the actor asks, "What do I want to get from or to do to this person at this moment?" the wants emerge. Perhaps the most all-encompassing of those wants suggested is "to perpetuate himself." Each of the other wants could come under this broad one. Even the act of dispelling loneliness by talking to the unseen and unhearing world could be seen as a device to reassure him of his existence, to tell himself to the world, as he does to the Girl later on.

Most importantly, such a motive could account for what happens in the play. The Girl becomes the vehicle for all the levels of self-perpetuation that develop in the play. And, finally, she does perpetuate the Young Man after his death by echoing his words.

At least we have come to the level of a working hypothesis. Under discussion and further analysis, the statement could be altered. Whatever statement is employed, it will have to account for everything the Young Man does in the play. The director can use it to clarify her own thinking and to divert the actor from purposes that run counter to the root action of the play; she may possibly suggest using the analysis process to guide the actor's work on character. But she does not want to impose the analysis on the actors. She should allow the actor the creative freedom to explore possibilities during rehearsal.

It may be difficult, for instance, for the actor playing the Young Man to consider the possibility that the play is about the Girl, that the attention should focus on her. But if this idea is given birth in the preliminary discussions of the play, he may see that the play is much stronger that way and, consequently, his role is also stronger.

What does the Girl want? She has stayed around the jail waiting for him to wake up because, while she was nursing him the night before, he said things in his semiconscious state that touched her. Maybe he said he loved her. In any case, she has deep stirrings from within that she never felt before in this place where she is ridiculed and exploited.

Let us list some possible purposes for the Girl and see if we can fashion a motive out of them:

- To see if he still likes her now that he is conscious
- To talk to him
- To make contact with someone
- To protect herself
- To come alive in a world where her human needs have been denied
- To help the man
- To strike back at her father
- To give herself to something beautiful
- To touch and be touched

All of the preceding statements are dimensions of the Girl's wants. There are, of course, other possibilities and other ways of phrasing the same possibilities. The importance of choosing the proper imagery should not be overlooked. Often a felicitous phrase can work over and over again to stimulate creative responses from the actors.

Of all the preceding phrases, perhaps the one about making contact has the most promise for a working statement of motive. The Girl remains behind to make contact with the Young Man, who seems to be her only hope of contact in her desolate world. As the play progresses, and she is made aware of her own worth by seeing herself through the eyes of the Young Man, her demands take on additional nuances. The possibility of the whole world is opening up to her.

At the end, deprived of the Young Man, she still utters her cry to the world. She has been changed by her encounter with the Young Man, but her motive is still to make contact. Now, however, she understands it in a larger context. Now she addresses her plea to the whole world. Keeping in mind this larger meaning for the word *con-tact*, perhaps we could say that her motive is "to make contact."

Here again we have just fashioned a working hypothesis to clarify our thinking. The final statement will be worked out by the actress, with the director's help.

The preceding analysis of *Hello Out There* is summarized in the play analysis form in Figure 2.6.

AVOIDING WORD-BOUND ANALYSES

Students tend to depend too much on the words of the script for locating key moments of the action. A play is more than just words. It is a complete action. Often important moments occur when no words are spoken.

A satisfactory solution in *Riders to the Sea* has the climax occurring when Maurya, kneeling at the foot of her dead son's body, slowly raises her bowed head to look at the heavens. In this moment Maurya has realized her victory over the sea; her subsequent speeches reveal a totally new attitude. The director who takes pains with this silent moment can prepare the audience for the full meaning of Maurya's final elegiac speeches. For example, it is possible to have her black shawl slip back onto her shoulders, revealing a burst of silver hair that wreaths her head like a halo as she looks heavenward.

In Tennessee Williams's *The Unsatisfactory Supper*, one director discovered that the best time for the catastrophe is at the moment when the screen door slams shut and Aunt Rose is left outside during the storm. Focusing on the literal and metaphorical reverberations of the screen door made an eloquent statement of Aunt Rose's rejection. Of course, once the director has made this decision, she must design the moment so that the proper emphasis is placed on it.

FIGURE 2.6   Play analysis form for *Hello Out There*

PLAY ANALYSIS FORM   NAME: _____

PLAY: *HELLO OUT THERE* _____

Do the analysis in the space provided below. Rationale is a
statement of the reason for your decision.

I.   Root conflict: *THE YOUNG MAN VS. THE GIRL.* _____
      Rationale: WHILE THE PLAY SEEMS TO BE ABOUT THE GIRL, THE YOUNG
      MAN INITIATES MOST OF THE ACTION. IT IS A DIFFICULT DECISION, BUT
      MOST OF THE TESTS FOR PROTAGONIST FAVOR THE YOUNG MAN.

II.   Root action: THE YOUNG MAN/ WANTING TO "SAVE" HIMSELF THROUGH THE GIRL,
                   Protagonist   *Protagonist's motive*
      TRIES TO CONVINCE THE GIRL OF HER VALUE AS A HUMAN BEING
      AND LOVER SO SHE WILL SAVE HIM SPIRITUALLY, IF NOT PHYSICALLY, /BUT, HOWEVER
           Protagonist's act   BY PERPETUATING HIM.

      THE GIRL   / WANTING TO OBSERVE AT A DISTANCE THE YOUNG MAN AND LIFE,
      Antagonist   *Antagonist's motive*
      TRIES TO RESIST HIS "BLARNEY" AND ITS DANGEROUS CALL
      FOR HER TO DEMAND SOMETHING FROM LIFE,   /RESULTING IN
           Antagonist's act
      HER MAKING A COMMITMENT TO HIM AND TO LIFE, WHICH
      SURVIVES HIS BRUTAL DEATH.
                   Resolution

III. Climax: *"HELLO-OUT-THERE! HELLO—OUT THERE!"* _____
      Rationale: WE KNOW HOW THE CONFLICT IS RESOLVED WHEN THE GIRL
      SPEAKS OUT USING THE WORDS OF THE YOUNG MAN. HE HAS GIVEN HER
      THE DESIRE FOR SOMETHING MORE. SHE HAS BEGUN TO ASK FOR HER
      DUE.

IV.   Inciting incident: *YOUNG MAN: "HELLO— OUT THERE!"*
      Rationale: THIS FIRST LINE OF THE YOUNG MAN CALLS OUT TO
      SOMEONE, AND THE GIRL, HIDING IN THE SHADOWS, HEARS AND
      RESPONDS. HER CLIMACTIC SPEECH ECHOES THIS SPEECH.

V.   Crisis: *THE GIRL: "PUT HIM DOWN!"* _____
      Rationale: THE GIRL'S DECISION TO FIGHT, TO STAND UP TO THE
      WORLD, SHOWS HER COMMITMENT TO THE FRAY. SOME KIND OF
      RESOLUTION IS INEVITABLE AFTER THIS MOMENT.

VI.   Catastrophe: *THE GIRL IS SLAPPED DOWN.* _____
      Rationale: SHE HAS MADE HER COMMITMENT IN STANDING UP TO THE
      MOB, BUT SHE IS IMMEDIATELY SLAPPED DOWN. HOW WILL SHE REACT
      TO THIS RESPONSE? WILL SHE CRAWL BACK INTO HER SHELL? OR WILL SHE
      CONTINUE HER AWAKENING? THE ANSWER IS THE CLIMAX, CAUSED BY THIS EVENT.

VII. Denouement(?):   *NONE* _____
      Rationale: THE CONFLICT ENDS AS THE PLAY ENDS. THERE IS NOTHING
      LEFT OVER.

KENNETH BURKE'S PENTAD
AND ANALYSIS

Kenneth Burke has developed a set of terms, called the **Pentad**, for use in clarifying and understanding an event.[3] The Pentad can be very helpful in analyzing an especially difficult moment in a play or in assessing a character's situation at a particular point in the action. The terms—act, scene, agent, agency, and purpose—imply five questions: What was done? (act); In what context was it done? (scene); By whom? (agent); With what was it done? (agency); and Why? (purpose).

Answers to these questions can give us some valuable, though rather limited, information about a play. The important point Burke makes is that the terms should be used not in isolation but as **Pentadic ratios**. Pentadic ratios, according to Burke, measure the extent to which one term affects and modifies another. The five terms yield ten ratios:

1. Act ↔ Scene
2. Act ↔ Agent
3. Act ↔ Agency
4. Act ↔ Purpose
5. Scene ↔ Agent
6. Scene ↔ Agency
7. Scene ↔ Purpose
8. Agent ↔ Agency
9. Agent ↔ Purpose
10. Agency ↔ Purpose

Because each side of the ratio interacts with the other, Burke calls this approach *dramatism*.[4] We can see, for instance, that the scene modifies the act if we consider going swimming. It means something quite different if we jump in a pleasant lagoon on a South Seas isle or jump into the icy waters near the Arctic Circle. The reverse is also true. Act affects scene. We think nothing of someone going swimming in the clear warm waters of the South Seas. But we question the sanity of one who dives among the icebergs. Likewise, the scene–agent ratio reflects mutual modification. No one objects if Mrs. Smith takes off her clothes in the women's locker room. But Mr. Smith stripping in the same scene could bring on difficulties with the law.

The agency, the instrument with which the act is performed, helps modify the act. The quality of the agency is directly related to the quality of the agent who uses it. Iago's use of the handkerchief to inflame Othello's jealousy is an example of an innocuous agency given great power by the skill and daring of the agent who uses it. Henry Aaron's baseball bat in the hands of Uncle George would probably yield fewer home runs—unless Uncle George altered the scene dramatically by inserting himself in the lineup of a Little League game.

Purpose is particularly important in evaluating an event. The law recognizes purpose as a mitigating circumstance in determining the seriousness of a crime. An unintentional killing may be classed as manslaughter, which carries lesser punishment. Certainly purpose can dramatically change the nature of an act. Consider the kiss as bestowed by a lover or by Judas Iscariot.

The act–scene and act–agent ratios can be illustrated in *Hello Out There* when we consider the phrase "Hello—out there!" as spoken by the Young Man at the beginning of the play and by the Girl at the end of the play. It is the "same" act, but it is rendered entirely different by the context (scene) and the agent, not to mention the different purpose in each instance of the act. Although it is obvious that the act is different in each case, we can illuminate the nature of the difference by examining the ratios as they apply in each instance.

A director can use the Pentad to illuminate a moment in a play. Hamlet virtually does a Pentadic ratio analysis in the "Now might I do it pat" speech, when he decides not to slay Claudius at prayer.[5] (In Chapter 4, the Pentad will be applied to character analysis.) In Act III, Scene iii, Hamlet says,

> Now might I do it pat, now he is praying,
> And now I'll do't. And so he goes to heaven, . . .

At this point, Hamlet is applying the act–scene ratio. If he does the act of killing while Claudius is at prayer, he will send him to heaven. According to Elizabethan thinking, when a man has just finished prayer, his soul is without sin. Would Hamlet revenge his father by sending his killer to heaven? Hamlet ponders:

> And so am I revenged. That would be scanned:
> A villain kills my father, and for that
> I, his sole son, do this same villain send
> To heaven.
> Oh, this is hire and salary, not revenge.
> He took my father grossly, full of bread,
> With all his crimes broad blown, as flush as May,
> And how his audit stands who knows save heaven?
> . . . And am I then revenged,
> To take him in the purging of his soul,
> When he is fit and seasoned, for his passage?
> No!

Hamlet goes right into the act–purpose ratio. He asks if he will accomplish his purpose by acting now. If Hamlet kills Claudius when he has just been purged of his sins, while Hamlet's father was dispatched without the benefit of cleansing prayer, will Hamlet accomplish his purpose? In answer, Hamlet cries, "No!" How then can the unfavorable act–scene and act–purpose ratios be rectified? Hamlet soliloquizes:

> Up, sword, and know thou a more horrid hent:
> When he is drunk asleep, or in his rage,
> Or in the incestuous pleasure of his bed—
> At gaming, swearing, or about some act
> That has no relish of salvation in't—
> Then trip him, that his heels may kick at Heaven
> And that his soul may be as damned and black
> As Hell, whereto it goes.

Hamlet's decision not to kill Claudius is based on his perception that the act in this scene would not accomplish his purpose. Unfortunately, for Denmark and Hamlet, not to mention several other characters, Hamlet's assessment was based on ignorance of the true situation. In the speech after Hamlet's exit, Claudius says:

> My words fly up, my thoughts remain below.
> Words without thoughts never to Heaven go.

Claudius was unable to pray because of his guilty conscience. Hamlet could have dispatched Claudius without fear of failing in his purpose.

As we see in this example, Pentadic analysis helps us to understand a moment in the scene. The director's task is to discover the necessities lodged in the form, so she can bring them to bear in her design of the production. If she uses the analytical tools provided in this chapter honestly and well, the action will emerge and the play will become her ally in the quest to do a powerful production.

EXERCISES

1. How can analysis help eliminate motion?

2. What is the difference between a "cycle of action" and a "beat"?

3. What is the difference between "action-centered" and "character-centered" analysis? Which is preferable? Why?

4. Give three tests for climax; three for inciting incident. On what are these tests based?

5. How does crisis differ from catastrophe?

6. The Pentad states that the elements of any event are constantly modifying one another. Using this Pentadic premise, show how the terms in each set modify each other: (a) character, motive, essence; (b) inciting incident, crisis, climax; (c) act, scene, agent; (d) motive, purpose, action; (e) root conflict, root action, resolution.

Group Analysis

Select a short one-act play. Each member of the group should prepare an analysis of the script using the *Play Analysis Form* (Figure 2.7). Bring two copies of the analysis to an analysis session. Give one copy to the leader and keep one for reference during discussion.

The purpose of the session is to determine the analysis that best accounts for all the elements in the play. Try to find the point of clash in each moment of the play and then determine how the points add up to a root conflict that accounts for everything in the play. See Figure 2.6, the *Hello Out There* analysis, for an example of a completed analysis. One member (preferably the leader) can put the developing analysis on the board. Members of the group should be willing to change their minds if better ideas are brought up in the discussion.

NOTES

1. For additional distinctions between poetic and rhetoric, see Roland M. Frye, "Rhetoric and Poetry in *Julius Caesar*," *The Quarterly Journal of Speech*, 37, no. 1 (February 1951): 41–48.

2. These terms were suggested by John Howard Lawson in *Theory and Technique of Playwriting* (New York: Hill and Wang, 1960), who adapted them from Aristotelian poetics. In some instances the definitions have been considerably altered.

3. Kenneth Burke, *A Grammar of Motives* (New York: Prentice-Hall, 1945), pp. 15–16.

4. See also John W. Kirk, "Kenneth Burke's Dramatistic Criticism Applied to the Theatre," *Southern Speech Journal* (Spring 1968): 161–77.

5. G. B. Harrison, ed., *Shakespeare: Major Plays and the Sonnets* (New York: Harcourt, Brace and Company, 1948), pp. 633–34.

FIGURE 2.7   Play analysis form

PLAY ANALYSIS FORM   NAME: _____

                                      PLAY: _____

Do the analysis in the space provided below. <u>Rationale</u> is a
statement of the reason for your decision.

I.   Root conflict: _____
        Rationale:

II.   Root action: _____/_____
                      Protagonist   *Protagonist's motive*

        _____/BUT,HOWEVER
                Protagonist's act

        _____/_____
        Antagonist   *Antagonist's motive*

        _____/RESULTING IN
                Antagonist's act

        _____
                        Resolution

III.   Climax: _____
        Rationale:

IV.   Inciting incident: _____
        Rationale:

V.   Crisis: _____
        Rationale:

VI.   Catastrophe: _____
        Rationale:

VII.   Denouement(?): _____
         Rationale:

CHAPTER
3

Action in Time
and Space

THIS CHAPTER is about translating an interpretation of a play into four-dimensional reality, about how to make conflict in action manifest itself in time and space. It develops and applies a visual aesthetics based on the principles discussed in Chapters 1 and 2.

While a director must remain open to contributions by collaborating artists, he should have the production plan firmly in mind before he begins rehearsal. We know, of course, that planning alone does not make a great production. The ability to make a plan come powerfully to fruition is the difference between a good director and a mediocre director. But having a plan based on an understanding of the dynamics of dramatic action is the first requisite for directing a successful production.

DEVELOPING A
PRODUCTION DESIGN

Why worry about having a theory of shaping an action in time and space? Why not just work out the action with the actors in rehearsal? Most theatre people who are eager to direct do not want to spend time at a desk staring at a script, drawing lines or moving figures around a model. Besides, a common belief is that geniuses of the theatre are consumed by divine fire, that their inventions are inspired on the spot during rehearsals. Such is not the case. We may not regard Thomas Edison as an artist, but he showed an understanding of the creative problem when he said, "Genius is one percent inspiration and ninety-nine percent perspiration."

Planning is necessary for successful directing for several compelling reasons. One reason is that working out ideas before rehearsals can save time. Actors, understandably, resent wasting their time re-staging the same scene over and over again. If a director is confused or uncertain about an aspect of a scene, it is much better for him to spend a long night in the study than for the whole cast to rehearse until two in the morning.

Perhaps the most glaring weakness of directors, even experienced ones, is conducting inefficient rehearsals. Most plays can be done in about thirty 3-hour rehearsals. Obviously there are exceptions to this figure, depending on the play and the directorial method. But if rehearsals are efficient, there is no need to rehearse casts far into the night or to spend three months in rehearsal. Wasteful rehearsals deteriorate actor morale. It is no accident that good directors are often blessed with good actors. A well-articulated plan for a play prepares the way for efficient rehearsals and can fire actors to a high level of creative activity.

A second reason for planning is that it can guide a production team to common objectives. If the director has done a conscientious analysis, which has evolved into a plan—a vision—rehearsals should be structured by it. So-called group efforts tend to muddy the vision.

Cast members often have strong ideas even if they know little or nothing about the play. While a director should always leave room in his plan for the actors' input, a production should exhibit the formal discipline characteristic of all works of art.

A third reason is that if a director does not have a clear idea of what he wants from the start, the actors (and the director) are more likely to develop a bad plan, one that they will later find difficult to abandon. Often the sheer weight of involvement of time and people will make a plan virtually impossible to reject. The temptation will be to "patch and fix," but such an approach is not likely to lead to a sound production.

To avoid the embedding of faulty first impressions, the director must come to the cast with a vision that will guide the actors' intuition. Otherwise the director might find it difficult to eliminate a pattern. Embedded patterns may continue to exert influence, sometimes in spite of actors' honest efforts to change.

A fourth reason is perhaps the most important argument of all for careful planning. A well-developed plan will help the director get his vision of the play across to the actors with a minimum of overt "directing." "The best director," English dramatist and novelist Somerset Maugham observed, "is the one who does least."[1]

By designing the movement (**blocking**) patterns prior to rehearsal, the director can free both the actors and himself from design problems, thus allowing him to concentrate on clarifying the action and improving his interaction with the other actors. This pre-designed blocking plan will result in more efficient rehearsals as well as provide a basic design for the production in time and space. Although it can always be adjusted to suit the specific needs of the action as rehearsals progress, the design provides a framework for powerful, well-conceived patterns that will bring out the action imaginatively and forcefully.[2]

A better performance is more likely to result if the director is not constantly interrupting the rehearsal to change this and that. If an actor is creative and gets the right start in developing his role, he should be doing things that are as good as anything the director can suggest.

Well-designed blocking patterns can be very helpful in allowing the director to influence without inhibiting the actor. The director can then assume his proper role of "audience of one."

Probably the most serious argument against designing basic movement patterns before rehearsal is the contention that it inhibits the actors' creative contribution to the production. But the ultimate goal of preblocking is to free the actor.

We ask actors, in realistic drama especially, to be true to life, to behave as if they were "living" the role. But a play is not life. It is a "closed" system, unlike life, which is an "open" system. A person in life is free to concentrate on the action of his life. He is creating it as he goes along. He is the author of his life. The actor on stage, however, is in a different situation. What the actor says, to whom he says it, and when he enters and exits are decreed. When he comes in, in addition to remembering his lines, he has to worry about how far he should come in and where he should be so that his exit will not be awkward. A character is not free. He must act, not as the spirit moves him, but as the author demands.

How do we release the actor from this bondage? How do we approximate the freedom of living, so that the actor can concentrate on the important element—the action?

Ironically, the director starts by constricting the actor's freedom. He provides movement patterns that the actor must learn by rote— just as he learns the playwright's words. If the director does the job properly, the actor soon realizes that the patterns merely form a *mold* for the action. Once he has learned them so they are second nature, he no longer has to worry about where he goes or when. He is free to provide the essence, the "soul" that fills the mold with the special meaning that comes from the action of the play. If, during this stage of free response, the actor makes some alterations in the basic patterns, so much the better. As the actor fills the mold in rehearsals, it finally breaks and allows the performance to expand beyond the confines of its original outline.

Some directors advocate allowing actors to "improvise" their movement patterns during the rehearsal period. This technique can be helpful in training exercises and may even be appropriate for a production under special circumstances. Preplanned blocking, however, is consistent with our philosophy of placing the emphasis on action rather than motion. Once we discover the purpose of a moment, we must design patterns that express that purpose. Randomness, or what we call motion, is not appropriate to artistic effort.

Freedom demands order. There is an old saying that if you put a horse in a pasture without a fence, the horse must be hobbled. But if you put a fence around the pasture, the horse can run free. Every artist needs to learn that even though the raw subject matter of art is chaos, the function of art is to create order and meaning.

The actor's task is to find the roots for each moment of his performance in the action. Most of the things an actor does in response to the action will be confined to a five foot diameter space that surrounds his body. The director's design for blocking should not penetrate that "five-foot space." The director preserves the actor's creative integrity in rehearsal by not invading that space unless the actor requests it, or it becomes absolutely necessary. Actors should not be treated as puppets or automatons.

A successful director creates patterns that will be responsive to the character relationships, that will be appropriate to the broad outlines of the action (the specifics should be left to the actor), and that will express the action clearly and powerfully to the audience. Given these patterns, the actor can concentrate on the essence of his performance: the interaction with the other actors at the point of clash.

A VISUAL AESTHETICS FOR THE THEATRE

What kind of planning should be done before rehearsals begin? Theatre practitioners tend to be so busy they have little time to write down their procedures or to articulate principles of their activity. Indeed, Stanislavsky blazed new trails when he examined closely the way directors and actors work and recorded his findings systematically.

But few have followed up on Stanislavsky's initiative in regard to developing concepts of visualizing the theatrical event. Many contemporary concepts of stage "picturization" are based almost entirely on aesthetic principles borrowed wholesale from other art forms. The work of Alexander Dean, professor and author, on stage composition, although helpful and thorough in its time, employed the principles of painting without adapting them to the dynamic nature of the stage event. As illustrated in Figure 3.1, directors were asked to think of the production as a series of static poses with people grouped in triangles for proper emphasis.

The idea of the stage as a picture frame came to us from Renaissance art theory and prevailed during the seventeenth, eighteenth, and nineteenth centuries. Today theatre architecture has escaped picture frame aesthetics, but staging theory has not changed essentially. We continue to use the old terms and concepts, even though they do not often apply to what we are actually doing.

Basic Dimensions of a Visual Aesthetics

When developing a new visual aesthetics for the theatre, we need to recall what we have already learned about the nature of the theatrical event. First, let us review what the theatrical event is *not*. It is not a painting, two-dimensional and static, relying on illusion for movement and depth. It is not a three-dimensional art form. Nor is it a series of sculptured images that remain stationary while the spectator moves. It is not space-bound or time-bound. The theatrical event penetrates the spectator's space. It may defy ordinary time patterns, even on occasion presenting the past, present, and future simultaneously. A theatre production is a dynamic process, or a flow of events—always moving, constantly happening. It is a continuum with the qualities of fast and slow, even stop and start, which are all controllable aesthetically. Thus time, the fourth dimension, is an important factor in a visual aesthetics for the theatre.

In preceding chapters we have maintained that conflict is the es-

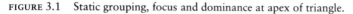

FIGURE 3.1   Static grouping, focus and dominance at apex of triangle.

sence of drama, and we have applied this premise to understanding drama as an art form and to developing a system of analysis. Applied to developing a visual aesthetics for the theatre, this premise leads us to the proposition that the purpose of staging is to clarify and under-score the conflict at every moment. Conflict can take many forms. The give-and-take of a scene requires that each side do its part in making the drama come to life. As shown in Figure 3.2, conflict can be interpreted as a form of cooperation. Without the counterforce, neither side can be maintained. Each side needs the other.

Kenneth Burke said that "form is the arousing and fulfilling of expectations."[3] In drama the conflict must be presented so that our desires for resolution are powerfully aroused. When resolution occurs, it must occur with such impact that the audience is fully satisfied. We are concerned, then, with the ways of representing promise and fulfillment visually. The psychic dimensions of promise must be made manifest in time and space. Relationships among the characters must be clarified visually at all times. The psychic **force field** that always exists between characters is altered subtly by each word or movement. Sometimes the slightest change in a movement pattern can indicate a profound alteration in the force field.

The psychic dimension of physical objects has been noted in other fields. Business psychologists, for example, have called attention to the effect of office furniture arrangement. A visitor may be asked to sit in a chair opposite a desk. The chair is cushioned so that the visitor

FIGURE 3.2   Conflict, in its many forms, is the essence of theatre.

sinks into it. The executive's desk chair, however, is higher. This height disparity, combined with the huge desk before which the visitor sinks, creates a psychic imbalance heavily in favor of the person behind the desk. If the visitor is aware of this situation, he may insist on standing or perhaps sitting on the arm of the chair to equalize the psychic disparity.

On the stage, relationships among characters are heightened because of the perspective afforded the audience. Two important factors in controlling the audience's response to action are **dominance** and **focus**. Dominance refers to the sense of strength or power a character receives from his position on stage in relation to other characters. Generally, the character who is in the upstage position will have a sense of dominance or strength, while the downstage character will feel vulnerable or weak (see Figure 3.3). The audience will perceive the relationship this way as well. An actor forced to attack from a weak position may find the moment impossible to play well without really knowing why.

Dominance also goes to the person who occupies the position of greatest height in the stage space. A standing character normally will

FIGURE 3.3   Dominance: Upstage figure has dominance.

be in a stronger position than a sitting one. Such may not be the case, however, if other psychic factors are in play. The king on the throne, for example, may be flanked by standing attendants who actually increase the sense of his power.

Focus refers to the point of attention of an audience. Although the character who has dominance most often has focus, dominance and focus are not the same thing. In Figure 3.4, the figure with dominance will probably not have focus. The dominant figure is directing her attention to the kneeling figure, which will draw the audience's attention to the same point. The kneeling figure is downstage, facing the audience with his strong "plane" (the face) to the audience. (We will discuss the term *plane* later in this chapter.) These factors—if not offset by other psychic forces—will draw the audience's attention to the kneeling figure; thus he has focus, but he does not have dominance. If the upstage figure in Figure 3.4 should suddenly make a menacing move, the focus would most probably shift to her.

In this discussion of the psychic dimensions of stage space we are isolating elements to clarify and study them, but on stage, of course, everything is happening at once. If all the elements of stage dynamics

FIGURE 3.4　The dominant figure does not have focus.

are not in concert, the result could be unwanted ambiguity or fuzziness. The director must continually be concerned about these matters. They are powerful tools for helping the blocking clarify the action. The psychic dimensions constantly support, or undercut, the relationships demanded by the action. The principles outlined earlier are as applicable to stage design as to directing. The physical stage can no longer be thought of as just a place where events happen. It must be responsive to the demands of the conflict.

A visual aesthetics for the theatre, then, must be based on the essential element of drama: conflict. What is dramatically engaging in a play is people in conflict. Similarly, what engages us in perceiving a visual arrangement is conflict, or, to use another useful term, contrast. The visual impact of a moment depends on how well the clash of forces, or the contrast, is emphasized.

In Chapter 1 we noted that professional football is very popular because the clash of forces is elemental and powerful, and because the point of conflict is sharply focused. Television makes it even more dramatic because the conflict can be emphasized by visual isolation. In replays the moment of clash is reexamined immediately, even in slow motion. TV football extracts conflict—the raw, essential element of the theatrical experience—and concentrates on it.

Conflict, Contrast, and Perception

In a sense we know all things by contrast. We discern their boundaries, and boundaries are the perceived contrast between a thing and that which it is not. If we want somebody to notice something, we make it stand out from its background. The chameleon hides by blending with its background. A person wearing a hat and topcoat and walking in a crowd of similarly dressed people can flow by without being noticed. An event occurring among similar events may pass unnoticed unless something is done to make it stand out.

Contrast is a form of conflict. The more two things are opposites, the more they contrast with one another. We see, therefore, that conflict, the essence of drama, is the principle by which we discern all things. It follows that things that are important in a theatrical production must contrast with their surroundings. Clarity, interest, and impact in the theatre depend on emphasizing the conflict, or contrast, between characters, attitudes, shapes, and events.

In a classroom exercise, a student director staged the confrontation scene between Willy and Biff in *Death of a Salesman*. Willy was on one side of the kitchen table and Biff was on the other. When the moment came for Biff to say, "All right, let's lay it on the line," he was to slap the rubber hose down on the table and confront Willy with the evidence of his cowardice in contemplating suicide. Hap and Linda were also there, standing behind the table. Biff and Willy were eyeball to eyeball across the table and the scene was acted according to plan. Somehow the scene did not come off. Observers could not tell for sure what Biff had done. Just whipping the hose out of the hip pocket and slapping it down did not provide enough emphasis. The movement seemed slight and too quick. The power drained out of the moment, and a sense of unfulfilled promise pervaded the audience.

After some discussion the director decided that Biff should be some distance from the table so that he would have to move several steps to slap the hose down, and that Hap and Linda should stand away from the table, taking positions to the left and to the right of Biff and Willy. Now the scene began to work because the confrontation had greater emphasis. The lengthened movements enlarged and strengthened the moment, and the two antagonists were isolated in the center, not lost in the crowd. By heightening the contrasts—that is, by changing the previous position and by creating a greater distance between the central figures and the background—the director made the scene more dramatic (see Figure 3.5).

Whenever a director wishes to sharpen the outline of, or to *point*, a moment, he increases the contrast between it and its surroundings. When pointing, the director uses the principles discussed in the next section to focus attention on a particular moment in the dynamic flow of the action so that an audience is sure to notice it and more likely to remember it.

FIGURE 3.5 Contrast for clarification. Foreground figures stand out when in contrast with background.

POINT, LINE, AND PLANE

The work of the Swiss painter Paul Klee is relevant to our purpose of developing a visual aesthetics for the theatre. While his field was not the theatre, and although his ideas cannot be borrowed wholesale, we can adapt his concepts to the needs of staging a play. They can help define and illuminate conflict in the four-dimensional structure of a theatrical production. Klee suggests that point, line, and plane are dynamic concepts that have psychic dimensions.[4]

Point

To Klee, **point** is a "cosmic moment," a potential source of power that is made kinetic (or active) by line. It is a moment of promise about to explode into some kind of directionality. This is a useful idea for the stage director. If we think of a character, who is in place and stationary, as a moment bursting with possibilities, we can use the character more effectively to orchestrate the audience's response. Figures on stage, even if they are stationary, are dynamic because they contain the sense of impending movement. The longer a figure possessing focus remains stationary, the greater is the audience's expectation of his moving. A pressure builds for the inevitable movement finally to happen. This dynamic pressure can be used by a director to intensify focus, or to underscore a key moment when the character finally moves.

In a London production of John Mortimer's *A Voyage Round My Father*, the curtain opened to reveal the main character stationary at center stage. He remained there for several seconds as the audience stilled to a hush of expectancy, waiting for that first movement promised by his presence on stage. One of the reasons for the audience's rapt attention was that, as their expectation increased, they began to wish for the movement they knew must eventually come. They were anticipating the potential movement becoming kinetic.

Point also comes into play when a figure moving with other figures on stage stops suddenly. His arrested movement can create a strong effect, reminding us that the stationary figure in contrast with moving figures can be loaded with power to clarify and underscore the action.

Line

Klee defines **line** as "force with directionality." He suggests that there is a purely psychic accompaniment to a line. Promise in line, as in point, projects beyond its actual physical presence. The psychic power of line can be useful to a stage director. As shown in Figure 3.6, when an actor moves, or even indicates an intention to move, he projects a line before him. When moving, he trails a line after him. The space the actor has just vacated is still "possessed" by the actor. It is part of the force field existing between characters that is constantly being altered by what they do and say. How one character deals with another character's line (his "force with directionality") can alter the force field dramatically.

The psychic power of line can also be significant in our perception of dominance, submission, and hostility. If one character projects a line of intentionality and another character cuts that line—even at some distance—a sense of hostility and confrontation occurs. When actors have been made aware of this psychic dimension of line, they become more sensitive to the subtle interplay of relationships that underlies movement.

A character's response to another character's trailing line can suggest aggression and hostility. One example is what we call a **hostile counter**. Most actors have been taught that an important aspect of stage deportment is to **counter** when another actor crosses in front of them. This means that when an actor moves in front of another actor, the latter moves a few steps in the opposite direction and, if he is not to take focus, directs his attention to the actor passing in front.

It should be apparent that the principle of conflict applies here. Two persons moving counter to each other are more dramatically interesting and allow more possibilities for the upstage actor to establish the proper relationship with the downstage actor. However, as shown in Figure 3.7, if the countering actor moves slightly downstage and cuts the downstage actor's trailing line, a sense of hostility is created. The knowledgeable director can use these psychic dimensions of line to develop a subtle awareness in the audience of hostility even when the speeches do not yet reveal it.

FIGURE 3.6 (a) Trailing line. (b) Projected line.

FIGURE 3.7   Cutting trailing line is a hostile counter.

Countering can also be used to control focus. Since the upstage actor has focus when he appears from behind the downstage actor, he may either return the focus by directing his attention to the downstage actor, or he may keep focus by directing his attention away from the actor, continuing his movement beyond the simple counter. By controlling focus in this way, the director underscores important relationships in the action (see Figure 3.8).

In Figure 3.8a, that the upstage figure is lifting a wallet might be apparent to everyone in the audience, however clever the pickpocket. If the lifting of the wallet is of special importance to the action, the director could point it by having it happen at the point of focus, just when the upstage figure emerges from behind the downstage figure. With knowledge of the principles of visual focus, a director can exert almost absolute control of the audience's point of focus.

Plane

Klee defines **plane** as "the tension between two lines."[5] When we perceive a figure as a single entity, we are perceiving its surface as a ten-

FIGURE 3.8 (a) Emerging actor has focus. (b) Counter, giving focus. (c) Counter, taking focus.

FIGURE 3.9   Plane gets power from size or surface interest.

sion created by the lines that bound it. These lines hold the plane intact so that we differentiate it from its surroundings. If we break or remove the lines, the tension is released. The plane ceases to exist.

Much in this concept is of use in the theatre. It not only can help us to discuss principles of staging that we have long used, but it can lead us to new ways of exploiting the actor and setting as plane. If the actor has visual impact as plane—a tension between two lines—then the more of him that is exposed, the greater the tension and the greater the impact on the audience. We have known, for instance, that an actor in profile does not have as much impact as an actor full front or full back. We now have the terminology to explain this phenomenon.

Planarity also has relevance to our concept of stage balance. The more tension or plane that is exposed, the more weight the actor or set piece has. Thus an actor full front will overbalance an actor in profile if both are the same distance from the center stage fulcrum.

Figure 3.9 shows that while a character creates psychic values of line and plane in her relationship with other characters, she also creates psychic values through her individual planarity. As a rule the front plane of a character is much more interesting than the rear. The front plane is accentuated by the face, which contains eyes and other features that reveal inner states of being. Sexual characteristics of a frontal plane can add psychic dimension. Clothing, too, is designed to create greater interest in the frontal plane. Of course, in special cases a rear or profile plane may carry greater psychic impact. In brief, the consideration of relationships on stage must take into account this impact of an individual's plane as well as the individual's interaction with other characters in time and space.

This interaction is affected by characters' positions in the three-dimensional space of the stage. Good stage blocking has three physical dimensions: depth, height, and width. We can think of the actor as a cube, having four "corners." In almost all instances subtly changing relationships are going on among characters. They seldom "face off" in a head-to-head confrontation. Actors should be instructed, therefore, to "play on the corners" of each other, except in moments of balanced confrontation (see Figure 3.10). Thus an actor will approach another actor from a slightly upstage or downstage position, depend-

FIGURE 3.10   "Playing on the corners" provides clarity and interest.

ing on his psychic relationship to the other character. If one character is on the attack, he will usually be using the upstage or dominant planes (unless the attack is so weak or doomed that a downstage plane is appropriate). In any case, the shifts in dominance must always support the demands of the action. If they do not, the sensitive actor will feel frustrated and inadequate, often without knowing why. This one technique leads to interesting and appropriate groupings without the necessity of continually making minor adjustments in the actors' positions. It provides another way to help actors create their own stage relationships without frequent interruption by the director.

Our reactions to the psychic dimensions of stage depth are not fully understood, but the following factors seem valid. The downstage actor is usually subservient, perhaps because he generally has his back partially to the audience. This means that he has less impact than the upstage actor who reveals the more interesting frontal plane. Even if each character has the same amount of planar tension exposed, the front-facing figure will seem to have more because of his "subjective" weighting.

However, if the downstage figure partially covers (stands in front of) the upstage person, the downstage figure will take visual emphasis because so much more of his plane is exposed. But the actor's sense of the situation will often still make the upstage figure dominant. Perhaps this is because as the downstage actor faces the upstage actor he feels more vulnerable with his back to the audience, especially if he is trying to project his personality forcefully.

These psychic dimensions are very important in planning movement. If the director places an actor in a weak position when the action demands a strong attack, the actor's performance will suffer and certainly the audience's perception of the action will be muddied.

Many productions, especially those that tour, must be capable of presentation in several kinds of theatres. A production may play in **arena** (stage in center, surrounded by audience) one night and in three-quarters (audience on three sides) or **proscenium** (framed stage with audience on one side) another. Good three-dimensional staging can readily be adapted to these changing conditions. Margo Jones points out in *Theatre in the Round* that good proscenium directors have little trouble directing in arena because good proscenium blocking is three-dimensional.[6]

THE FOURTH DIMENSION: THE FLOW THEORY

A production does not exist in three dimensions only. The fourth dimension, time, is always present. The dynamics of time as it affects our perception of events on stage, in concert with other elements, plays an important role.

We can illustrate this idea by referring to *Siddhartha*, a novel by the twentieth-century German novelist Hermann Hesse. In his search for the secret of life, the book's main character repeatedly finds himself at a river. As he crosses back and forth on a ferry, he feels deeply that the river holds some clue to the mystery of existence. Finally, at the climactic moment, he wades into the water and realizes that the river is a metaphor for existence. When one is in the river at a given moment, one becomes part of the flow—one is simultaneously in the beginning of the river and at the end. When one is in time at any point, one is part of all time: Each moment of existence has as one of its dimensions all of time—thus, no moment in time is ever complete until all time has run out.

Analogously, according to the **flow theory**, each moment of the flow of action in a play has as one of its dimensions all of the action. A play begins at its source and flows like the river until it reaches its fruition. As we manipulate this flow, we create currents, pressures, eddies, and counterflows that illuminate the action of the play. This concern for time as a controllable dimension of space can help the director to design dynamic blocking.

Thinking in terms of flow leads us to consider new ways to describe the dynamics of a production. One of these is the idea of vacuums. Physicists tell us that nature abhors a vacuum; what they mean is that the pressure of the atmosphere will immediately rush in to fill a vacuum (unless it is protected by a powerful container). Theatre audiences, too, abhor a vacuum—what we might call a psychic vacuum— and they desire that it be filled. A director can make use of psychic vacuums in order to achieve maximum audience involvement. Creating vacuums can bring dramatic intensity to talky or fundamentally static scenes.

Counterflow is related to vacuums. Counterflow enhances conflict by arousing a desire for a certain movement and then causing the character to flow against that desire. Let us imagine this sequence. Aunt Martha in Joseph Kesselring's *Arsenic and Old Lace* picks up a candelabra from the table and establishes her intention of taking it to the sideboard. The audience begins to participate in the expectation of that movement. But she stops to emphasize a point, returning to the table. She creates an interesting flow against the intention, and a vacuum begins to develop in the area of the sideboard. Perhaps she starts again, her projecting "line" sweeping out from her to the sideboard, enhanced now by the desire of the audience. Halfway there she stops again, turns and flings a speech back against the psychic flow, before she continues her cross to the sideboard, fulfilling, at last, the expectation of the audience. If the fulfillment of the audience's expectation comes on a climactic speech, so much the better. Emphasis is achieved here in a dynamic rather than a static way. A production, as we have noted, is a constant flow with highlighting achieved by stopping, starting, accelerating, slowing, or changing direction. Each represents some form of counterflow.

In other words, we point up a moment by using conflict (contrast) to illuminate its boundaries. Vacuums are created out of the flow and enlarged with time; they take into account the four-dimensional nature of the theatrical event. In a well-orchestrated production, psychic demands grow and subside continually as the audience is drawn into the action.

Imbalance: Creating
the Demand for Flow

Imbalance is dramatic because it frustrates the natural desire for balance. In a sense, imbalance creates vacuums, which demand to be filled, thus generating conflict and tension. These vacuums draw members of the audience into the action by causing them to wish for the redress of imbalance. The audience feels frustrated when the wish is denied and rewarded when the wish is granted.

Designing the movement of a play consists in managing imbalance–balance situations in order to create a variety of promise and fulfillment patterns. Failure to promise anything leads to boredom; failure to fulfill promises leads to anger and a sense of bad art.

In one production, a long opening scene that was jammed with exposition was played by two characters who remained comfortably seated the entire time. As the scene progressed, it became apparent that the characters had settled down for a chat and had no intention of moving. In this staging of the scene, the words seemed to lack interest or power. The staging contained few possibilities for making a physical statement in support of what was being said. The director failed to give the actors the opportunity to use the dynamics of flow. The scene was static.

On this point we can learn a good deal from watching television. In most soap operas very little, if anything, is happening. The plot moves with agonizing slowness so that the writers are not sorely taxed to invent daily episodes. All kinds of staging tricks, however, are used to give the illusion that something is happening. The scenario goes something like this. Mrs. Y answers the door. She is startled to see Mrs. X outside. Upon invitation, Mrs. X enters, crossing Mrs. Y, who stares appraisingly after her while the camera comes in for a close-up. Mrs. Y recovers her composure to ask if Mrs. X will have tea. Mrs. X pauses a moment as if lost in thought and then turns suddenly to refuse the offer. (Close-up on her troubled face.) But Mrs. Y insists, saying that she has tea prepared. Mrs. X counters that she is staying only a minute. This goes on, with cameras switching back and forth, in and out, developing a manufactured tension until, when Mrs. X finally accepts a cup of tea, we have the illusion of a climactic moment, as if something important had really happened. The pleased, triumphant smile on Mrs. Y's face explodes in a close-up as she leaves the room. Immediately the camera shifts to a close-up of Mrs. X, who, left alone, allows extreme agitation to show on her face, and we are off again on another manufactured action.

In much the same way that the clever manipulation of the camera in a soap opera can give the illusion of promise and fulfillment, the director of a play can use imbalance–balance on the stage to heighten the action. Of course, the end result of a soap opera is often anger or frustration, because we are promised so much and usually given so little. The stage director often has a stronger action to develop.

The visual and psychological forces in the stage space strive for balance. Balance results when wishes are fulfilled. Balance is non-dramatic because it is static, not demanding anything. Conflict, which arises from the absence of fulfillment, is dramatic (see Figure 3.11). Motive dies when a goal is reached. When the cause of a conflict is removed, the motives that powered the action no longer exist, and the action disappears.

Movement: Managing the Physical and Psychic Dimensions of Flow

The tendency among some directors to create pretty pictures often leads to static, undramatic staging. Scenes ought to be flowing events (except in well prepared contrasting moments) in which each moment emerges from the previous and gives birth to the following moment. This is also true of crowd scenes. Scenes in which people are grouped in obviously posed positions are now regarded as old-fashioned and tend to be static. The director must orchestrate flow, not make pictures. A play, after all, is a happening. The power in staging results from the effective clarification of conflict in the flow of the action.

The quaint, archaic flavor of Russian film director Sergei Eisenstein's classic film *Tsar Alexandre* comes from his having constructed scenes as static compositions, which were then filmed. Usually there is a moving element in the center of the composition, but the background tends to be frozen. When a background element does move, it

FIGURE 3.11   Balance is undramatic; imbalance is dramatic.

is only in a repetitive pattern that falls within the boundaries of Eisenstein's tolerance for the values of the "painting."

Faced with the problem of filming the battle scene (the high point of the film), Eisenstein had to abandon his usual method of composition and use hand-held cameras, which moved in and out of the flow of the action. The difference is startling. Suddenly the film breaks its moorings and the action flows freely and powerfully.

In his early films Eisenstein borrowed the techniques of painting—without sufficient modification—to provide a basic aesthetics for using the camera. But in his later work, he led filmmakers away from this inappropriate aesthetic. Filmmakers have since developed their own set of principles, and at present directors of stage drama can learn more about their business from filmmakers than they can from their own theoreticians.

One key to successful staging, as we have seen, lies in the effective use of elements of movement. The nature of a conflict at any given moment can be pointed up through some aspect of movement. Movement executed, movement threatened but not taken, and movement implied in the context of a situation can help illuminate the conflict.

In a production of William Inge's Bus Stop, a fight between the cowboy, who was played by a lean, six-foot-six actor, and the sheriff, who was played by an equally powerful six-foot-six man, was promised throughout the production. Their size created an awesome spectacle on stage, which the director exploited. He created moments when the impending confrontation was foreshadowed in the movements of the two. For instance, in the play the cowboy wants to leave the restaurant, the scene of the action, but the sheriff does not want him to leave. In this production the sheriff pulled a chair from one of the tables and put his foot on it as he discussed the situation with the cowboy. It was not lost on the cowboy or the audience that the chair was directly in the path to the door and that the sheriff without saying so was implying that if reason did not work, muscle would.

In a production of Hamlet, the director wanted to clarify the sinister nature of Claudius' court by having one of the courtiers constantly spy on Hamlet. This was a nice idea, but it had the potential to be overstated, interfering with the main action of the play. The director used the psychic dimensions of flow to solve the problem very effectively. At the end of the opening court scene, the court, except for one courtier, exited left, trailing after the king. The courtier moved right, against the flow of the crowd, finally emerging alone to make his way to the exit. The audience watched this minor character because of his counterflow without realizing the significance until he paused at the exit (breaking the rhythm established by the rest of the court), turned, and, before closing the door, looked intently at Hamlet, who was alone left center. This counterflow and the breaking of the rhythm at the exit combined to leave a strong impression on the audience.

In addition to being concerned with the actor's movements in relation to other actors, the director must also be concerned with the actor's movements as they reveal individual character traits, psychological as well as physical. We have seen that the actor has value in space as point—a cosmic moment bursting with potentiality. We have also discussed the actor's value as line—the psychic power of projected intentions and the psychic possession of space in his trailing line. Teachers of stage movement theorize that the psychic center of an actor is roughly in the area of his sternum: If an actor moves so that this area of him leads all the rest, he will be more powerful in his physical statements. Just as the director uses the psychic dimensions of movement in planning the staging of a play, so, too, he must make his actors aware of these individual physical dimensions in order for them to improve their nonverbal communication.

A young director was working on *A Streetcar Named Desire*. In trying to make Stanley appear very physical and masculine, he directed him to swagger and to take languorously confident positions on stage. The result unfortunately was ludicrous because his suggestions caused this particular actor to lead with his hips, giving his movements an unmistakably feminine quality in spite of all his efforts to do the opposite. The psychic dimension of his attack on space projected female characteristics. Given this attack, the director's and the actor's efforts were unable to solve the problem.

Movement for the director is the art of managing the physical and psychic flow of a production so that the action—the point of clash—at every moment is clarified and reinforced. If he does this well, he will help his actors to find their characters while remaining true to the action.

BLOCKING: DESIGNING MOVEMENT TO SUPPORT ACTION

The principles of a visual aesthetics discussed here can be applied to a production at any time and at any place. We have seen that the principles apply to planning the production before rehearsal, to solving actor problems in rehearsal, as well as to aiding the work of the designers. Now we will apply these principles to the difficult task of planning the movement for the production **prompt book**. (The prompt book is a notebook containing the script in which the director records his plans for the production.) The purpose of planning the movement, or *blocking*, is to clarify the conflict at every moment in the play. We advocate that this be done prior to rehearsal and recorded in the prompt script for use in rehearsal. (See Chapter 5, pp. 162–165 for an illustration of a prompt book.)

Developing a Floor Plan

Before a director can begin planning his blocking design, he must have a **floor plan**—a plan telling him how much space he has on the floor of the setting and where things are to be placed in that floor space. If a director has not learned how to read floor plans well, he works under a serious handicap. It is most distressing to design a plan for a scene only to discover that the scene will not play in the space provided.

Reading floor plans requires an understanding of scale. How many characters will fit on a four-by-eight platform? Can characters move easily between a couch and a chair? How much space does the average person require? Inexperienced directors try to save space on the blocking diagram by making the character symbols smaller. Unfortunately, this does not work when you finally have to deal with real live people. As a rule of thumb, a grown male measures about eighteen inches across the shoulders. The symbols should be scaled for about eighteen inches at their widest part. (A quarter-inch scale is common for prompt scripts, but scales ranging from three-eighths inch to one-half inch can be used, depending on the size of the stage space.)

In the staging for the moment in *Bus Stop* mentioned earlier, Bo, the cowboy, has just been told by the Sheriff that he cannot take Cherry away if she does not want to go. Bo says that he will do as he likes and makes a step toward the door. The Sheriff pulls out a chair from the table and puts his foot on it. He suggests calmly that Bo think it over. Bo stops as he realizes the Sheriff is between him and the door, and Bo's friend Virge gets off his stool in case there is trouble.

This is a major confrontation. But an experienced director would know that the tentative floor plan and the design shown in Figure 3.12 are giving Bo even more trouble than the Sheriff. Because the exit is up center (up center doors should be avoided unless the advantages are overwhelming), Bo has to play his big moment facing away from the

FIGURE 3.12   Tentative floor plan and blocking for a moment in *Bus Stop*.

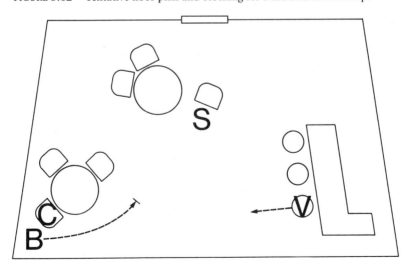

audience. He is upstaged. The actor's face, his most useful instrument for conveying inner emotions, needs to be in view of the audience as much as possible—especially during crucial moments. Also, Bo is in a weak position downstage of the Sheriff. Although we know that the Sheriff is going to beat Bo when they finally come to blows, we do not want to give it away too soon.

Bo is not the only one in trouble here. The Sheriff is too. Bo is partially covering him, and Virge getting off his stool covers him still further. The characters are in each other's **depth space**—the space that downstage actors or objects command in the upstage planes. It fans out in a V-shape, possessing more and more space the further upstage one goes (see Figure 3.13).

A good way to test for depth space is to stand upstage of another person and note how much of the audience you can see. When you can see all of the audience, you are completely out of the other person's depth space. Note also that if you move directly downstage, you can move out of the depth space because you are moving down to the narrower part of the V.

When consulting with a designer on the setting, the director must

FIGURE 3.13   Depth space must be considered when blocking.

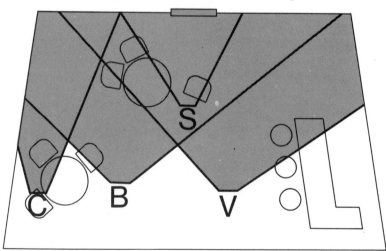

be aware of depth space. If two major pieces of furniture are in each other's depth space, it will be difficult to play a scene using both of them at once. The director must head off such potential design problems in the early planning stage before the designer has begun to build the set.

How can we solve the problems in the scene from *Bus Stop*? First, we need to redesign the floor plan so we get the characters out of each other's depth space. Putting the outside door down right will cause us to rearrange the furniture in the restaurant that serves as a bus stop.

In this revised floor plan shown in Figure 3.14, Bo and the Sheriff are on a nearly horizontal plane. They are more open to the audience, out of each other's depth space. Virge is out of their space, too, if he comes off his stool left. If Bo moves slightly right center on his confrontation with the Sheriff, he opens up Cherry quite a bit so that her reaction to the moment can also be registered by the audience. Though Cherry is still partially covered, at this moment she is not a key figure in the action. However, if the director wanted, she could rise and move down left a few steps, thereby calling attention to her reaction. The director must decide if Cherry is concerned for Bo in spite of

FIGURE 3.14   A new floor plan for *Bus Stop* creates new depth space values.

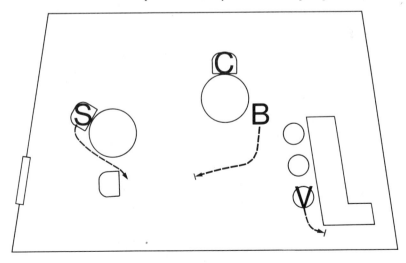

her exasperation with him. Or does the director want to keep the focus sharply on Bo and the Sheriff? If so, Cherry can remain seated and her reaction will not be given focus. While Bo is in a slightly stronger position in the stage space, the Sheriff can offset this somewhat by his relaxed confidence.

Planning the blocking before rehearsals begin gives the director the opportunity to make decisions about how he wants to control the focus and to underscore the action. The director puts to use his knowledge of stage dynamics. The actors, meanwhile, are not burdened by the many concerns of the director. They learn the blocking as they learn the lines. If they find they are enjoying their interactions with the other characters, so much the better for their eventual performance. They may not be fully aware of or understand all the director has done to create their feeling of well-being and power. Good craftsmanship makes art invisible. If the director creates patterns that are responsive to the character relationships in general (not having a dominant character in a weak position, or an attack pattern in a retreat situation), the actors will not be inhibited or hindered by preplanned blocking.

Floor plans provide a shape for an action. They should be designed to create the right spaces and relationships for the particular action of a particular play. The director should look at the high points in the action and make sure that the floor plan supports and enhances these points. That the space is a plausible room, restaurant, or peasant hut should be a secondary consideration. If the director feels the action needs five levels, the designer should provide a five-level peasant hut. Support the action first, then make the space plausible.

Blocking and Conflict

The director can help himself to respond to the conflict in a scene by remembering that most scenes are built on attack–retreat patterns. Often scenes are subtle "chase" scenes. One character is attacking; the other is defending, retreating, or counterattacking. How the characters use the space, the furniture, and each other to attack and retreat makes up the bulk of creative blocking.

The argument has been advanced that there are moments in some plays—love scenes, for instance—that do not have conflict as their essence and that blocking should clarify moments of togetherness as well as conflict. This does indeed raise an interesting point. In keeping with our philosophy, we insist that scenes without conflict are undramatic. Does that mean love scenes are undramatic? On the contrary, love scenes can be very dramatic, if the director realizes that the basis of courtship is conflict. What makes lovers ardent is the limited accessibility of the loved ones. When a motive is fulfilled, it dies. Many people have learned to their sorrow that love diminishes, and perhaps even dies, unless motives of courtship are continually renewed.

One of the greatest love scenes in all of drama is the balcony scene between Romeo and Juliet. But young actors have difficulty understanding why the lovers stand around spouting poetry at each other. If they do not understand the motive for the poetry, the scene will lack conviction and authenticity.

When one aspiring Romeo was asked by the director, "What do you want?" Romeo replied, "To make love with Juliet." And to the same question Juliet responded, "To make love with Romeo."

"Fine," said the director, "go to it. Don't bother with all the poetry nonsense. We'll do an improv that gets right to the heart of the matter. I mean, if both of you want the same thing, it's silly to stand around talking."

This remark left the actors confused. Finally, Romeo suggested that he could not just grab Juliet. He really loved her and wanted her to love him. Juliet, too, said that she did not want Romeo to think that she was an "easy sexual conquest. This was love, not just a physical encounter." The actors were getting somewhere. They were beginning to understand the frustrations of desire that had to be overcome, to understand why they had to court each other. They had to feel their way emotionally and psychologically in order to make clear how profound and beautiful their passions were. A crude or callous misstep could ruin everything. Both thought the other so beautiful and so pure that they were afraid to give way totally to their physical passion.

Now the actors had the basis to act out a good love scene. Each had to overcome several obstacles to the successful consummation of the eagerly desired union. Each had to let passion out carefully, lest the very power of it should frighten or appall the object of affection. The pure love they felt for each other provided mutually inhibiting motives. Passion and purity warring within them and between them created a powerful source of drama. Each had to subdue the other, to create a willing victim. The dramatic interest in the love scene comes from this struggle.

The important point, then, is that even togetherness, if it is dramatic, must be based on conflict. The director's goal remains the same: to illuminate the conflict at any given moment in the production. Blocking should reveal the psychological conflict of a dramatic moment by manipulating the flow of physical elements in space and time.

Ibsen's Hedda Gabler is a woman who is trapped in a hopeless marriage and forced to deal continually with people she cannot stand. In one production the essence of her dilemma was captured by the blocking. The characters onstage are discussing Hedda as they wait for her to come downstairs for her first entrance. Suddenly Hedda appears, not in the main room, but in a foyer at the foot of the stairs. She is unseen by the other characters, but the audience watches as she stiffens at the prospect of encountering these people. Her whole body contorts as she runs her hands through her hair, pulling it away from her head as though trying to tear it loose. After a moment, she recovers and, reasserting her icy calm, enters the sitting room. The exposition is practically complete with this one physical evocation of the inner Hedda.

The Cherry Orchard, though seldom done effectively, is a superb play with subtle interpersonal relationships. The conflict between the beautiful but ineffectual aristocracy and the efficient but coarse peasant class must be revealed at all times. At one point the characters gather in the garden on a warm spring evening. The sounds and fragrances evoke a mood that causes the characters to stop talking about their problems and to drift into a lovely melancholy reverie. The few gold coins that Luba has left on her lap slip to the ground. The sound of distant music and the fading light of evening make a perfect accompaniment to this scene of arrested beauty.

Then the servant Yasha slips to his knees and, aware that the others are not watching him, snatches up the forgotten coins and slips them into his pocket. His scrambling, in contrast to the serene inactivity of the others, and the distinct impression, lost on Yasha, of his groveling at Luba's feet serve to point out the difference in values and quality of life.

Whatever is demanded by the script in any scene—love, hate, anger, or indifference—should be designed into the movement patterns by the director. The purpose of blocking, after all, is to give physical manifestation to character relationships in each confrontation. If the director does this well, it will stimulate the actors to a deeper understanding of the moment, without the director's further intrusion. Insofar as the director does not do this well in his blocking, changes will have to be made in rehearsal, and the actors may find the blocking patterns troublesome rather than helpful.

Blocking and Arena Staging

The principles of blocking just discussed apply with a few variations to arena staging. Good proscenium staging, as we have noted, is three-dimensional; the actors are playing on the corners. Arena staging should be designed and blocked on the diagonals. While a room on an arena stage may appear to be square or rectangular, the furniture and other set pieces should not be arranged that way. The real arena space is configured on diagonals that extend from the vomitories (entrances). These principles also apply to three-quarter stages, where the downstage areas have spectators on the sides. The point here, as in all staging, is to have a floor plan that will allow the audience to see the actors without the actors getting in each other's way.

In arena staging the actors' depth space extends on stage from the point of view of the audience behind them. The fewer members of the audience located behind the actors, the more open and visible the production will be. In Figure 3.15, we have some severe problems. Because the furniture is related to the "walls" of the space (a perfectly natural thing to do), the actors are working in each other's space. Character A has his back to the audience behind him, and he is covered by Character B from view of people in back of B. Character C is preventing the audience behind him from seeing what is going on between A and B. When the actors relate to the furniture, they are relating poorly to the audience. When they relate to each other, they are also relating poorly to the audience. Let's change the floor plan.

FIGURE 3.15   Arena set configured on the walls of square room.

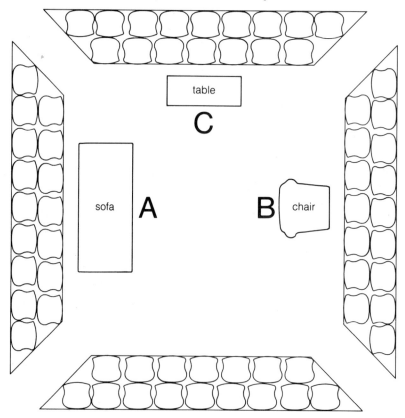

The new floor plan shown in Figure 3.16 has better relationships for the arena stage. The diagonal configurations in a square set will, after brief acquaintance, seem appropriate to the audience and in time, if not at once, to the director. Diagonal configurations look better and better after one adjusts to the idea that the design need not be dictated by the shape of the room.

The dynamics of the floor plan are much improved. The characters are much more open to more of the audience. Playing on the diagonals provides fewer blocks and allows the audience to feel that the action is always being played to them. Some directors chalk or tape diagonal lines across an arena set to help the actors play on the diag-

FIGURE 3.16   Arena set reconfigured on the diagonals.

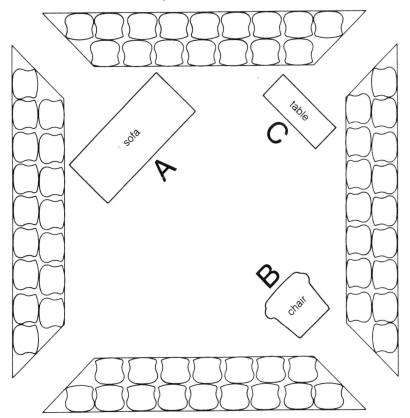

onal during rehearsals. When the actors "play on the corners," as they should in good proscenium theatre blocking, they will be on the diagonals in arena staging.

Blocking and the Actor

Remember that the director, in preparing the blocking, should not intrude upon the creative province of the actor. The director's concern is with broad movement patterns, not with the gestures and nuances of the actor's performance. As a rule of thumb the director should not intrude upon the actor's "five-foot space," a cylinder five feet in diameter that surrounds the actor. The actor carries this space around with him. It is the actor's domain, the area of his creative contribution. The director observes and comments as an "audience of one." Of course, what the director does in his blocking pattern can influence the actor within his space, either stimulating creative responses or hindering them.

Often a director can design movement patterns that will not only stimulate the experienced actor, but may help a neophyte actor find a credible performance. These patterns contribute to the creation of verisimilitude—the illusion of reality—which will help the actors to perform well. In real life, things do not usually happen one at a time. Several things are going on at once. When an actor has so much to do that he has no time for "acting," only for "reacting" to the stimuli that surround him on stage, his performance will become more authentic. The contrived, the cliché, and the self-conscious will disappear.

The stage context can be enriched by finding secondary or even tertiary patterns of activity to highlight key moments in the throughline (main action) of a scene. Weak or inexperienced actors often want to stand on the stage and speak words at each other. They are too troubled by the basic task of saying the right words at the right time to give attention to other details. But verisimilitude demands a complex of activity. Actors must invent, or be given, things to do. These activities can help the inexperienced actor to understand that a performance is not just words but a series of acts.

One director, for instance, found an effective way to use a secondary pattern of activity to add dimension to a domestic quarrel scene. The husband and wife argued as they went through the ritual of preparing the bed for sleeping. Removing the spread required teamwork, a special pattern of activity well rehearsed after years of practice. This evidence of their working together as an efficient team in the midst of an argument underscored the basic strength of their relationship and provided comic comment. At a key moment the ritual of folding the spread brought them face to face, and they became aware of the ironic disparity between their secondary pattern of activity and the main line of the argument.

An actor can use the secondary pattern of activity to point a moment by applying the techniques of contrast and counterflow discussed earlier. If he is lighting a cigarette while carrying on a conversation, for example, he can dramatically arrest the process to clarify and deepen his reaction.

Developing more than two simultaneous patterns of activity usually provides a comic effect. Adding a tertiary pattern (the pot boiling over while the roast is burning and the phone is ringing) calls extra attention to the patterns. When we focus on *motive*, the situation is usually serious. When we focus on *mode*—not what is done, but the way it is done—the effect is usually comic.

These patterns of activity must be appropriate to the action of the scene. They must grow naturally out of the situation or the activity will seem contrived, superimposed on the action.

Inappropriate blocking can divert focus from the point of clash and damage the scene. Early in Ibsen's play *When We Dead Awaken*, the husband and wife are engaged in a scene that reveals their deep frustration and dissatisfaction with each other. The director of a production had the husband buried in his paper, ignoring the wife, while the wife looked out at the far-off mountains to "symbolize" her yearning to be out of the relationship.

The scene was a failure. Neither the actors nor members of the audience could get into it. The activities were supportable rationally, but not theatrically. Ibsen had written a domestic battle scene. The characters needed to do things to each other—to evoke a response and to express their anger and frustration with each other. To do so, they must interact. They cannot ignore one another. The activities provided for the actors led them away from the "space between" and away from pursuing the vital question, "What do I want to get from or to do to this person at this moment?"

We see, then, that the visual aesthetics based on the principles of flow can be applied specifically to the task of clarifying and enhancing the conflict at each moment in the course of a production. The more appropriately these are applied, the more powerfully the director can use his craft to bring out the soul, the inner meaning, of the play in time and space.

The building of a prompt script with movement patterns carefully designed is important to this process. Much can be accomplished by the intelligent design of elements. The design of the action is far too important to be left to the vagaries of inspiration during a blocking rehearsal.

The secret of effective staging is to find ways of illuminating the conflict at every given moment of the action. Anything that intensifies the audience's perception of conflict will make the staging more dramatic. In particular, the intelligent use of point, line, plane, balance, and movement in clarifying conflict will help the director exploit the dramatic potentialities of the play.

EXERCISES

1. Give three reasons for preblocking.

2. We argue that preblocking, while seeming to add restraints to the actors' freedom, actually increases freedom. Explain.

3. The blocking theory is based on the premise that conflict is the essence of theatre. How is this premise related to blocking?

4. The blocking theory is called the "flow theory." Why?

5. Line, point, and plane are related to each other in staging theory. How do they affect each other on the stage?

6. Why is a character upstage of another perceived to be in the stronger position?

7. What has the fourth dimension to do with staging theory?

8. This chapter holds that the basic purpose of blocking is to reveal the action at every moment. Why? How?

GROUP PROJECT

One good way to learn something is to teach it. Each group member should pick one of the following concepts to explain to the other members in a four-minute oral presentation. The concept should be "taught," or explained, as though other members had not heard of it before. The underlying principles should be brought out in each instance. Members can ask questions about each presentation so that misunderstandings can be cleared up. (Members can grade the presentations to test their ability to evaluate "auditions." Making clear notes and rendering judgments from brief presentations are techniques the director must learn.)

Concepts

1. The case for designing movement patterns (blocking) before rehearsals begin. Illustrate.

2. "Flow theory," the dynamics of staging. Illustrate.

3. The role of conflict in a visual aesthetics for the theatre.

4. "Line theory," illustrating the power of the psychic dimension of line.

5. "Plane theory," illustrating the psychic dimensions of stage planes and the surface plane of the actor.

6. The power of imbalance and creating vacuums in staging.

7. The purpose of blocking. Discuss principles and illustrate.

8. Illustrate the difference between dominance and focus, showing the principles involved.

9. Discuss primary, secondary, and tertiary patterns of activity and their role in staging.

10. Discuss the role of counterflow in creating dynamic blocking. Relate it to the basic action–conflict theory.

11. The value of three- and four-dimensional staging.

12. Discuss the principle of "playing on the corners." Illustrate.

13. Discuss "countering," illustrating the principles involved and its value in orchestrating the audience's attention.

14. Discuss blocking and the actor, showing the difference between designing the action and designing a performance. Show why blocking that is responsive to action is helpful and why invading the actor's "five-foot space" is harmful.

NOTES

1. W. Somerset Maugham, *The Summing Up* (New York: New American Library, 1958), p. 94.
2. Even the British director Joan Littlewood apparently used a "prompt book" for her improvisational techniques. See Clive Godwin

and Tom Milne, "Working with Joan," in
Directors on Directing, ed. Toby Cole and
Helen Chinoy (Indianapolis, Ind.: Bobbs-
Merrill, 1963), pp. 390–401.

3. Kenneth Burke, *A Grammar of Motives* (New
   York: Prentice-Hall, 1945), p. 136.

4. Paul Klee, *The Thinking Eye: The Notebooks
   of Paul Klee* (New York: Wittenborn, 1964),
   p. 125.

5. Klee, p. 125.

6. Margo Jones, *Theatre-in-the-Round* (New
   York: Rinehart and Co., 1951), p. 116.

CHAPTER

4

Working with Actors in the Search for Character

THE MOST important of the director's challenges is working with actors. No matter how well the director has designed the action in time and space, the production may fail if she cannot lead the actors to a creative and powerful evocation of the action of the play.

The techniques for working with actors are as varied as the personalities of directors and actors. A director should use techniques that suit her own personality and her own natural way of relating to people. Because of their personal nature, these techniques cannot profitably be codified into rules of behavior.

Not everyone can be a good director. Something in the nature of a particular human being fits her for the task of guiding other human beings to create a coherent statement of a work of art. But talented people who have that special something may fail at directing because their goals are self-destructive. Though specific techniques are personal, goals are based on aesthetic criteria that transcend personal techniques. In this chapter, therefore, we will discuss a director's aesthetic goals in working with actors.

Both the director and the actor are artists who require freedom to pursue their creative objectives. Interference must be minimized. Their interests are conjoined in an effort to make the action of a play come to life in space and time. The precise relationship between the director and actor must be determined by the particular director and actor, and the conditions under which they rehearse. The most competent and experienced actor still needs the director to function as a perceptive, intelligent, and articulate "audience of one." The director may, however, go further and attempt to help the actor overcome obstacles in her development as an actor or in her work on a particular role.

The director has the responsibility for communicating an overall vision of the play to the actors. She may even make changes to accommodate the needs and contributions of the actors; ultimately, however, a single vision must prevail if the artistic product is to have clarity and coherence. The director serves as final arbiter.

Many directors, especially neophytes, are eager to establish their authority early in the actor–director relationship. Taking the title literally, they immediately begin to "direct" the actors. However, the director's first task is to receive, not to give. She should study the actors carefully and come to understand what they are trying to do. She must be extremely receptive in early rehearsals. Once she has done them the courtesy of watching and listening and trying to understand them, she has earned the right to make suggestions.

If the director does her homework and makes her vision of the play clear at the initial cast meetings, she will accomplish two things. She will begin to develop a natural authority with the cast because of her strong commitment to the play, and she will establish ideas about the play that should lead actors in the right direction in early rehearsals without interruption from the director. If she accomplishes these two goals, the director is then free to make contact with the special talents of the actors.

The early receiving period can set the stage for a solid and productive relationship with the actors, who may, if they understand the director's intentions, appreciate the director's efforts to understand them. And if the director has, indeed, come to know the actor's talents, her subsequent direction will be more efficient.

WHERE IS CHARACTER FOUND?

An actor faces an awesome responsibility at the beginning of rehearsal. In a few weeks, she must discover a performance that will capture the essence of the character she is to portray. A good actor soon learns that character cannot be "made." Character must be "found." The question then becomes, Where can character be found? Under what rock will the actor find her character?

An actor must find the wellsprings of character, the inner source that powers what the character says and does in the play. Once the play has been analyzed and understood, the director's primary responsibility is to assist the actor in the quest for character. She must be concerned, therefore, with acting both in theory and practice. She must, in short, know where character is found if she is to help the actor find it.

Nearly 2400 years ago in his *Poetics*, Artistotle said that character is subordinate to action—that is, character exists for the sake of the action, not the reverse. Today, under the influence of psychology, we tend to forget this fundamental truth of the theatre. Actors and directors often get so involved in examining the mysteries of psycho-

"Character is a
motive happening."

logical motivation that they fall into the trap of doing *character-centered*, rather than *action-centered*, productions.

Stanislavsky inadvertently contributed to this tendency by emphasizing the importance of psychological investigation of the inner self in preparing for a role. Although Stanislavsky steadfastly maintained the primacy of action, his interpreters frequently have not. This is not to suggest that introspection is useless. Nor should we cast aside what help the psychologists can give us. The object is to maintain focus on the real source of character in drama—the action.

Character Defined

Everything in our philosophy of play direction has developed from the premise that action, the conflict of mutually opposing motives, is the essence of drama. It follows that the definition of character should relate to this essential premise.

To explain what follows, we must first point out that characters in plays—as well as people in life—do not act without motive. They act only when they want something they do not possess or when they want some condition to be other than it is. To understand a character, we must discover what she does not have that she desires. When we find that, we have found the source of motive.

At the heart of the play is a root conflict that establishes and maintains the frustrations of desires that create motives. Characters do not "create" this conflict; they act in response to it. They are, in a sense, created by it. A necessary precondition for an act is the absence of a desired object. Therefore, if we ask which comes first, the character or the conflict, the answer must be the conflict.

Accordingly, we define character as an individual locus (or center) of motives. We saw in earlier chapters that the quest for the meaning of a play is the quest for motive. We now apply this fundamental principle to character. The quest for character is also the quest for motive. Stanislavsky and most contemporary theorists agree that motive, or "want," is at the center of understanding character. Character is a motive happening.

If the source of character is action, then the place to look for character is in the action. Nearly all contemporary theorists mention the importance of action in drama, but they fail to carry out the implications of accepting the primacy of action. Consequently, actors tend to think of character as a collection of characteristics that accrue around a body and a mind—and, perhaps, a spirit. However, the conflict theory developed in Chapter 1 holds that character is found, not within the individual, but in the clash between that individual and all she encounters. Character is indeed found in the action.

Can this be true? If we are to create lifelike characters on the stage, should we not create them in ways that reflect our conception of human existence? Can we believe that our own essence exists, not within us, but somewhere out in the space between ourselves and the rest of the world?

Some of the most advanced statements in criticism and theology, as well as contemporary physics, have argued that the world is a contingency function, each element modified by every other. All forms, even life itself, have been described as the product of the conflict between order and chaos, or form and disintegration. Form exists as an ideal of order, which struggles to maintain its perfection against the disintegrative forces of entropy.[1]

The theatre is not life, but it is the "mirror of life." If we are to create believable images, should we not reflect the most advanced concepts of what life is? The more we know about how we exist, the better we will be able to mirror it in the theatre.

What is a human being, this form we mirror in our work? The answer to that question will lead us to some basic premises about acting and the search for character.

Living Is the Battle Against Dying

Death can be defined as a void, a nothingness, or the absence of meaning and order. Life is the struggle against death. Encountering the void, life reacts against it. This moment of reaction is the power source of a living being.

A fetus is one with the mother in the womb. At the moment of birth, the child is ejected into a black and meaningless world—a void for her. This encounter with death—with nothingness—creates a profound trauma of rejection. The baby takes a deep breath and cries out. At this moment the child's life as a spiritual creature begins. She commences the desperate struggle to get back to the state of oneness from which she has been ejected.

This absence of the womb, this "fall from grace," creates the primary motivating force in human beings. To escape death becomes an overpowering goal. From the moment of birth we begin to push back the void of meaninglessness, replacing it with the light of perception and understanding. Surrounded by death (the unknown), we struggle to expand the boundaries of life (meaning). The process continues throughout life.[2]

Who we are and the quality of our life depend on the nature of our struggle with "death," the mysteries that surround us. We should look, then, to the struggle occurring in the "space between" us and all that we encounter to determine our character. This may come closer to describing the way people happen than the psychological study of personal characteristics. Certainly the idea that character is found in the space between us and our environment is relevant to the premise that action, the clash of motives, is the source of character in the theatre.

This premise has important implications for our methods of rehearsal and performance. Many of the methods used in the past may have been less productive because they ignored the primacy of action. Much is still to be done in developing new techniques based on the action emphasis and in adapting traditional techniques to it.

The Void, Absence, and Premotive

We already noted that the perception of the void, of the absence of the womb, gives rise to the first act of life. The desire to breathe and to cry is preceded by the confrontation with the void. Nature's abhorrence of a void is seen in a child's reaction to it. Motive is born in the moment of this response to emptiness. Thus a necessary precondition for motive is absence—the absence of something desired. If our acting is to be true to life, we must be "born" into our character just as we are born into life.

> **"Premotive: the profound awareness of the absence of the desired object."**

Paradoxically, the birth trauma, when life begins, is also the perception of the absence of life. The reaction to this first awareness of nothingness, or nonlife, is the vigorous rejection of nothingness, the profound desire to live. The actor needs to find this "life force" in her role; she needs to find the absence that forces her character to act the way she does.

Actors need to understand that birth is not just a moment at the beginning of life. Birth continues throughout life. We constantly encounter death (meaninglessness, mystery), and we constantly react against it. We are "born" continually and we "die" continually as we battle to overcome the unknown and to understand ourselves in the universe. The actor must find the birth of each moment in her performance. She must discover what makes the character want what she does—what causes the motive that leads to each act. She must find the **premotive**, *the profound awareness of the absence of the desired object.*

It is generally believed that acting starts with motive and that poor acting is a product of insufficient concern for motive. We suggest, however, that we have not gone far enough when we stop with motive. Just as a human being lives by reacting against the absence of meaning or fruition, so the stage character must "live" the same way.

Our work with actors suggests a series of steps that will lead to successful acting. There is, obviously, the physical activity, that which is most apparent, or the surface of an event. If an actor does only this, her work will be hollow. Actually, only motion, not action, occurs. Thus we can say that if an actor starts with the physical activity, she plays in motion.

If an actor starts with motive, however, purpose is added to what she does. We understand what she is doing, but it lacks profundity. We are aware that it is a manufactured act. It does not draw us into the event with enough force to register only the event without making us aware of the manner of doing it. Starting with motive, the actor plays in act. We are seeing patterns, not essences. Another step is necessary.

The actor who starts with premotive, or a deep perception of the absence of what she wants, plays in motive. This is the acting of genius, of a performer who sweeps us along with her from essence to essence so that we respond directly to the event, not to the process of her performing an event. In short, the actor who gives the most profound performance must pass through the superficial stages to get to the premotive stage.

A good actor, as Stanislavsky made clear, comes as close as possible to treating the imaginary conditions of the play as if they were real. The premotive helps us to apply the magic *if* in our work. Premotive leads the actor to concentrate on the unfulfilled wants, which impel character, and makes it easier for the actor to animate the given circumstances.

If an actor or character, for example, must deal with the circumstances of her mother's death, should she think of the "fact" of the mother's death or should she think of the loss of the mother's presence—what it means in many intimate ways for her not to be there? The latter approach, as good actors know, offers greater potential for making the circumstances of the situation spring to life.

If on a hot summer afternoon a man rouses himself from his front porch to walk across the street for an ice cream cone, we propose that he does so, not because of the ice cream cone, but because of the absence of it. If someone brought him an ice cream cone, he would not take his walk. He has the ice cream cone, but he does not cross the street because it is the absence of the cone that made him act. If he had just eaten three ice cream cones and was satiated, he would not cross the street because the absence of the ice cream cone would have so little significance it would engender no motive.

The point here has been made before in several contexts: Motive exists in the absence of achieving a goal. When a goal is achieved, motive dies. Thus to concentrate on a goal is to concentrate on the death of motive. But to concentrate on how much one wants the goal, how deeply one feels its absence, is to concentrate on the life force of motive.

Once an actor finds her motive, she must go even further in rehearsal; she must plunge into the absence that powers the moment so that she can act with strength and conviction. She must, in short, move from motive to premotive to find the source of her performance.

Character and Action

To guide her search for premotive, the actor should fashion a preliminary statement of the character's primary motive in the play. The statement, which should derive from the action, may be altered by the rehearsal process. In helping the actor shape the statement, the director suggests the right places to look for the motive. This effort provides a format for later interaction between the director and actor. When the actor has designed a satisfactory motive statement, the director then helps her move beyond it to premotive.

Character, which we have defined as the "locus of motives," can be compared to a locomotive that gets its power from a transformer, which is comparable to action in the play. A play takes the life struggle and converts it into a specific action from which character is powered. Just as the locomotive cannot use power that has not been converted by the transformer, so the character will not function well unless the life force has been channeled through the action of the play. Actors often make the mistake of seeing characters as "life-types" and set out to construct characters from characteristics of these types. Unfortunately, much of the work of the followers of Stanislavsky has encouraged the characteristics approach to character. It may, indeed, be useful for actors to study life-types, so as to increase their general knowledge of the human condition; when creating character, however, they must go to the specific action of a specific play to find it.

If an actor is not plugged in to the power source of a character, she will find frustration at every turn. If the actor has discovered the true power source, however, and has begun to respond to it emotionally, she will be infused with creative energy. She will have taken the first step to banish cliché acting, which is a step toward true artistry.

Finding the Power Source in the Space Between

Since action, the clash of motives, is the essential element of the theatrical event, we propose that character must be found in the action. More specifically, character is found in the space between the character and all that she encounters at each specific moment of her life on stage. Thus the actor cannot find her character in her own mind or emotions entirely. She must leave the haven of her own interior monologue and venture into the world of interaction. As illustrated in Figure 4.1, character is found at the point of clash—at the precise point where the purposes of a character encounter an object or a character in her surroundings. The function of rehearsal is to discover the point of clash for each specific moment. Since this discovery depends on the interaction of two or more characters, actors must move outside themselves; they must leave introspection and go into the space

FIGURE 4.1   Character is found in the space between, at the point of clash.

between to find the truth of each moment of the action that controls the play.

It is difficult to accept the premise that one cannot control absolutely the creative process. But a true artist in any field knows that creating a work of art always requires a humble surrender of the artist's self to the demands of the form. So also in acting, the actor surrenders a portion of herself and realizes that her character must in some measure be created by those she encounters in the scene. Because this self-surrender is not easy, requiring a deliberate embracing of "death"—the absence of control or of knowing—the actor will tend to avoid it. She will try to find the keys in her own mind or in the mind of the character. This will carry her focus offstage, not in the moment. She will not be in the space between and will not be searching for the point of clash. Consequently, she will probably not find the source of power in the scene; she will not directly contact the action core of the scene.

This question of where actors hunt for the "keys" that will inform their performance is vitally important. Actors tend to focus on something safe, something that will not change with each moment of their performance. Left to their own devices, actors will continually shift their focus to offstage keys.

In *Macbeth*, Macduff receives the news that his wife and children have been slain by Macbeth (IV,iii).[3] In the famous scene, he is griefstricken, while Malcolm and others try to use this information to inflame Macduff to be their ally in defeating Macbeth.

MALCOLM: Be comforted.
   Let's make us medicines of our great revenge,
   To cure this deadly grief.
MACDUFF: He has no children. All my pretty ones?
   Did you say all? O Hell-Kite! All?
   What, all my pretty chickens and their dam
   At one fell swoop?

In one particular performance the actor playing Macduff chose to make the line about children refer to Macbeth: "Macbeth has no children." But Macbeth is offstage, and, besides, he may have (or have had) children. (Lady Macbeth says she has nursed babies.) The important point is that the actor is using an offstage key. Macbeth is not there. Malcolm is. This young prince is trying to tell Macduff to turn his grief to revenge. But Malcolm has had no children and is little more than a child himself. The actor playing Macduff can use Malcolm to give depth of meaning to his speech. Malcolm is there; something is going on between them. To key the speech, the actor should use the space between himself and Malcolm, not an absent, intangible Macbeth. Another actor playing Macduff may perhaps be tempted to key his speech on his lost and distant wife and children. But again they are an offstage key. Macduff must wrestle with his grief in front of these men. They, in turn, are trying to use his grief to manipulate him. The keys are onstage.

The director can help actors by encouraging them to shift the focus out of themselves and into the space between. She can do this by asking one fundamental question: What do you want to get from or to do to this person at this moment? This question drives the actors to the heart of the moment and leads them to the point of clash, the power source.

If an actor happens to respond, "I don't want to get anything from or to do anything to anyone at this precise moment," the director can respond, "Fine, let's cut the speech. If action is essential to drama and this moment has no action, let's cut it." When given this option, an actor will usually find a point of clash.

In a love scene an actor might respond to the question by saying, "I want to marry her." The director's response might be, "How can you do that? Where's the minister?" The actor replies, "Well, not this very minute!" This exchange illustrates another common error: The actor is not truly in the moment.

To help actors, the director should ask questions and avoid suggesting options. Telling them what to do may cause the actors to depend on the director for inspiration or may lead to prolonged debates that take up rehearsal time. Asking questions does not usually provoke debate because the director has only stimulated inquiry, not taken a stand on a point. The freshest work comes from the actor's personal reservoir of talent. The director can, however, stimulate the actor's own inspiration by asking questions that get her out of herself and into the space between. In fact, the director will almost always be helpful if she asks one question over and over again: What do you want to get from or to do to this person at this moment?

Actor-Puppet vs.
Actor–Human Being

The actor who has found the right motive source for her character and has gone beyond it to the deep emotional responses of the premotive can lay aside the tricks and stock responses she once thought constituted acting. The performer's **actor-puppet** consists of all the tricks and protective devices learned when she was young and playing roles that were too difficult for her. The **actor–human being** consists of the real living self that has grown into maturity but is still hidden by that old actor-puppet shell that is no longer needed. Once the actor has developed a valid methodology and has been encouraged to believe in it, she can throw off the actorish "husk" and bring herself as a human being to bear on the role.

The director helps the actor find the basic motive of the character, which grows out of the root action. She helps the actor–human being in her battle against the false actor-puppet, and she points the actor toward the emotional riches of the premotive. She must do all this subtly, allowing the actor maximum freedom to find her way without overt interference. Above all, she must make sure that the actor's concept of motive is appropriate to the total production concept. Keeping the actor in the space between will help ensure this.

Burke's Pentad and
Action-Centered Character Study

Kenneth Burke's Pentad of act, scene, agent, agency, and purpose is a particularly useful tool for character analysis.[4] Because it emphasizes the interaction of the five elements, the Pentad continually focuses attention on the action of an event. Used as ratios, the elements modify each other and, in a sense, seek to merge with one another.

The Pentad can be used by the director in her own preliminary character studies and can be used by the actors as a way to clarify their work on character and to communicate with each other and with the director. Pentadic analysis is not a complete methodology. It provides a stimulating point of attack. It can guide but not replace the actor's own human responses to the motives of characters.

Definition of Pentadic
Character Analysis Terms

While the discussion in Chapter 2 introduces the Pentad as a tool for analysis of the play as a whole, here we make specific application of the ratios to character analysis.

Act stands for what a character actually does and says. The mere act of a character is not very illuminating until it is given added dimension and meaning by the impact of the other elements of the Pentad. Sometimes, however, an actor can isolate for close study an act of a character to make certain that it is being given enough value. A listing of what a character does from moment to moment focuses attention on those moments and helps the actor get beyond generalizations to specific motivations. Then each moment can be analyzed in terms of the Pentadic ratios.

Scene is the context in which a character acts. This context includes the situation, the setting, what has gone before, and what is in prospect after. It includes the physical setting (scenery), the time setting, and the psychological dimension. The final nature of the scene is also determined by the impact of the other elements on it. The Girl's cry, "Hello—out there!", as we noted in Chapter 2, has a much different impact at the end of Saroyan's play than the Young Man's cry at the beginning of the play. The events of the play have altered the context, so that the identical words by the girl (a different agent) become a significantly different act. Certainly modifications occur in all the other elements too. None of the ratios exists in isolation.

Agent refers to all the personal characteristics of a character—

her biography, whether she is attractive or ugly, and the other physical traits that are relevant to the action. Under this term, too, are
included psychological characteristics (mean, suspicious, greedy, trust-
ing, and so on). All characteristics are modified by the impact of the
other elements of the Pentad. Thus, a limp, a squint, or another such
trait must be a product of all the Pentadic elements, not just superimposed by the actor because it is an "interesting" characteristic.

In a production of Peter Shaffer's *The Royal Hunt of the Sun*, the
actor playing Pizarro developed a fascinating limp involving the whole
hip area. However, the effort of producing the limp through the whole
production prevented him from giving full energy to the essentials of
the action. A large part of his actor–human being was always required
to maintain the manufactured limp. The result was a weak performance. This performance placed too much emphasis on an agent characteristic at the expense of other elements of the Pentad.

Agency is defined as anything the character uses to accomplish
her purpose. It may be a physical or metaphysical agency—a knife or
an argument, a look or a word. Here again the nature of the agency is
modified by the impact of the other Pentadic elements. As previously
noted, Iago's use of the handkerchief as the instrument of Othello's
downfall is an example of how a seemingly innocuous thing can become a terrible weapon in the hands of a cunning agent.

Purpose applies to the conscious goals of the character: what she
professes to want or what she believes she wants. Purpose must be
clearly distinguished from motive, which is the deep-seated driving
force that makes a character happen the way she does. We have already noted (Chapter 2) that character controls purpose while motive
controls character.

Sometimes purpose runs counter to motive, and it then might be
a means of measuring insanity. A person whose consciously expressed
goals (purposes) that are opposed to her subconscious but controlling
want (motive) would be living in a self-destructive way. The greater
the battle within the self, the more disturbed the character is. All the
purposes of a character must be subsumed under one motive, which
should account for everything the character does and says in a play.

Purpose of Pentadic Analysis:
To Clarify Motive

The quest for character is a quest for motive. The Pentadic ratios provide excellent tools for charting the clash of forces that reveal the basic motive of a character. The convenience of the terms should not, however, lead to their becoming too important. They can help an actor get at essentials of a character. They can help her solve a specific problem with character. But they should never become so important or ritualized that they stifle creativity. Analytical tools can be dangerous when they shift emphasis from goals to methodology. When this happens, art begins to die. The great value of Pentadic analysis is to stimulate the actors and director to creative thinking about character. A secondary value is that a common vocabulary is acquired for talking about character.

The first value needs some explanation. Everyone should approach the elements of the Pentad with as few preconceived ideas as possible. A danger is that an actor will decide what the act is and what the scene is, throw them together as a ratio, and write it down on paper. This denies much of the main value of using the ratios to stimulate new ideas by examining the clash of elements. One should allow for free association. Elements of the Pentad should keep changing value as the analysis progresses. At the end of the process, the actor or director might write out the ratios to help clarify her thinking.

Example of Pentadic Analysis

Here is an example of how the free association phase might proceed and then lead to a written statement in the analysis of the Girl in *Hello Out There*.

What does the Girl do? What is her act in the play? How does the scene impinge upon this?

Specific acts: Girl stays behind in the jail; hides in shadows; answers Young Man; comes out of hiding; expresses her interest in him; believes in him; offers to help him; offers to get him a gun; offers to kill herself if he is taken; says she loves him; leaves to get gun; returns and finds him shot and cries; attacks mob; is thrown to the ground; rises, after all have gone, and says, "Hello—out there." This list of acts is quite short. The actor playing the role might list several more specific acts to help her get deeper into a moment-by-moment analysis.

Scene context: Matador, Texas; lonely, cold, unfriendly, and hostile atmosphere of ridicule and exploitation; Girl in context of "outside, looking in," yearning. New scene element: attractive Young Man spoke warmly to her when she nursed him and says she is beautiful; he says they are a team, an "in crowd" of two.

Girl reacts against scene initially by staying behind; she shows a certain rebelliousness in even speaking to prisoner; she has chance to be part of something with Young Man. Girl also a product of the scene: lethargic, hopeless, an acquiescent victim.

Girl's rejection of empty loneliness of Matador scene turns into acceptance of the alternative context offered by the Young Man: love, acceptance, success.

What act accounts for what the Girl does in the play? The Girl falls in love with a man? No. There is more to the play than that.

What scene impinges upon the act? General statement of context: loneliness, exploitation, yearning.

Act statement: The Girl reaches out for life—at first, tentatively, and then more forcefully.

Act–scene ratio statement: In an atmosphere of loneliness, exploitation, and yearning, the Girl reaches out for life (love?) at first tentatively and then more forcefully.

The process is not finished. Many avenues of investigation stimulated by the process need to be explored. Nevertheless, we already see that numerous aspects of the Girl's motivation have been revealed by an examination of the act–scene ratio.

This approach to one ratio illustrates the function of ratio analysis. As the director or actor examines each of the ten ratios, she will undoubtedly uncover insights that will affect her understanding of a character.

In time it will not be necessary to go through a long, formal analysis. When a person gets accustomed to applying the ratios, the analysis occurs as a mental process without the necessity of much paperwork. Indeed, once one develops the habit of "thinking" ratios, the process goes on continually, almost subconsciously. In the beginning, however, written analyses are helpful. For some they will always be preferable.

A creative person asks more questions than the noncreative person. Pentadic analysis provides a framework for asking many questions about character. If the questioner possesses sensitivity and intelligence, the questions should lead to a deeper understanding of character.

REHEARSALS: THE QUEST FOR MOTIVE

If the director is well prepared for rehearsal, she has made her decision about the basic motive of the play. Her rehearsal task will be to help the performers and other stage artists connected with the production to bring that motive to fruition.

We usually start on a play from the outside and work inward. We encounter first the words of the script. We study these to discover the acts they clothe. Next, we examine the acts to find the motives that lie behind them. Having discovered the motives, we now possess the essence of the play. We then encourage the actors to break through motive to the premotive, so that they can express that essence with power.

The Director's Role in Character Study

The actor's fundamental task in rehearsal is to find the motive of her character and then to search for ways to manifest it in her acting. The director can help the actor accomplish this. In doing so, the director will make certain that the actor does not develop a pattern of motivation that is irrelevant to the action. She will also make certain that an actor's first impressions of a character are appropriate to the character's true function in the play. False first impressions are very difficult to eradicate. Therefore, the director must study the characters before she meets with the actors in rehearsal, even before she has her casting sessions.

The director may write carefully considered character briefs for the use of the actors in auditions. These should suggest motives compatible with the director's vision of the play. They can provide a guide for the actor's initial work with the role during the director's receiving period.

These briefs should be broad enough to allow the actor freedom to do much of her own work on the character. Statements about the characters can serve to stimulate the actors to productive creative work on the role, especially if the imagery is vivid. Elia Kazan's notebooks are excellent examples of the effective use of character study by a director.[5] The notes on Stanley Kowalski from his original production of Williams's *A Streetcar Named Desire* are insightful.

Action Rehearsals

Since we believe that character is found in the clash of motives, then the place to look for character is obviously in the clash. But, traditionally, we have sent actors home to work on their roles in the hope that they would bring ideas back to rehearsal to be tried out. This means that an actor may come to rehearsal with preconceived ideas that she hurls at the other actors' preconceived ideas. Each actor tends to think that she must construct her role by herself and bring it to rehearsal, if not ready-made, at least fairly well formed.

This traditional approach may, if actors experiment in rehearsal and if action shapes characterization, allow roles to be brought in line with the motive of the play. Often, however, the actors' private work is so strong an influence that actors are unable to deal effectively with what is actually happening in a scene. Sometimes the action is realized imperfectly because what finally evolves is a compromise between the actors' private conception of their characters and what the action demands. Improvisation can help—but only when used to illuminate the clash of motives in the action.

In short, many contemporary acting techniques are not well designed to find character in the space between. Actors are not sufficiently open to the action. Their private work may obscure forces that should be discovered at the point of clash.

One effort to remedy this condition is called **action rehearsal**. Actors are requested to respond to the total action situation as honestly as they can. If their response fits the one called for by the script, we may assume they are perceiving action in a way appropriate to the play as a whole. But if their honest response is far from what the script suggests, they are misreading the other actors' roles, misunderstanding or misrepresenting the given circumstances, or misinterpreting the speech. Each of these possibilities requires a different kind of adjustment. But an adjustment in each case must be made in what is happening between characters. The actors should work in the action, not be locked into their own self-centered responses.

If, for example, we have a situation where George comes in on John after an all-night party and performs an act that is indicated by the words "Good morning," the actor who plays John must open himself as fully as possible to this situation and respond. If John replies, "Good morning," because that is precisely what he feels like doing, he is reacting openly to the meeting. But what if John is supposed to say, "Go to hell"? Should the actor say, "Go to hell," even if he really feels like saying, "Good morning"? Of course not. If what is happening between them leads to a pleasant greeting, that is better than to deny the action situation by mindlessly repeating the words of the script or by manufacturing an act internally that does not grow out of the moment.

The actors should review the circumstances and alter each other's purposes until they create a clash that leads to the response the playwright wrote. Maybe John did not consider the given circumstance that George had spent the night with John's girl. If altering the given circumstances in this way leads John to the right response naturally, then the problem is easily solved. But usually the problem is more complex. Perhaps the way George says the line inhibits John's response. Or maybe the actor playing John says that he would not react the way the script demands to what George did. His personal reaction would be different. How? Why? How can the situation be altered so that John can bring his actor—human being into play the way the playwright seems to suggest?

If this approach does nothing else, it indicates that actors should respond honestly to what is actually happening in the scene. They should not manufacture responses without really understanding the action. If they are not responding the way the script suggests, they should alter their perception of the action, not just their reading of the lines.

An actor will sometimes come to a director with the complaint that another actor in the scene is "not giving her enough." She wants the director to intercede. Usually what Actor 1 wants is a different response from what Actor 2 is giving, so Actor 1 ignores what Actor 2 is doing and responds as if Actor 2 were giving the "right" response. However, if Actor 1 is properly in the space between, she must respond to what is actually there. In fact, the best way for Actor 1 to alter the input of Actor 2 is to respond fully to what Actor 2 is doing. If it is wrong, it will probably become apparent. Consequently, the scene evolves as it should through the interaction of the two characters who create each other out of the clash.

Sometimes action rehearsals can be used to find out why puzzling aspects of a scene are there. In an acting class performance of the last meeting between Nina and Treplev in Chekhov's *The Seagull*, the actor playing Nina could not understand why Nina said she was going to leave three times, yet each time came back to say more. It seemed the most common melodramatic technique, like the dying diva in opera.

The solution to the problem was for the actors to respond to the actual action situation. If Nina felt like leaving, she should do so. For several run-throughs Nina would leave when she felt like it. Either the first or second time, she would go, and the scene would stop. Finally, during one run-through the actor playing Treplev began to respond to the situation more fully. As Nina began to leave, she sensed a desperation in Treplev. Was it the actor begging her to let him finish the scene? Or was it the character begging his beloved not to go? The actor playing Nina stopped in the middle of what had, by now, become her exit pattern. Slowly, warmly, she came back, her face full of compassion for this poor child.

At that moment the scene assumed new depths. The actor now understood why she came back and why she said what she did during the rest of the scene. She was not talking about her art alone when she talked about acting; she was talking about his *and* hers. She was trying—and failing—to help a young man who is doomed, just as she is doomed. But she could not give him the one thing he needed—her love. From that moment of understanding the nature of the action, the actor playing Nina gave the scene greater depth. The hint of melodrama evaporated, and moments that had seemed contrived now began to ring true.

In this case the actors kept returning to the clash in the action for inspiration. They put aside theories about motivation, forgot their biographies, and found the truth in their mutual struggle. If actors can learn to rely on the action for inspiration, their actor-puppets peel away and their actor–human beings emerge.

We have suggested ways that action rehearsals can be used to help actors find the soul of a moment. In the first example we saw that actors who respond honestly to the action situation, even if it deviates from the script, may be working more efficiently than actors who repeat a prepared response over and over again just because the script demands it. This open response to the space between can force modifications in the given circumstances and in the actors' perceptions that will lead to the true power source of the scene.

In the Nina–Treplev example, the actors used the action rehearsals to find the truth of a puzzling moment. Playing the clash and allowing for honest interaction led them to find the truth that might have remained obscure if they had continued to force the moment to happen in spite of the promptings of their instincts.

In each case, getting in the space between and responding honestly to what is actually in the interaction are the keys to solving problems. Of course, there are difficulties in getting actors to allow their actor–human beings to respond to the playwright's situation. Much attention needs to be given to developing an uninhibited response that remains focused on action and does not degenerate into personal exhibitionism. Young actors with newly developing craft may need the intervention of a sensitive teacher-director.

These ideas are not presented as startlingly different. Good teachers and directors use some form of them. For example, Stanislavsky's work on the "magic *if*," "given circumstances," and "through line of action" is relevant.[6] Such methodology, however, must be employed conscientiously and consistently and should be directly related to the basic premise that all drama grows out of the clash of mutually opposed motives. Whatever methodology a director uses, the purpose of rehearsal should be to discover character from the action.

One method that has worked with considerable success in rehearsals as well as in acting classes is the evocation exercise (described in the Group Exercises at the end of this chapter). Because each actor does not know what to do but must find that out from the other actor, the participants are forced into the space between. After some experience with this exercise most actors become much more flexible and responsive to the moment. They learn how to find their keys in the action.

Improvisation as a Device
for Character Study

Improvisation is a spontaneous performance; that is, dialogue and movement have not been predetermined. It allows actors to respond directly and honestly to motives. It will often reveal motives that were

not perceived initially. The key to improvisation, as with almost everything in acting, is motive. Without a clearly defined motive, the improvisation will have little value for the actor. When actors begin
"scripting" an improvisation—just saying words without doing acts—
it usually means the conflict has not been clearly established.

In an acting class, the students were given this situation: A woman
and her husband's brother are alone in her home; they have fallen in
love and are facing the consequences of this fact. An improvisation
based on this scene did not work, because the actors had no conflicting motives. They wanted each other, but they had to discover the
need for conflict, even in a love scene. Once they saw that their relationship involved a moral question and several other frustrations of
their passion, the conflict began to emerge. Because each became less
available, even the love motive became stronger.

In another instance, an actor was puzzled about why John Proctor in Arthur Miller's *The Crucible* told his wife about the affair with
Abigail. An improvisation of the confession was staged, and it was
discovered that Proctor confessed because he had to share his guilt. It
was not just "goodness" that moved Proctor to confess; it was his inability to bear the burden of guilt alone. This discovery sharpened
the actor's perception of the role and clarified Proctor's motive for
self-punishment.

In brief, improvisation can help clarify motive and can help an
actor get into the space between. When there is no script in which to
hide, she must listen and respond to her fellow actors. The evocation
exercise is specifically designed for this purpose. The kind of action
rehearsal described earlier is also an improvisation, but it is based on
the script.

If improvisation is used as a rehearsal technique, the director
should make certain that the situations are related to the action of the
play. It can be counterproductive if an actor makes "discoveries" that
are not related to her character's function in the play. Sometimes an
actor will spin out a litany of subtleties and crosscurrents that may be
plausible for a person of the age and background of the character, but

if they are irrelevant to the action, these features will diminish the power of the characterization. This is not to say that an actor should avoid complex detail in her characterization. Each detail, however, should be tested by weighing its relevance to the action.

THE DIRECTOR AS ADVISOR
TO THE CREATIVE ACTOR

Perhaps the greatest problem for a director is the director's commonly perceived role as an authority figure with the power to interfere in the actor's creative process. Most actors have worked with directors who have, at least in the actors' view, hindered their creativity. Creative people tend to distrust authority figures. This may be partly because institutions usually make life difficult for the creative person. Parents, teachers, and directors have provided the young actor's main experience with authority, an experience that has sometimes been unpleasant.

The director must perceive, and work to allay, the fears and suspicions that arise when the actor struggles to create a role. An actor is often insecure in the early stages of work on a role. She may need the director as a scapegoat if the role proves too difficult. In this case she can blame the director for failure to do a role well. The director should understand this and not expect absolute rapport with a cast until the early fears have been dissipated by successful rehearsals. The

"Good criticism always says yes."

actor's ego must be left intact. The director should try to establish her credentials by an in-depth commitment to the play, not by emotional browbeating of the actors. Even being well prepared and fully committed can be frustratingly ineffective because the actors may not have the background or prescience to appreciate the quality of the director's work. Because of this, the director may be tempted to bulldoze the actors. She should resist this as much as possible, although an occasion may arise when the director will be forced to impose some control over an actor for the benefit of the whole cast.

The director should try to foster an environment that allows honest discussion of problems that actors encounter, without bringing into question the actor's worth as an artist. One approach is to make clear to the actors that the director considers them professionals, and respects and even admires their talents. This requires initial effort and thereafter constant reinforcement. Of course, the director should avoid excessive or unwarranted praise. Nothing is more destructive than dishonesty. It should be possible to respect and admire dedicated effort even if the result is not highly polished. No one is ever finished as an actor. The greatest are always learning more about their art.

If an actor is a serious artist, she will be pushing herself to the limits of her creative abilities. She will be operating at the outer edges of her talent, where the going is always rough. She will, therefore, constantly need reassuring. If an attitude of honest, mutual respect is established, it will be much easier to discuss problems openly and constructively.

A Creative Atmosphere

A creative atmosphere is necessary for the best theatre work. What is a creative atmosphere? Simply stated, it exists when the actors have the freedom to fail. Creative activity means bold experiments, some of which will fail.

The way to combat a negative, uncreative attitude is to cultivate the ability to say yes to all things. Art always says yes. Good criticism always says yes. Productions or performers should be criticized in a creative atmosphere as part of a growing, developing process. But the criticism should never say, "That is bad." It should say, "This scene lacked clarity because . . ."; or, "I have been trying to understand why I do not believe your affection for Hamlet is genuine in this scene. Have you considered . . . ?"

When a critic joins any artist in an honest attempt to solve the problem of art, she is saying yes. She is saying yes to the artist by helping her in her work, and she is saying yes to art by joining in the glorious effort to make meaning out of mystery. She is saying yes to the light rather than cursing the darkness.

Communication

In our discussion of the relationship between the director and the actor, we said that the director is responsible for "receiving" the actor in the early rehearsal period. This means that the director has the obligation to watch and to listen carefully in order to make sure she understands what the actor is trying to do. She must make an effort to understand the actor's particular talent. Only then should she offer positive criticism.

But this relationship is complicated because the actor will probably not tell the director when she is misunderstanding her; often she does not even realize it. The communication gap widens inexplicably. Sometimes an actor will do amazing things—things that defy all common sense—because she thinks the director told her to do them. There is nothing more depressing than to find direction coming back in hideous distortions. But it is one of the hazards of the art and ought to be anticipated and dealt with magnanimously.

Finally, the director must never compromise her professional standards. She must continually seek perfection, even while knowing that absolute perfection is unattainable, and she must inspire her actors to make a like commitment. This shared commitment will enhance the communication process.

PREPARING FOR PERFORMANCE

Preparing the whole production for performance is discussed in Chapter 5. Certain attitudes, however, should be instilled in the actors throughout rehearsal to prepare them for a good opening performance. Initially it is important to draw a clear distinction between rehearsal and performance. Rehearsal is for experimentation and discovery. Performance is when the discovered essence of a role is adapted to the changing conditions of each encounter with the audience and with the other performers.

Preparing Roles in Breadth and Depth

Many new directors find that no matter how hard the company works in the rehearsal period, the play does not seem ready by opening night. They feel that if the play were put back into rehearsal after opening night, they could really get the production in shape. Even when the cast seems well prepared, something is missing that only an appearance before an audience can clarify. Unfortunately, in amateur theatre it is seldom possible to put the production back into rehearsal after opening night. Frantic notes and cast meetings may help, but they can confuse the actors. If the production is fundamentally strong, the cast learns from its encounter with audiences, and performances improve. If the production is marginal, the encounter with the audience often disorients the cast, and performances get worse instead of better.

Designing a rehearsal schedule with an early preview for a limited audience and a subsequent week of rehearsal before the public opening is one solution. But this requires a longer rehearsal period and makes insupportable demands on most theatre organizations. The best solution is to design rehearsals so they prepare the actors for the encounter with the audience—so they are ready to let the audience participate in the production.

> "There is an additional
> cast member on opening
> night: the audience."

Such a design, however, is often frustrated by the actors' desire to find the one right way to do things in rehearsal. But there is no one right way to do a role. It must change each night depending on the audience and the way the other actors perform. The performance must remain true to the basic motives of the play, but it must allow for a wide band of possibilities in accomplishing these motives. If the actor develops her role in a very narrow way during rehearsal, the audience's response during a regular performance will often throw her off the path. Once off the path she is working in uncharted territory and at the mercy of an audience that may lead her to gross distortions of her intentions.

When the actor has discovered the basic motive of her character and has found her impulse in premotive, she must use the rehearsal to explore the boundaries of her performance. Given a particular scene or encounter, the actor should explore different approaches to accomplishing the motives of the character. By exceeding the boundaries in rehearsal, the actor finds out where they are. She finds out how far she can go in any direction and still remain faithful to her role. In this way the actor develops the role in breadth as well as depth. She can then handle the unpredictable input of the audience without getting out of the designed limits of her performance. She is strong in performance because she is never forced to travel in strange waters. Perhaps the most important single factor in a strong professional performance—as opposed to a weak, uncertain amateur effort—lies in having rehearsed the cast in breadth as well as depth.

In rehearsal the cast should be reminded constantly that there is an additional cast member who will not appear until opening night—that is, the audience. If the cast does not make room for this additional character, the audience will either be kept out of the performance by the cast, or it will force its way among them and disturb their performance. Either alternative will lead to a weakened production.

To encourage flexibility, the director can insist that if the actor is doing the same thing more than twice in succession in rehearsal, the actor is not "working" at that moment. Even if she has found what seems the best way to do something, the actor should experiment with other possibilities to clarify the moment and to avoid getting stale with the constant repetition of the same response to a point of clash. Often the actor will find that the assumed best way is not the best after all. By experimenting, she may find an even better response. If not, she can always return to a previously successful response, and she will tend to be much surer in the moment, having investigated other possibilities.

In rehearsal an actor should learn to treat her performance with a certain amount of irreverence. She should be prepared to take a response that pleases her very much and "turn it upside down" just to see what happens. If an actor begins to think of her performance as a sacred ritual, a set of responses that become untouchable, she will become enslaved by the performance instead of becoming master of it.

The actor must develop a sense of trust in her own intuition, an understanding of her own psychic response to the encounter with the action, so that she knows when something feels right. The director can help by encouraging this self-direction and providing evaluation from the audience's point of view. Neither a director nor an audience should determine the actor's performance. The actor must learn to use the input from other actors, the director, and the audience in designing a performance. Ultimately, however, the performance is a personal expression of the actor's intuition and she must bear the consequences of pleasing or displeasing the public.

One aspect of effective directing is developing in actors the attitudes discussed in this section. The goals are clear, but the methodology depends on the complex blend of personalities involved in a rehearsal situation. Each director must find a methodology compatible with her personality, and she must be prepared to adapt the methodology to each actor and each play.

Ensemble: Playing in Context

Ensemble playing is a natural outgrowth of finding character in action and in developing a performance in breadth. Ensemble means that actors are giving and taking from each other. Ensemble playing begins in rehearsal, where the actor seeks her character at the point of clash with the other characters. She listens and watches and, if creative, she is excited and moved to fresh responses throughout rehearsal. Nothing is fully anticipated. Everything is open to possibilities that arise in the moment. A cast that is working well in ensemble may go into an improvisation spontaneously by carrying out the implications of something that happened by chance.

Great acting creates anew each performance. Seasoned actors know they can never repeat a performance. It is gone forever. In ensemble playing the production changes as the actors respond to every nuance of each other's performance, as well as to the reactions of each audience. If the motives have been clearly perceived and rehearsed in breadth as well as depth, the performance will keep its spontaneity and freshness while remaining true to the action.

"Root, Not Result"

The most fundamental principle of directing is encapsulated in this statement, one of the enduring truths taught by Stanislavsky: Directors should direct "root, not result."[7] What he means is that directors should approach actors from the point of view of basic motives rather than the outward manifestations of motive. Directors should not, except when all else fails, give actors a specific line reading or show a precise movement. They should talk about actions, not motions. They should clarify the motive by asking the question "What do you want to get from or to do to this person at this moment?" and let the actors discover the means of expressing the motive. In this way actors maintain their creative integrity, and the chances for a successful performance are enhanced.

"Result" directors can be found everywhere in the theatre, especially in the amateur theatre. Directors who tell actors "what they want" at this or that moment are asking for specific results rather than helping actors find their own personal way of expressing the action. Result directors themselves often do not search for the action. They think theatre is doing speeches and movements. That an inner soul infuses each word and movement of the production has not occurred to many of them. Some result directors are seasoned "professionals." Having directed a show successfully once, they try to repeat the show the same way over and over again. Producers often demand result directing for tours of successful Broadway shows. They ask a young director or former stage manager to reproduce the directing of the original production. Dull and lifeless touring productions result and give theatre a bad name in communities all over America.

Preblocking and the Actor

The arguments in favor of preparing a prompt script containing a design of movement patterns have been presented in Chapter 3. They will be reconsidered here only in regard to the director's relationship to the actor. Most experienced actors appreciate receiving a blocking pattern from a director. They know that when a director has taken the trouble to prepare a prompt script, the prospects increase for successful rehearsals.

The most important value for actors is that preblocking, properly designed, frees them from the unnatural burden of being "open" in a "closed" system. Because actors are not free, as in life, but locked into a form created by the playwright, director, designers, and others, they should welcome a prearranged movement pattern. Once the patterns (blocking and dialogue) are learned, they are free to concentrate on the action, where the essence of their role is to be found.

Actors should try to learn all of the patterns by approximately the tenth or twelfth rehearsal. The blocking and dialogue should first be learned as neutral patterns that will finally be shaped by the encounter with the action of the play. That is to say, the dialogue should not be "performed" in the pattern-learning process. It should be learned as words, which will be given their proper meaning in the action rehearsals that follow. Likewise, the assigned movements should be learned as patterns, which will be infused with meaning and brought to life later in the rehearsals. The actors should be assured that any patterns they find troublesome can be changed in later rehearsals if, after the action has been investigated more thoroughly, the patterns remain troublesome. When actors stop being open to change, they stop rehearsing.

Directors would do well to minimize their interference in the early rehearsals. Much can be said for allowing assistant directors to conduct these rehearsals, but their interference must also be minimized. This leaves the actors free to learn patterns without concern for characterization and action problems.

During this time the director can study the actors closely so that she will understand them better when work on action commences. She should fight against the temptation to interfere when an actor seems headed in the wrong direction. If she thinks the actor is far off base, she may suggest changes to her after a rehearsal session. In this way the director avoids intruding in the actor's first tentative efforts to feel out the role. Most of the things the director may believe are wrong the actor probably also senses are wrong. If the director points these out early in rehearsals, it may exasperate the actor and diminish her eagerness to experiment. The more the actor discovers on her own, the more she will like the role and the greater will be her enthusiasm for the production. Preplanning and preblocking help make this possible.

The director's responsibility to the actor is to provide her with an order that allows her to rehearse unhobbled. This order consists of a plan for the production based on an analysis of the action. It provides a pattern of movement to support the pattern of words appropriate to the meaning of each moment of the play.

The actor will have a better chance of interacting meaningfully with fellow actors if her face is not buried in a text, or if she is not constantly diverted from the point of contact by worrying about where she is standing and when she should move or sit. Thus in pre-planning the director provides the means to free the actor from these concerns so that after about ten pattern rehearsals, she can concentrate entirely on the action. As the actor plunges into the action, she will begin to discover the essence of her performance—the conflict that creates her character. Her early concern with patterns—the words said, the movements made—will fall away like a chrysalis and what remains will be a performance born in the moment, nurtured in the space between, and living in truth.

EXERCISES

1. Where is character found? What has that to do with conflict?

2. What is premotive? How does it differ from motive?

3. What does the space between have to do with acting?

4. We suggest in this chapter that an actor should not make up her mind about her character before she comes to rehearsal. Why not?

GROUP EXERCISES

A. Mirror Exercise

The purpose of this activity is to help the participants to understand the space between. Group members pair up two on two. They face each other and begin slowly to mirror each other's movements. Each participant must try to be completely in the space between, neither leading nor following. If the activity is successful, the participants will achieve the sense of being controlled by a power between them that does not come directly from either of them. The leader can pass among them gently altering the input and response until each pair has achieved the space between. Actors who are flexible and responsive will be more successful with this exercise. Those who are not will be helped to discover their own personal barriers to free interaction.

B. Evocation Exercises

These exercises will give actors additional training in learning how to find the space between in an action. They can be used at the beginning of rehearsals as "psychic warmups" to accompany the physical warmups. Two people are chosen from a group. One is sent out of the room while the other is given an act to evoke (for example, to cry, dance, lie down, or tell a joke). The absent actor returns (while the other is sent out) and is given a different act to evoke. The actors then improvise a scene to evoke the required response from each other. As members of the group become proficient, the leader can introduce variations, such as sending in other actors to join the scene at intervals.

The rules of the game require that the actors may not ask for the desired act, may not do the act to encourage imitation, and may not deny or resist any lead offered. Dialogue may be used. As soon as one participant senses what the other wants done, she should do it. It is not a contest, but an exercise in connection and cooperation. As actors gain experience, they soon turn aside from the obvious and create deep and complex interactions.

NOTES

1. See "Action in the Universe," Chapter 1.
2. These ideas are rooted in the phenomenological thought of Sören Kierkegaard, Martin Heidegger, Jean-Paul Sartre, as well as Carlos Castaneda and Kenneth Burke, among others.

3. G. B. Harrison, ed., *Shakespeare: Major Plays and the Sonnets* (New York: Harcourt, Brace and Company, 1948), p. 857.

4. Kenneth Burke, *A Grammar of Motives* (New York: Prentice-Hall, 1945), p. xv. The Pentad is introduced in Chapter 2.

5. Elia Kazan, "Notebook for *A Streetcar Named Desire*," in *Directors on Directing*, ed. Toby Cole and Helen Chinoy (Indianapolis: Bobbs-Merrill, 1963), pp. 364–79.

6. Constantin Stanislavsky, *An Actor Prepares*, trans. Elizabeth Reynolds Hapgood (New York: Theatre Arts Books, 1936).

7. Constantin Stanislavsky, "Creative Work with the Actor," in *Directors on Directing*, ed. Toby Cole and Helen Chinoy (Indianapolis: Bobbs-Merrill, 1963), pp. 109–10.

CHAPTER

5

The Director
and the Production

IN MANY respects the weeks before rehearsal are at least as important as the rehearsal period itself. During this time of early study, the director "finds" the play and develops a vision of the production.

GETTING READY

In some cases, finding the play means literally finding a satisfactory version of the script to be used in the production. Finding a strong dramatic translation of a foreign play or the best edition of any play issued in several editions is the first order of business. Some translations of Molière's plays, for instance, are stodgy and self-consciously literary. Molière was anything but a stuffy academic. Richard Wilbur's delightful rhyming couplets seem to capture the flavor of the original French verse. The punctuation in some editions of Shakespeare is misleading, and the footnotes are sometimes wrong-headed. Careful consideration of the translation or edition at the outset is vitally important to the final success of the production.

Readings

In preparing for later work, a director must begin by reading the script several times. Although he may become impatient with repeated readings because of his eagerness to start designing the production, he can strengthen motivation by giving himself a new task each time. After the first get-acquainted reading, the director might use the second reading to break the play into cycles of action. Finding where each minor conflict begins and ends provides useful information about the play. Comparisons based on the number of these cycles in each act often reveal interesting structural patterns. The director will usually find that this approach to his reading helps him to understand how the author's mind functioned while he was writing the play, why he put things where he did, how he set up the ending of each act, and even, sometimes, what was added for technical effect and what might be extraneous to the root action.

A third reading might be devoted to exploration of some of the problems that emerged from the second reading. How can conflict be clarified in static passages? What confrontations demand special staging conditions? How does the setting help or hinder illumination of the conflict?

A fourth reading might be given over to "what-iffing" the play. In this reading the director can turn things "upside down" to get a fresh perspective. What if the play did not occur in the interior setting suggested? What other settings are possible? What if it were done without intermission or with one more or less than specified? What if the relationships between the characters were supported by expressionistic or other kinds of staging? Sometimes one might even ask, "What if the hero were seen as the villain or vice versa?"

There is always the question, What if certain scenes of the play were eliminated or if others were added? Many other "what-if" questions can be raised about a particular script. Even the most preposterous possibilities can be considered. The idea is not to brutalize the script but to get into a creative frame of mind about it. The director should allow his imagination free rein. He should consider ideas that may seem absurd and, indeed, may later be rejected. These readings

> ## "The director should be in a creative state of 'I don't know.'"

will open his mind to possibilities inherent in the script that may be obscured by first impressions. But the director must never forget his obligations to the script and to the necessities inherent in its form. All ideas must ultimately be validated in the light of a thorough script analysis.

Analysis

After the free-wheeling early readings, the time comes to examine the structure of the play very closely. At this point the director should be in a state of healthy confusion, a creative state of "I don't know," because he has become aware of many questions about the play but few of its answers.

This is a difficult condition for anyone. If the basic life quest is to fill the void with meaning, a person may feel very uneasy in the absence of answers. John Keats, the English poet, referred to this state as one of "negative capability."[1] For him this was a highly creative state of mind. One must be open to all possibilities, but it requires great personal sacrifice. To court death—the absence of meaning (answers)—is very frightening. Most people embrace the nearest answers and hang on for dear life. Those who do, however, are not artists. They are too "safe." The true artist experiences "death" by not knowing until the answers inherent in the form are revealed to him. If the answers do not come, he goes on suffering. As the ancient Greeks tell us, this creative suffering is the way to knowledge and wisdom. The tragedies of Aeschylus, Euripides, and Sophocles give testimony to this artistic credo.

The structural analysis described in Chapter 2 treats a play's form as a unique event. The analysis charts the effects of the beginning of the play on the end and vice versa. Each part has an influence on all other parts. Values are not superimposed on the form from outside. The parts are studied to determine the particular way they combine to make the play. The contemporary term for this approach is **phenomenology**. Phenomenology holds that "everything necessary for understanding (or describing) a form is contained within it."

Jerzy Grotowski, a twentieth-century Polish director, talks about the importance of "contiguity" in guiding the actor's performance. This means that the actor will allow each moment to trigger the next moment. As each moment touches (is contiguous to) the next moment, it ignites it. The actor should work to remove everything that might interfere with this direct experience of the moment (the *via negativa*).[2] The director can use this idea to help him follow the text as each moment happens and to avoid superimposing ideas upon the script.

The more open-minded a director is in his analysis, the more he will be able to see the action for what it is. He will avoid being influenced by preconceived ideas. For this reason it is best to do the analysis before reading published critical commentary on the play. Much criticism tends to be external. It places a play in historical context by comparison and contrast with other plays or conventions of the theatre. Often it categorizes and cubbyholes the play as a completed structure with little concern for its internal relationships. This kind of criticism may fail to capture the special qualities of the play and indeed may not discover what gives it its vitality.

A director is concerned with the particular happening that is the particular play, the way the opening moment moves into and impinges upon the next moment and so on throughout the play. As an artist himself, he is concerned primarily not with the rhetoric of the play— what "lesson" it has for mankind, what politics it espouses, or similar questions. These concerns constitute the play's **theme**. A play may have a theme that is important or valuable to society, but it is not a major concern for the director. He is looking for the structural essence of the play so that he can bring it to life in time and space efficiently and powerfully. After he has grasped essences, he can consider the rhetorical implications of the play. But these implications should never assume primary importance. A director should find the solution to the mystery of the play inside the play.

The director may find it helpful to read literary criticism about a play, but he should do so only after the internal necessities of the play's form are understood. Literary commentary can then be seen in proper relation to basic structural considerations. This is not to suggest that the director should cultivate literary ignorance. What he knows, of course, will not hurt; the way he uses his information may. Proper value must be placed on what is read.

Study of the historical period, for instance, is very useful for period plays. Often aspects of the action cannot be fully understood unless seen from the perspective of the play's historical context. In this connection the role of the **dramaturge** is becoming increasingly important in the contemporary theatre. The dramaturge, who is usually a historian or literary scholar, can research the social and literary conventions of a period and provide study materials for the director, designer, and the cast. Often the dramaturge attends rehearsals and acts as a consultant to the director on matters of style or advises on questions of historical detail. Sometimes the dramaturge contributes to the director's analysis of the script by supplying information about the author, literary conventions, or attitudes of the time.

Arthur Miller suggested that we ignore the autobiographical implications in *After the Fall*. Perhaps so, but that does not mean the director should be ignorant of who the characters represent. Once the director understands as much as he can about the subtle pressures that may have been acting on Miller as he wrote the play, he can decide for himself how important to make them in his treatment of the play.

Style

Style is a major concern for many directors. The term, however, means many, often ambiguous, things to different people and must therefore be used with caution. Directors are aware that a seventeenth-century play ought to look different on stage from a twentieth-century play, and that a certain type of play (a melodrama or a comedy of manners) ought to exhibit distinguishing features. These differences are often referred to as "style."

In this day of "charismatic" directors, a director may want to put the stamp of his own personal "style" on a production. At times directors and actors talk about "stylized" acting. This usually refers to a self-conscious aping of characteristics that someone has decided should mark all productions of a particular era, playwright, or genre. These concerns with style may lead the director to impose features on a play before he has discovered the inherent action, or it could call undue attention to external characteristics that obscure the action.

It seems clear that style has come to mean so many things that it runs the danger of meaning nothing at all. A functional definition of *style*—one we can employ without getting embroiled in all the specialized uses of the term—is necessary. We propose the following: Style is a characteristic way of doing.

If we observe enough instances of the recurrence of something, we may cite these as evidence of a characteristic way of doing. Thus one can speak of a Shakespearean style. But it is important not to let this evidence of similarities obscure the most crucial consideration: the unique way a particular play happens. The production choices should be determined by the action, not some preconceived idea about the "style" of a playwright, an age, or a director. Each play has its own root action. If you discover the particular action of *Tartuffe* and design a production to support it, you will have found an appropriate style for *Tartuffe*.

Script Revision

The director bears an almost sacred responsibility to the script he is interpreting and translating into a four-dimensional medium. Before deciding to change or cut a script, the director should be absolutely certain he has made the effort to understand and appreciate the script as it is written.

Nevertheless, some plays undoubtedly should be cut. The published version of a script often contains material the author could not get into the original production. Cutting should be based on the interpretation that emerges from a careful analysis, which should expose what does not contribute significantly to the development of the action. Even though a scene has good dramatic moments, a director may still decide to cut it if it does not fit tightly into the total structure.

Playwrights, especially inexperienced ones, tend to include more exposition than is necessary. When writing a play, an author has a total experience in mind, but he usually writes about only a segment of that experience. Exposition that concerns a part of the total experience not relevant to the action of the play should be cut. Also, exposition that functions just to reveal character should be closely examined for possible cutting. What a character does in the main action and how he does it should provide adequate information about the character. Cutting character-expanding exposition is difficult, but we must always remember that the theatrical event is based on action. The character will usually be stronger if he "does" himself instead of "talking" himself.

The script, of course, is the heart of the theatrical event, and, as noted earlier, it must be respected by the director. The current idea that a new script is "work in progress" and may be tampered with by everyone who comes in contact with it can be damaging to the play and is ultimately inimical to the best interests of all. Yet, the theatre is a collaborative effort. No playwright, not even Edward Albee (who demands a no-cut agreement in his release statement), ought to insist that every word of his play be in the production script. While we can appreciate the playwright's desire to protect himself from indiscriminate tampering, the realities of stage practice require that the director have some freedom with the script. A good script is never fixed in production. It takes on new life and meaning with each new cast and production staff. Shakespeare's plays have managed to survive quite well thousands of interpretations. His plays remain box office attractions partly because one can see *Hamlet* over and over again without exhausting the possibilities for fresh new angles in a production.

In the contemporary theatre two hours of actual performance

time seems about right. With an intermission or two an audience is released within two-and-a-half hours. Although certain scripts run longer, the director should keep in mind that this comes close to the limit a modern audience ordinarily will endure before time begins to exert a negative influence on the production.

If a director is undecided about whether to cut a scene and the action analysis does not resolve the question, playing time becomes a factor. Most of us have seen productions that might have been successful if they had not dragged so far beyond the fatigue threshold. Often the last ten minutes of a production can sway an audience to a favorable response, even if there have been difficult moments earlier in the play. If the last ten minutes come too late, this fact alone can prevent the audience from fully appreciating the production. Of course, a truly great performance or production may hold an audience spellbound for three or more hours. The acclaimed English production of *Nicholas Nickleby* ran more than eight hours in two sessions.

The New Script

The playwright has an obligation to be well schooled in the demands of the stage, so that he does not invite script tampering by displaying his ignorance of basic stage practice. In recent years, however, many playwrights have come from literary or academic backgrounds. They have not grown up in the theatre as Shakespeare or Molière did, for instance. Out of this condition was born the need for close collaboration—almost coauthorship—between directors and playwrights. T. S. Eliot and Christopher Fry, writers with little or no theatre background, wrote their plays in collaboration with a director. Norman Marshall describes the relationship between T. S. Eliot and his British director, E. Martin Browne:

> A few months later [Eliot] . . . sent Browne the first
> draft of *Murder in the Cathedral*. It was little more
> than a scenario submitted for criticism and advice.
> . . . When writing his next three plays, *Family*

> *Reunion, The Cocktail Party,* and *The Confidential
> Clerk,* Eliot followed much the same procedure, be-
> ginning by sending his producer [director] the first
> rough outline and afterwards constantly seeking his
> advice during the writing of the play.[3]

Elia Kazan's collaboration with Archibald MacLeish in the revising of
J. B. is well documented by MacLeish himself, who gave Kazan much
of the credit for the final version of the play.

While these are examples of productive playwright–director relationships, the current trend in which every neophyte director thinks
of himself as the savior of the play, and whole companies are formed
to "develop" plays probably works against the creation of first-rate
plays. More plays are likely to be diminished or destroyed by this
"committee action" than are improved.

Some directors are reluctant to direct new scripts. They feel inadequate to cope with sailing in uncharted waters. This is particularly
unfortunate in the academic environment, which should be producing
the new plays the commercial theatre is financially unable to produce.

Keeping in mind his responsibilities to the script, even though it
may still be in manuscript form, the director should prepare himself to
be an effective collaborator with the playwright in producing new
scripts. Suggestions for revisions must be determined by the pragmatic
needs of staging. All changes should be based on strong reasons growing out of the demands of the action, not on personal preference or

> # "Stage setting establishes
> # a shape for action."

whim. Analysis isolates the root action of a play and provides a rationale for appropriate changes. Sometimes a joint analysis of the forces at work in the play will help stimulate the playwright to rewrite.

Many times a playwright gets caught up in the plot of his play and does not carefully consider the full significance of the action, even though he is aware that action is driving the plot. Once he realizes what the action is, he may be able to create a better plot to reveal it more effectively.

What the playwright intended when he began to write his play is only peripherally relevant. What he has actually written is the important consideration for the playwright and director. Analysis may reveal that the action of the play is not what the playwright thought. The playwright usually appreciates intelligent criticism, especially if what he has actually produced is better than what he intended.

When writing a play, an author would do well to start with an action, proceed to plot, and then flesh it out with dialogue. Composing in this fashion can give the playwright a surer control of structure. He may also have more freedom in writing dialogue if he has established the boundaries of a confrontation by setting up action cycles first. At least, with the kind of analysis proposed here, the director has a terminology and a critical basis for discussion with the playwright.

DESIGN CONCEPT

A stage setting establishes a physical shape for an action. The setting should grow out of the demands of a particular play. Designers should design not rooms or backyards but spaces for a particular action indicated by an analysis of the play.

When working with designers, the director should develop his blocking concepts around the high points in the action and try to create images that will illuminate the conflict clearly at these points. The designer can then design a basic set for these high points. The lesser moments can be adapted to the basic set. Adaptability, therefore, is an important requisite of a set.

The Director and the Designer

The director must be careful not to intrude into the artistic province of the designer. Early in their meetings, however, the director has the responsibility of making his ideas for the production clear to the designer. If the director can communicate these ideas with vivid imagery that helps clarify his concepts but does not demand specific design elements, he allows the designer to function as an artist in his own right while directing his thinking along ways appropriate to the director's idea of the play's action. The best atmosphere for a successful production allows all the collaborating artists to work freely in response to a well-articulated production concept.

The director, of course, must remain open to suggestions about the controlling concept. Help from any source ought to be appreciated. However, the director must have completed his analysis and must have developed a fairly complete controlling concept so that a clear sense of direction emerges from the design conferences.

Talks should continue until the director is sure that the designers are understanding his ideas. He should give the designers plenty of opportunity to react. Often their responses will give clues to areas of misunderstanding. If frank and open discussion does not resolve disagreements, the director's position should prevail. The production must have a sense of direction. It cannot be tugged one way and then another without adverse affect on the entire collaborative process.

Giving designers something in writing is a good idea. A copy of the analysis on the brief form might be very helpful in clarifying the director's point of view. A written analysis, character description, or design statement gives them a reference to keep the director's ideas from being forgotten during the designers' subsequent work.

The first necessity is a floor plan, so that the prompt book can be started. A floor plan should be ready at least two weeks before rehearsals begin. The vertical treatment does not have to be complete by this time. The need for changes in the plan may arise as the director preblocks the show, but such changes should be minor and kept to a minimum. Of course, exceptions to this pattern may occur. If something does not work, it must be changed. But everybody should try to meet a timetable similar to the following one. Obviously, each theatre or production team will have its own variations on the pattern.

Steps in the Design Process

1. *Script Reading.* By studying the script, the designer anticipates the director's input. He considers the historical and cultural setting, writing style, aesthetics, and practical demands, but he does not develop specific design ideas until after the first conference.

2. *Director Conference.* The designer learns the director's interpretation for the entire production. He discusses the production schedule, the limitations of the physical plant, and like matters and encourages the director to express his feelings about the play.

3. *Preliminary Sketches and Ground Plans.* The designer tries to capture on paper the spirit of the production as to line, color, and mass. A floor plan is devised from preliminary sketches. The director reacts. The director and the designer continue to meet at this stage until they agree on a design concept that reflects the director's intentions and pleases the designer. The director, who should be able to read floor plans, must have a clear idea of space needs; he should note traffic flow patterns and consider the playing of key moments in the script.

4. *Renderings and/or Models.* The renderings may be freehand perspective or drafted in perspective. The model must be drawn to a specific scale. Settings gain in clarity if the model is made with extreme accuracy.

5. *Construction Drawings.* Construction drawings are the blueprints for all parts of the scenery. The plan, side, isometric, section, and exploded view may all be used. A detailed enlarged view may be required. These drawings, which take

considerable time, are drafted to scale with accuracy, neat-
ness, clarity, and completeness.

6. *Painter's Elevations and Color Swatches.* The painter's elevations differ from the earlier drawn elevations. They are to
scale, serving as a guide to the scene shop painters and detail artists. The actual quantitative formulae are given for
colors.

7. *Costume Designs and Makeup Charts.* The costume plates,
prepared by the costume and makeup designers with precise guides and charts for makeup, are to the costume and
makeup department what the construction drawings are to
the carpenters.

8. *Light Plot.* A description of the lighting, including an instrument schedule and a ground plot of areas, is in the light
plot. A complete cue sheet for the production is a must. It
should be prepared by the director and designer before the
first technical rehearsal. The levels can be modified during
the technical rehearsals.

9. *Sound Effects.* The manual and recorded effects are specified. A cue sheet specifying each sound cue is provided.

10. *Properties.* Properties are of two kinds: hand and set.
Objects, such as pictures on a wall, that are not handled
by actors are set props. Objects, such as umbrellas, that
are handled by actors are hand props. Set props may include very large items such as tree stumps, lampposts, and
the like. The production team should make clear which
hand props are the responsibility of the prop department
and which are the province of the costumer.

11. *Final Dress Rehearsals and Costume Parade.* The production is rehearsed to discover any flaws in stagecraft. Cue
schedules are fixed, curtains determined, and other technical matters are tested for the last time.

12. *Rehearsal Performances.* All elements of the production are
in place and operating as they will on opening night. A
small rehearsal performance audience is invited, and the

technical support retreats "behind the scenes" so that crews and technicians can rehearse their functions under performance conditions.

A director would do well to train himself thoroughly in the technical phases of the theatre. A director should know what can, or cannot, be done technically on stage. If he does, he will not ask for the impossible. If a technician says something cannot be done, the director will know if it is truly impossible or just beyond the technician's present means or desires. Directors must be able to speak the language of designers and technicians if they are to be fully efficient in dealing with them.

PROMPT BOOK

The prompt book, or prompt script, is the director's working draft of the script and contains his notes about character, sound, lights, and other matters. It contains the preplanned movement patterns, as well as the list of cues for the stage manager. It contains, in short, the director's complete plan for the production.

In addition to these practical matters, the prompt book serves an important function as the "bible" of the production. It reassures the actors that what the director asks is not a whim, but has been carefully thought out and committed to paper. The prompt book can also serve to remind the director of his original inspirations while he is in the heat of rehearsal.

The prompt book should not be regarded as sacred by the director, even if it seems so to the actors. The director should be prepared to change preplanned patterns and ideas if something better develops in rehearsal. The better the preplanning, however, the fewer the changes.

Blocking should be entered in two forms in the prompt book. It should be written out on the text page and diagramed on the floor plan page (see Figure 5.1). This double-check on the director's intention leaves little chance for confusion. The double-entry system is especially helpful if the assistant director or stage manager is giving the cast the blocking patterns.

The Assistant Director or Stage Manager and the Prompt Book

Many directors may not want to relinquish rehearsals to an assistant. The chance for constant interaction with the cast may be more important in a particular director's mind than the opportunity to observe the actors and learn about them from an "objective" distance. In any case, a director can probably accomplish all of the following major objectives without using an assistant. Prevailing practice may favor less use of an assistant than suggested here. However, allowing the assistant to conduct the pattern rehearsals has several important advantages. Since the assistant will be working with the prompt book, the director is free to study the actors as they learn the blocking patterns and the lines. This receiving period (discussed in Chapter 4) prepares the director for his later work with the actors.

Directors may also find that any attempt to work with the actors in this early period—especially if the actors are expected to learn all patterns by the tenth rehearsal—will seem more like interference than help. Because actors are struggling for lines and movement patterns, it is better if they do not have to worry about character or action problems. Some directors may be tempted to move hastily beyond the actors' present concerns. If the director begins making character suggestions too soon, while the actors are still working on patterns, he may inhibit them, or, even worse, he may impose his interpretation of the role on them and thereby impair their later creative work.

If rehearsals are turned over to an assistant, who has the responsibility for seeing that the actors learn the movement patterns and lines accurately, many of the false starts and downright misinterpretations may be corrected without the director's intervention. If actors have a good idea of the basic motive of the play and their characters, they will usually work out of false starts. Bad moments generally come when they are concentrating on movement and lines rather than action. After about the tenth rehearsal, the cast should begin work on action. By then actors are ready for the director, and the director is ready for them.

Obviously, this method requires that the director have a good assistant director or stage manager. Such an assistant should have had some training and experience in directing and should have a personality forceful enough to keep the cast to the prompt book. If the director explains to the cast that the assistant is a director and will be given great responsibility in the rehearsal period, a strong working relationship between the cast and assistant can be established during the first ten rehearsals. The assistant's position of responsibility forces him to become deeply involved in the production and to become thoroughly knowledgeable about the play's design and intentions. This background makes him a valuable helper in the later stages of rehearsals. Many times an assistant will be able to clear away a communication block between a director and a cast member and contribute to the solution of other problems.

Of course, the director must make certain that an assistant understands his role and that it is consistent with the director's objectives. If the assistant begins interfering with an actor's interpretation in the early rehearsals, serious difficulties can develop. The assistant must have the prompt book before rehearsals begin so that he can study the blocking. Usually the director can intervene if it becomes apparent that the prompt script has been misinterpreted.

A director must always be present in the theatre during the early rehearsals. There may be times when special business will take the director out of the theatre, but these occasions should be few and brief; otherwise, the whole rehearsal process will suffer. Not only will the director be unable to study the cast as he should be doing, but the cast may think the director is not interested in them or that he is shirking his responsibilities.

Learning the dialogue and movement in early rehearsals requires the actor to understand that his lines and blocking are patterns, neutral words, and movements. They will be given their proper signifi-

> ## "Lines and blocking are patterns, given their proper significance when the actor concentrates on action."

cance later when the actor concentrates on the action. The actor must not set such strict patterns that they will resist any change later. If the director suspects that this is happening, he should immediately discuss the matter with the actor.

Some directors have the cast sing or chant lines so they will not develop interpretive patterns while they are learning the lines. Since meter is so important to the proper performance of Shakespeare, a director might do well to have the cast chant the lines in iambic pentameter during the learning process. This will help to instill the feel for the meter that a Shakespearean cast must have if they are to do a credible performance. It will also help the cast avoid making interpretive decisions about the lines before they have had a chance to probe for meaning in rehearsal.

Prompt Book Format

Figures 5.1 and 5.2 show an opened prompt book. The 8½-by-14-inch sheets provide plenty of room for notes. If the script pages are all pasted in the middle of the page, the prompt script will have a huge lump in the middle, which will make it difficult to handle. This can be avoided by pasting the script pages alternately on the left and right side of the 8½-by-14-inch page. It also helps to put cardboard spacers in the binding. Seven or eight of these inch-wide strips punched in the same places the paper is punched will provide enough filler to offset the extra thickness caused by the pasted script pages. Obviously, these are not necessary with scenes or short one-act plays.

The left-hand page (the back of the previous page) contains a dittoed (or photocopied) quarter-inch scale drawing of the set floor plan. As a rule, a quarter-inch scale will allow the whole set to fit on the page. (Smaller sets may use three-eighths-inch or larger scale.) The drawings must be in accurate scale or the blocking will be off. A director must know how to draw and read floor plans in scale. (See the discussion of developing a floor plan in Chapter 3.)

The pages can be fastened on the narrow edge in a legal-size binder. Two scripts are required for pasting (or taping) in the prompt book, unless the script pages are photocopied on the prompt book pages. In the latter case the page can be tacked down and copied on one side, then released and copied on the other side. While considerably more expensive, photocopying makes for a very professional-looking book.

Blocking is done on the right-hand page, either to the right or left of the text depending on which offset is being used. A line is drawn from the instructions to the precise point in the text where the blocking is to occur. The blocking is then diagramed on the facing page copy of the floor plan. Each character is given a symbol, and this symbol is placed on the diagram at the point where the character was at the end of the previous page. The direction of movement is indicated by lines with arrows. A short cross line indicates where a movement stops. Sometimes a character may move three or more times on the same page and have cross lines for the termination point of each movement.

In Figure 5.3 note that Bo (B) has two moves. He breaks away from the confrontation with the Sheriff (S)—after a significant pause—and moves down near Virge. Two cross lines show that Bo stops twice.

Note, too, that no extra marks appear on the diagram. Young directors are often tempted to do a "good" job and add different colors for each character, put numbers on the diagram to correspond to numbers in the text, and so forth. These extra marks get in the way and cause confusion. Colored lines and extra marks also make recording the blocking much more difficult. When a scene goes well, the director is thankful for a simple notation system that keeps the process of

FIGURE 5.1   Sample prompt book.

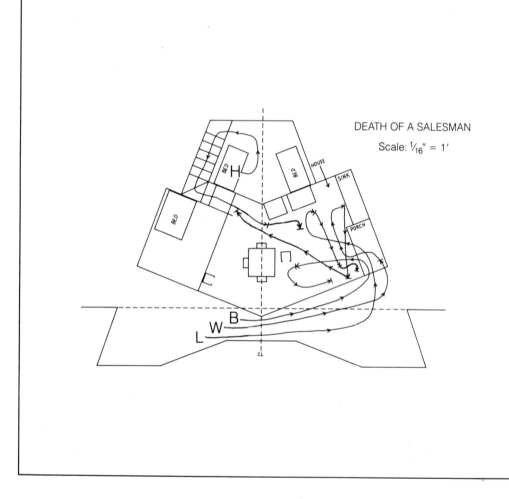

WILLY. (~~Crosses above past BIFF.~~ *More harshly now.*) Don't bother me, will you?

BIFF. (*At* R. *of* WILLY, *holding him by the arms. Shakes* WILLY. LINDA *crosses* D. *to* L. *of* WILLY.) What do you mean, you don't want to see her!? You don't want them calling you yellow, do you? This isn't your fault, it's me, I'm a bum. Now come inside. (WILLY *pulls against him, silent.* LINDA, *behind* WILLY, *puts hands on his arms.*)

LINDA. Did you plant, dear? (~~WILLY *pulls away and enters kitchen. She tries to follow him, but BIFF stops her in front of porch. WILLY crosses, puts hoe by door to bedroom, seeds, flashlight on shelf.*~~

ACTION #38

WILLY GOES IN, PUTTING HOE BY PORCH RAIL OUTSIDE AND GOES TO SINK, PUTS SEEDS AND FLASHLIGHT ON SINK COUNTER — SILENCE — LINDA HURRIES AFTER WILLY TO U.L.C. IN KITCHEN; BIFF FOLLOWS LAST. BIFF SPEAKS AS HE ENTERS DOOR AND X'S TO L. OF TABLE. AFTER BIFF ENTERS, WILLY X'S D.L.; LINDA X TO HIM. HAP DOWN STAIRS TO U.C.

BIFF. (HAPPY *comes downstairs in his shirt sleeves.*) All right, we had it out. I'm going and I'm not writing any more.

LINDA. (~~Going to WILLY, who has crossed to D. R. of kitchen. BIFF enters kitchen, closes door.~~) I think that's the best way, dear. 'Cause there's no use drawing it out, you'll just never get along. (~~She wipes his hand with her handkerchief.~~ WILLY *doesn't respond.* HAPPY *crosses to refrigerator.*)

BIFF. People ask where I am and what I'm doing, you don't know, and you don't care. That way it'll be off your mind and you can start brightening up again. All right? That clears it, doesn't it? (WILLY *is silent and* BIFF *goes to him,* ~~crossing below table.~~) You gonna wish me luck, scout? (*Extends his hand.*) What do you say?

LINDA. (*Above* L. *of* WILLY.) Shake his hand, Willy.

WILLY. (*Turning to her, seething with hurt.*) There's no necessity to mention the pen at all, y' know. . . .

BIFF. (*Gently.*) I've got no appointment, Dad.

WILLY. (*Erupting fiercely.*) He put his arm around . . . ?

BIFF. Dad, you're never going to see what I am, so what's the use of arguing? If I strike oil I'll send you a check, meantime forget I'm alive.

WILLY. (*To* LINDA.) Spite, see?

BIFF. Shake hands, Dad.

WILLY. Not my hand.

HAP COUNTERS BIFF'S X

BIFF. I was hoping not to go this way.

WILLY. Well, this is the way you're going. . . . Good-bye. (BIFF *looks at him a moment, then turns sharply and goes toward* ~~kitchen~~ Stairs.

163

FIGURE 5.2 Sample prompt book, continued. Note that floor plan displays new positions for actors.

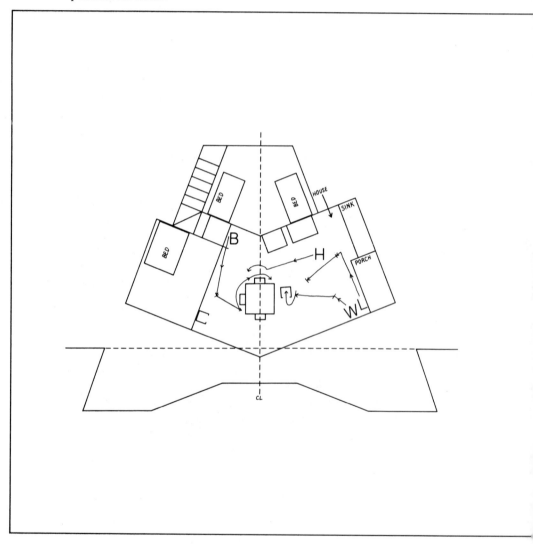

164

door. WILLY *stops him with:*) May you rot in hell if you leave —— WILLY X A FEW STEPS TO L.C. BIFF this house!   FROZEN AT FOOT OF STAIRS.

BIFF. (*Turning.*) Exactly what is it that you want from me!? —— BIFF Xs FEW STEPS D.S.

WILLY. (*~~Crosses to n. of table. LINDA crosses u. R.~~*) I want you to —— WILLY X TO L. OF TABLE; HAP know, on the train, in the mountains, in the valleys, wherever you   COUNTERS L.; LINDA Xs UPSTAGE go, that you cut down your life for spite!   TO U.L.

BIFF. No—no . . .

WILLY. Spite, spite, is the word of your undoing, and when you're down and out remember what did it. When you're rotting somewhere beside the railroad tracks, remember, and don't you dare blame it on me! . . .

BIFF. I'm not blaming it on you!

WILLY. I won't take the rap for this, you hear?

BIFF. That's just what I'm telling you! ———————————— TO R. OF TABLE

WILLY. (*Sinking in chair R. of table.*) You're trying to put a knife in me, don't think I don't know what you're doing!

BIFF. (*Crosses to ~~above~~ table.*) All right, phoney! Then let's lay it on the line. (*He whips rubber tube out of his pocket, puts it on table.*)

LINDA. Biff! (*She moves to grab hose, ~~but BIFF holds it down with~~ —— Xs FEW STEPS C. ~~his hand.~~*)

HAPPY. (*Crosses to ~~L. of~~ BIFF.*)   u.c.   You crazy!!

BIFF. Leave it there! Don't move it! (LINDA *above* R. *of* WILLY, *puts her arms around him.*)

WILLY. (*Doesn't look at it.*) What is that?

BIFF. You know goddamn well what that is.

WILLY. (*Caged, wanting to escape.*) I never saw that.

BIFF. You saw it, the mice didn't bring it into the cellar! What is this supposed to do, make a hero out of you? This supposed to make me sorry for you?

WILLY. Never heard of it.

BIFF. There'll be no pity for you, you hear it? No pity!

WILLY. (*To* LINDA. *Starts to rise.*) You hear the spite!

BIFF. (*Grabs* WILLY, *pushes him down.*) No, you're going to hear —— BIFF Xs AROUND U.S. END OF the truth, what you are and what I am!   TABLE

LINDA. Stop it!!

WILLY. Spite!

HAPPY. You cut it now! ————————————

BIFF. (*To* HAPPY.) The man don't know who we are! The man is —— H. TO U.R. OF TABLE AS BIFF   BLOWS THROUGH HIS MOVE.

FIGURE 5.3   Blocking diagram for *Bus Stop* scene.

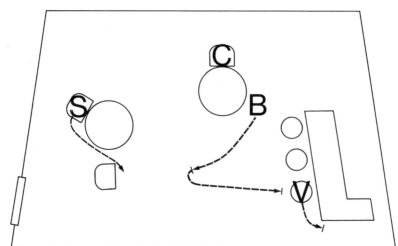

recording from interfering unduly with the process of creation. When the director is trying to read his "inspiration" of the night before, he appreciates the absence of various unnecessary symbols on the page.

Usually one page of the standard acting edition of published scripts will be about right for one prompt book page. However, if a lot of movement is blocked, the diagram gets cluttered. In this case we can tape another floor plan drawing over the first one for a continuation of the blocking. The added floor plan can be cut down so it covers as an overlay only the set area. Diagrams can be numbered to indicate which comes first.

It is usually necessary to cut manuscript (8½-by-11) pages into two or three segments—one segment to each page of the prompt book. If there is too much script, the diagram will look like a "can of worms" to the assistant. It may even be indecipherable to the director himself after he is away from it for a few days.

PREBLOCKING

The arguments in favor of prerehearsal blocking are discussed at length in Chapter 3. We are convinced of its value. Here we shall deal with some of the mechanical problems of preblocking.

Visualizing the action can be difficult at first, but it gets easier with practice. Preblocking, however, is never easy. It is lonely, demanding, exasperating work. The only thing that keeps a director at it is the knowledge of how much it improves the rehearsal process. When the problems of the script have been studied and resolved into spatial concepts before rehearsal, the director is much better equipped to help the actors, and rehearsal becomes a more stimulating and rewarding activity. Even if a director decides in a particular instance that giving the actors preblocking may be inhibiting, he should still preblock it for himself. There is no better way to understand the values and subtle rhythms of a script than to labor through preblocking.

Joan Littlewood, the British director, was well known for her improvisational techniques in preparing for a production. But two of her actors remember, as they tell us in *Directors on Directing*, that she had a "book" that she consulted from time to time.[4] Even though it was her practice not to tell the actors directly where to move, her improvisations were designed to achieve predetermined effects.

Of course, some occasions may be served better by avoiding preblocking. Some special two-person scenes that require close personal interaction between the actors may be effectively rehearsed by letting the actors improvise and feel each other out before the blocking is set. And a single-person scene is perhaps best left to the actor. The director may say at this time, "Use area, ending up down left." Then the director can pick up again with the preblocking patterns. In both these instances the decision is based on the particular nature of the scene and actors.

The director should make sure he thoroughly understands the space relationships in the floor plan of the set. Perhaps he should even lay out the relationships in full scale in his study. Experience in drafting and set designing can help the director to visualize how much space a human being requires.

The director must know how many actors can occupy a certain size platform comfortably if his blocking is going to be effective in the theatre. Nothing is more disheartening than to arrive at the blocking rehearsal only to discover that the blocking will not fit the set. Using objects in rough scale to represent actors can help, but the director must simply learn through practice to visualize an actor in a particular stage space of a certain theatre. It is worthwhile to sit in the empty theatre and study the stage. View it empty and then with actors and objects on it at different levels, and fix it in memory so that it can be brought back to mind in the privacy of the study.

In addition, the director should know how to render a simple mechanical or freehand perspective quickly and accurately. If he is not sure of a relationship, he can sketch it from the floor plan, thus saving time and mental anguish. In any case, he must be able to visualize the setting before designing the blocking.

Blocking should not be forced. If a scene is not clearly envisioned, it is better to take a break and think about it in a different atmosphere than to do uninspired blocking, which will have to be erased and done over. When the vision comes naturally and clearly, the blocking will usually go fast enough to make up for lost time.

The process of blocking will be made easier if the director remembers this guiding principle: Stage movement should illuminate the conflict at any given moment in the play. If the director turns always to the point of clash for his inspiration, the blocking will be crisp, appropriate, and imaginative. Blocking that comes from the action will stimulate the actors and help to create productive and enjoyable rehearsals.

TRYOUTS AND CASTING TECHNIQUES

Casting is a vitally important part of directing. Its value cannot be overstated. Decisions made in casting can haunt a director for the life of the production. The amateur director usually has a great advantage here: He can choose his cast on the basis of ability instead of box-office appeal or the whim of a producer.

The best methods of auditioning are very personal. The director must usually meet the potential performer in a highly charged competitive atmosphere. He must discover somehow who is lurking there behind the facade that actors erect at tryouts. To do this requires the application of the director's unique personality. Though the goal to cast the best possible actor for a particular role is universal, the application of auditioning techniques is as varied as individual directors. The following techniques have been used with success, though each director will undoubtedly want to make his own modifications.

Preparing for Auditions

Information Cards

Each aspirant should fill out an information card that gives his experience, address, and telephone number. Sometimes an actor's experience can be decisive in a difficult decision.

Character Description Handouts

Handouts with a description of the characters, based on the director's analysis, should be available. The actors' response to this will give the director a way to determine how they will react to directorial suggestions. The handouts may also prevent a promising aspirant from taking a completely wrong approach that would put the director off and possibly cause him to reject the right actor who made the wrong decision.

The handouts should also identify the selections that will be used in the auditions. These should be available as early as possible before

> ## "Use code words to trigger the memory of the whole reading."

auditions so that the actors will have the opportunity to prepare. By preparing or not preparing, the aspirants tell the director something about their attitude.

Conducting Auditions

"Preaudition" Auditioning

The director should make a point of being around before the tryouts actually start, handing out cards, talking with people, and using any excuse to make contact, especially with newcomers. Some of the trying out occurs during this period, when there is an opportunity to talk with and observe the applicants while they are off-guard, being themselves. At this time the director can form a valuable impression of the real person to compare with the actor person who will usually be present during the audition.

Taking Notes

The director should take careful notes during an audition, remembering that they must effectively bring the reading to mind hours afterward. Most directors find it nearly impossible to conduct tryouts and still take enough notes to describe essentials. A good plan is to use code words to trigger the memory of the whole reading. The best code word is often the first thing that flashes into a person's mind as he watches and listens to the reading, no matter how irrelevant it seems. The director will associate the code word with his impressions at the time of the reading. Seeing the word later can bring the reading vividly to mind, whereas a laborious attempt at a full description may have little value. A few code words can capture the reading and still leave most of the director's attention for the actor. Most actors have en-

countered directors who spend nearly all of the time during an audition hunched over their notebook, writing furiously and seldom looking at the actors. Not only is this insulting to the actors, but there is a
good chance the director will miss something important.

Writing down a few identifying characteristics about unknown
actors can also be useful. Here again the first things that come to mind
can trigger recall, no matter how unflattering they might be. The point
is to be able to bring a person clearly to mind later when casting decisions have to be made. As the rehearsal period advances, the notes
may be destroyed, but not before the director has gone through the
receiving period with the actors. The notes may remind the director of
something that will assist him in working with the actor.

Directing During Auditions

The director should not hesitate to give directions during the audition, especially with actors he does not know. It provides a good opportunity to test an unknown actor's response to suggestions. If an
actor performs the same way each time no matter what the director
has told him, it must be assumed that he does not take direction well.
Other factors should also be considered, but if the actor responds
similarly in several different contexts, the director can conclude that
he will be difficult to direct. The director is trying to find out not if the
actor is a puppet, but if he is receptive to suggestions. Can he consider
suggestions thoughtfully in order to accept or reject them? Or does he
just ignore them?

The actor usually brings his actor-puppet to auditions and puts
him on display. By the end of the rehearsal period, however, the director wants the actor's human being to be playing the role. Thus, even
though the actor is showing his actor-puppet, the director must observe his actor—human being. This is indeed a difficult problem, and it
emphasizes the director's need to penetrate the audition as much as
possible.

Releasing "Totems"

Directors often need to help actors overcome personal acting
problems so they can appear at best advantage in the auditions. One

major problem is misplaced tension. Inexperienced actors often have a lot of creative energy that they do not know how to put into the performance. But the energy demands expression, threatening to burst out uncontrollably. In order to avoid losing control, the actor often pours this energy into some part of his body. This will manifest itself in rigidity of the arm, neck, or leg. One can actually feel the tension by touching the area. In a sense, the actor has made a **totem** of a portion of his body. Just as a primitive tribe puts all the "evil spirits" into the totem to rid society of them, the actor gets rid of those "evil" energies he does not know how to use by putting them into a part of his body, where he intuits they will be hidden. That area usually becomes racked with tension, diminishing the actor's creative energies. If the director can get the actor to relax the totem area, the energies will be released and will be available to the actor in his interaction with others. Eventually the actor will come to understand that instead of tucking the energy away, he would be better off to discover how to use it beneficially.

The techniques for getting an actor to relax are as varied as the personalities of actors and directors and the ambience of the audition hall. Some directors can go onstage and penetrate the auditions very effectively. Others have found that their presence is intimidating. Most totems can be released by touching the area, but this is not always advisable or proper. If an actor's totem is in his right arm, shaking hands may release it without calling undue attention to it. Sometimes the actors can be put through exercises, ostensibly to release general tension, which will free the affected area. If the director discovers that the actor seems to be locked into his tensions, it would be better to cast someone else.

Augmenting Auditions

Individual Interview

Although an interview can be very profitable, open auditions are usually preferable because the contrast between the actor's performing puppet and his real self is brought into clearer focus. Also, the actors can be stimulated to better auditions by watching each other perform. But there are times when the performance situation is too threatening for good communication between actor and director. Indeed, for the director who knows how to get the best out of it, both public and private aspects of the actor can be revealed in a personal as well as in an open audition.

Some people, however, are very charming in close personal contacts but drained and dull in public. The actor must be a person who expands, or becomes larger, onstage rather than one who diminishes. The director needs to find out about this public personality; such a task is more difficult in the personal interview.

The Best Audition: Performance

The best audition is to have seen the actor in performance. Whenever a director watches actors whom he may some day cast in a production, he should study all the performances. He may see something that will help solve his own casting problems in the future.

Callback Session

It is often useful to have a callback session. Here the tentative cast can be seen together to try out the blend and to check further the actors' abilities. Also, more time can be spent with the most promising candidates.

Casting Dangers

Faulty judgments about an actor's talent, character, or intelligence are dangers that derive from the director's personal inadequacy in perception at the time of auditions or the particular ambience of the moment. Even the most brilliant directors have made errors in judgment at auditions. A few common errors, however, are so universally encountered that they can be discussed here.

Some people read well from the page. They seem glib and confident. The director's first response is to be delighted with his good fortune. But he must find out if the actor has depth and flexibility. If he is just a glib reader, he may be no better on opening night than he was at tryouts.

On the other hand, the poor reader may be prevented from revealing his true strength in a tryout based on the reading alone. If the director suspects this problem, he may use improvisations based on situations in the play. Without the burden of reading, the actor may blossom. However, usually the person who has difficulty reading has not read much. This suggests a narrow cultural background that may prevent him from finding all the dimensions of his role.

During his initial preparation the director may have set his impression of what each of the characters looks like. This can be dangerous. First, it may cause the director to cast a weaker actor because he resembles his own preconception. Second, it may cause the director to try to impose his idea of the character on the actor. This will impair the actor's creative response. Later, it can lead to tensions in the rehearsals. The director should concentrate on motive and leave his conception of the physical traits of character deliberately vague.

Lee J. Cobb's performance as Willy Loman in *Death of a Salesman* will be remembered as one of the greatest performances of the American theatre. Cobb was stocky in build and of medium height. According to a much circulated story, Arthur Miller visualized Willy as a tall thin man, resembling Miller's own father. A famous poster did depict Willy as a tall thin man with sample cases in each hand. Miller acquiesced in director Elia Kazan's choice of Cobb; two weeks into rehearsal, however, when the producer became alarmed at Cobb's rehearsal techniques, he found Miller a ready ally in demanding Cobb's removal. Kazan eventually won the battle and the rest is history. Now it is hard for us to visualize Willy Loman other than as Cobb depicted him on the stage and on television.

The point is that the director should always cast the best actor in the role, even if he does not look the role. Sometimes height and other factors in cast balance will make this difficult to do, but the production will ultimately be served best by having the best actors in the main roles.

REHEARSAL

Perhaps the least developed aspect of the director's work is rehearsal theory. Often rehearsals are haphazard affairs, inefficient and self-defeating. Even experienced directors will sometimes cling tenaciously to rehearsal techniques they have used before, even though they waste time and mislead the cast. Unwillingness to experiment with rehearsal techniques is probably due to a director's reluctance to depart from familiar methods because he fears losing control of the rehearsal situation, and because the production must be ready for that inexorable opening night.

Rehearsal techniques, like all other techniques of play production, should be built on a basic theory that will achieve clearly delineated goals. Experimenting with individual techniques in applying the theory should be standard operating procedure for any director.

The actual process of rehearsing—what the director does each moment behind the closed door of the rehearsal hall—is much more difficult to discuss. Each director will develop his own method of achieving the goals. This method should be based on his own personality. Very few methods will not work if pursued with intelligence, patience, and a measure of charm. The absence of these qualities in the director probably contributes as much as anything to the failure to rehearse well.

One problem plaguing many directors is the tendency to talk too much. Nothing is more likely to create tedious and inefficient rehearsals than the proliferation of talk. Whether it takes the form of directors' erudite lectures or "speeches to stimulate" or certain cast members' need to "talk things out," the impulse to talk rather than to do should be stifled as much as possible. At first these "talks" can leave everybody with an exciting sense of accomplishment, but there is usually little residual effect. Furthermore, the enshrinement of talk as a legitimate rehearsal activity is ultimately destructive.

Purpose of Rehearsal

The purpose of rehearsal is to discover the best means of illuminating the action of a play and to perfect the performance of that action in time and space. With regard to actors, this quest includes finding the motive of the characters and perfecting the means of expressing the motive.

Specific rehearsals and groups of rehearsals have special functions (pattern, action, continuity, and so on). These will be defined and described later in this chapter. However, the best way of achieving the underlying purpose of all rehearsals is to get the actors to go into the space between, to investigate that space thoroughly, and to discover what the encounter with other characters and the physical setting leads them to do. The actors perfect their performance out of this encounter in the space between.

Number of Rehearsals

The number of rehearsals required depends on several things, including the nature and length of the play, and the method of rehearsal. Most contemporary plays can be rehearsed in about thirty, 3-hour sessions. Although many stock and professional rehearsal periods run 8 or more hours, experience suggests the optimum rehearsal segment is around 3–4 hours. It is better to have two 3½-hour rehearsal segments than one 7-hour rehearsal, for instance. Special problems, such as technical rehearsals, may require a longer session.

The famous Stanislavsky production of *The Seagull* was done in twenty-six rehearsals. But Stanislavsky's production of Byron's *Cain* opened to dismal failure after 160 rehearsals. Success depends, of course, not so much on the number of rehearsals but on how efficiently they are used. Casts can go stale or lose their confidence if rehearsals accomplish very little. In general, a 3–4-hour session including a 30-minute warmup is a good rule.

Cycles of Action

Rehearsals should be arranged according to a play's cycles of action. The director's analysis should have already determined the cycles by the time the rehearsal schedule is made up. Treating the play as a continuum of cycles of action serves to focus the cast's attention on action as the important element.

Rehearsing action cycles rather than using the formal act–scene divisions helps the director break the rehearsals into manageable segments. Rehearsal segments should be roughly the same length, but it is unwise to have actors stop with a cycle of action incomplete, or, worse, start in the middle of one.

Most plays have around thirty cycles of action. The basic premise is that each cycle marks one complete minor conflict in the development of a play's root conflict. Deciding where cycles of action begin and end is not always easy. Sometimes it is a choice among two or more possibilities. Sometimes one cycle begins before another has ended. Sometimes a cycle ends and the play drifts a moment before a new cycle begins. These "interludes" are identified and noted in the action schedule. Sometimes a cycle is a half-page long; sometimes it is five pages long. Figure 5.4 is an action schedule from a production of *Death of a Salesman*.

Schedule Design

We recommend that plays be rehearsed in segments. Depending on the length of the play, the script can be broken into three or four rehearsal segments (see Figure 5.5). Extremely long plays might be broken into five segments. Most contemporary plays can be rehearsed in three segments. The director must be careful to break the play into nearly equal segments, taking care not to split a cycle of action between two

FIGURE 5.4   Cycles of action schedule for *Death of a Salesman*.*

Action	Characters	Pages	Title
1	Willy, Linda	7-11	"I Came Back"
2	Biff, Happy, Linda, Willy	11-14	
3	Biff, Happy	14-18	"The Dreams"
Interlude 1	Willy, Hap, Biff	18	
4	Willy, Hap, Biff	18-22	
5	Willy, Hap, Biff, Bernard, Linda	22-24	
6	Willy, Linda (Woman)	24-27	
7	Willy, Woman	27	
8	Willy, Linda, Bernard (Woman)	27-29	
9	Willy, Happy	29	
10	Willy, Charley, Hap	29-31	
11	Willy, Charley, Ben	31-33	
12	Willy, Ben, Linda, Biff, Hap, Charley	33-37	
Interlude 2	Linda, Willy	37-38	
13	Biff, Linda, Hap (Willy)	38-42	
14	Biff, Linda, Hap	42-45	"Willy's Dying"
15	Linda, Hap, Biff	45-48	
16	Biff, Hap, Linda, Willy	48-50	
17	Willy, Linda (Biff)	50	

END OF ACT ONE

Action	Characters	Pages	Title
18	Linda, Willy	51-54	"It's Changing"
Interlude 3	Linda	54-55	
19	Willy, Howard	55-59	
20	Willy, Howard	59-61	
21	Willy, Ben, Linda (Hap, Biff)	61-63	
22	Bernard, Willy, Linda, Biff, Hap	63-65	
23	Willy, Jenny, Bernard	65-69	
24	Willy, Charley	69-72	
25	Stanley, Hap	72-73	
26	Miss Forsythe, Stanley, Hap, Biff	73-76	
27	Hap, Biff	76-77	
28	Willy, Biff, Hap, Stanley	77-80	
29	Young Bernard, Willy, Biff, Linda, Hap	80	"Biff Flunked Math"
30	Willy, Biff, Hap (Woman)	80-83	
31	Woman, Willy, Biff, Hap, Miss Forsythe, Letta	83-84	
32	Willy, Woman, Biff	84-86	"Boston"
33	Willy, Woman, Biff	86-88	"Cataclysm"
34	Willy, Stanley, Waiter	88-89	
35	Linda, Hap, Biff	89-91	
36	Willy, Ben (Linda, Biff)	91-93	
37	Biff, Willy	93-94	
38	Biff, Willy, Hap, Linda	94-97	"Guts Ball"
39	Willy, Linda, Hap, Ben	97-99	
40	Linda, Biff, Hap, Bernard, Charley	99-101	

* Page references are to *Death of a Salesman*, Authorized Acting Edition (New York: Dramatists Play Service, 1952).

FIGURE 5.5   Rehearsal schedule for *Death of a Salesman*.

No.	Day	Date	Time	Place	Actions	Purpose
1	Tues	Jan 13	7:15pm	301	Whole play	Read and discuss
2	Wed	Jan 14	7:15	301	Segment 1	Block
3	Sat	Jan 17	9:00am	301	Segment 2	Block
4	Sat	Jan 17	1:00pm	301	Segment 3	Block
5	Sun	Jan 18	7:15pm	301	Segment 4	Block
6	Mon	Jan 19	7:15	West	Segment 1	Patterns
7	Tues	Jan 20	7:15	West	Segment 2	Patterns
8	Wed	Jan 21	7:15	West	Segment 3	Patterns
9	Thur	Jan 22	7:15	West	Segment 4	Patterns
10*	Fri	Jan 23	7:00	West	Run-through	Patterns
11	Sat	Jan 24	9:00am	West	Segment 1	Action
12	Sun	Jan 25	2:00pm	West	Segment 2	Action
13	Sun	Jan 25	7:15pm	West	Segment 3	Action
14	Mon	Jan 26	7:15	West	Segment 4	Action

Break, Regional Festival**

No.	Day	Date	Time	Place	Actions	Purpose
15	Sun	Feb 1	7:00pm	West	Run-through	Continuity
16	Mon	Feb 2	7:15	West	Segment 1	Action
17	Tues	Feb 3	7:15	West	Segment 2	Action
18	Wed	Feb 4	7:15	West	Segment 3	Action
19	Thur	Feb 5	7:15	West	Segment 4	Action
20	Fri	Feb 6	7:00	West	Act One	Action Continuity
21	Sat	Feb 7	9:00am	West	Act Two	Action Continuity
22	Sun	Feb 8	7:15pm	West	Segment 1	Action
23	Mon	Feb 9	7:15	West	Segment 2	Action
24	Tues	Feb 10	7:15	West	Segment 3	Action
25	Wed	Feb 11	7:15pm	West	Segment 4	Action
26	Thur	Feb 12	7:00pm	West	Costume, Dress, Tech	
27	Fri	Feb 13	6:00pm	West	Whole Play Continuity	
28	Sat	Feb 14	6:00	West	Dress Rehearsal	
29	Sun	Feb 15	6:00	West	Dress Rehearsal	
30	Mon	Feb 16	6:00	West	Final Dress Rehearsal	
31	Tues	Feb 17	6:00	West	Rehearsal Performance	
32	Wed	Feb 18	6:00	West	Rehearsal Performance	
	Thur	Feb 19			Opening Night	

Segment 1: Actions 1-10, pp. 7-31
Segment 2: Actions 11-18, pp. 31-54
Segment 3: Actions 19-28, pp. 55-80
Segment 4: Actions 29-40, pp. 80-101

* Whole play rehearsal indicated by underlining.
** A break is often necessary during the rehearsal period.

rehearsals. When determining the equality of segments, the director should consider crowd scenes or other difficult staging factors so that each segment takes approximately the same amount of time to rehearse. Nothing is more frustrating than to dismiss the cast early on one segment while another segment never gets finished in a single rehearsal.

Another factor in designing a schedule is the convenience to the cast. If starting a segment one action later allows an actor to be excused for an entire rehearsal, it is considerate to do so. Sometimes, however, a cycle of action is so long that to move it with another segment would seriously unbalance the rehearsal time. In this case the interests of the whole company must come before the convenience of one actor.

While directors often prefer to rehearse otherwise, we recommend that the segments be rehearsed in chronological order. There may be some convenience in doing all the scenes with a particular set of characters at the same time, but the damage done to the perception of continuity and structure is often quite severe. Moreover, by moving through the play a segment at a time, the director provides a sense of continuity so that scenes are rehearsed at regular time intervals. An actor can find it disconcerting that a particular scene has not been rehearsed for ten days.

A sense of order prevails when an actor knows that he will rehearse three segments of the play twice and then have a continuity run-through so that he can get a feel for the whole structure. It is poor practice to come up to dress rehearsals without having had a run-through of the whole show. The director is wise to schedule one or two to-be-announced rehearsals at key points to allow for extra run-throughs or rehearsals with problem actions or special actor problems.

Because members of the cast are equal partners in this creative endeavor, they have a right to be informed of the director's plan for

> "The rehearsal schedule should be distributed at the first rehearsal, and every effort should be made to follow the schedule."

the rehearsal period. The rehearsal schedule should be distributed at the first rehearsal, and every effort should be made to follow the schedule. If the director must make a change, he should consult the company and announce it as far in advance as possible.

Types of Rehearsals

Pattern

The first series of rehearsals may be called **pattern rehearsals**. In these sessions, usually about ten, the cast learns the dialogue and movement patterns of the production that the playwright and the director have provided. There will usually be one rehearsal for orientation and read-through. If it is a three-segment play, three rehearsals are needed to put in the blocking for the whole show, followed by three rehearsals to run the lines and blocking without scripts. Next, depending on the director's feeling about the play, one or two rehearsals can be scheduled for a complete run-through. Sometimes it is good to schedule a to-be-announced rehearsal before the run-through to pick up on problem scenes that the actors have not learned well enough. With this method the patterns in a three-segment show can be learned within ten rehearsals. The actors can put aside their books and concentrate on each other as they probe the action in the space between.

It should be impressed upon the cast that when learning movement and dialogue they are learning just patterns, not essences. They are learning words and movements. What the patterns really mean will be discovered in the action rehearsals when the actors seek the essences that lie beneath the patterns.

A director or assistant director needs to help the cast learn movement patterns as efficiently as possible. If the cast tries to write blocking in their scripts as they actually walk through the scene, the blocking tends to be too sketchy and often indecipherable. The cast should sit to write the blocking for a rehearsal segment and then walk through the blocking twice before the rehearsal ends. Translating the written instructions into kinetic activity during the same rehearsal helps the cast remember the blocking. Failure to have at least one walk-through of new blocking is counterproductive. The cast will almost certainly have to be given the blocking again at the next rehearsal.

Action

The second series of rehearsals should be devoted to the action. (These were discussed in Chapter 4.) At the beginning of action rehearsals the actors must know their lines and their basic movement patterns so that they are free to concentrate on the conflict, the action of the scenes. The director, who may have left the pattern rehearsals to his assistant, now becomes directly involved in the rehearsals. Here the actors can put aside the technical problems of words and movements and concentrate on getting into the space between so they can give life and meaning to the patterns.

Continuity

Approximately one-third of a play's action cycles (one-fourth, rarely one-fifth, if a play is long) should be rehearsed in each rehearsal session. After the first or second round of action rehearsals (perhaps after both), the play should be put together so that the cast can become aware of continuity and discover the problems that arise from integrating rehearsal segments. These sessions are known as **continuity rehearsals**. A complete run-through is desirable, but if that seems unwise, the play can be done in two parts. If possible, the break should come at an act division. Otherwise, one can make an interval based on the cycles. It is important, however, to return to the smaller rehearsal segments after a run-through.

During continuity rehearsals some directors will be giving attention to tempo, pace, and rhythm. One problem in discussing these terms, however, is that the terms are not universally understood. Directors and actors often use *pace* and *tempo* interchangeably, sometimes confusing both with *rhythm*. The following definitions have considerable currency and provide a clear distinction among the terms.

Tempo refers to how fast or slow a scene is played, the speed at which things happen.

Pace refers to the relationship between the flow of the production and the demands of the action. If an actor allows a scene to "break" because he fails to pick up a cue, the pace would be bad. A long pause may be quite appropriate to the flow of the action at a certain moment and therefore the pace would be good. The pace of a scene depends on the flow not being broken, or artificially manipulated. If an actor waits too long, the scene may "hit the floor" and "break." If an actor keeps firing cues regardless of the demands of the action, the pace may be artificially fast. Some directors, aware of the need for a fast tempo in a comedy, will superimpose a flow that is too fast for the action. The production will not be paced well because the flow is not rooted in the action.

Rhythm refers to the regular or irregular recurrence of something in the flow of a scene or a performance. Rhythm creates expectation based on the audience's perception of the presence of a pattern. A good way to understand rhythm is to play a drunk. The drunk "steps on the cracks" between the normal rhythms of the human flow. By denying the normal recurrent patterns, we become aware of them as they beat in the flow of the action. A director who is sensitive to the power of this rhythmic flow can consciously use it to enhance the performance.

Most directors used to plan "pacing" rehearsals or beat "tempo" during rehearsal. These techniques are fading away as the focus on action provides built-in pacing and tempo, avoiding the danger of superimposing an artificial pattern on the production. Most problems with pace, tempo, or rhythm can be traced to a deficiency in playing the action.

Technical

Toward the end of the rehearsal period we come to what has traditionally been called **technical rehearsals**. At this point the director's attention focuses on the many technical details of the production. A danger here is that the director's relationship with the actors may fall apart. Actually, the last several rehearsals should be the most productive for the actors. They should have developed to the point that they are ready to rehearse almost entirely on their own. Because knowledge of their characters is now well advanced, they can try the bold experiments that will lead to a deep and flexible performance. Above all, they should not be dully repeating the same patterns over and over again.

The cast must be made aware of its responsibility to continue to experiment during these last rehearsals. The technical rehearsals should interfere as little as possible with the actors' main concerns. For this reason, a good plan is to avoid rehearsals completely devoted to technical matters. It is unnecessary to have a full evening devoted to hours of standing around while the technicians try this cue or that refocusing.

Technicians and designers can bring in technical support a little at a time during three or four technical rehearsals prior to the final rehearsal performances. They should be consulted when the rehearsal schedule is being constructed so that the published schedule has been approved by all concerned. Needless to say, the technical staff should get several copies of the schedule when it is distributed. If the run-throughs are underlined or set apart by asterisks, the technical staff can readily see when it would be appropriate to have the running crews come into rehearsal to get familiar with the show. Experience has shown that the actors' rehearsal need not be interrupted or abrogated by technical problems at the crucial final rehearsals, if the director and technical staff have planned together and communicated well.

This method requires close collaboration among the designers, the technicians, and the director. It means that the director must sit down with the designer and technicians and work out a base setting for all the cues in the script before the technical rehearsals. This can be done effectively if the director knows the fundamental principles and terminology of lighting and sound and if he has prepared himself for the collaborative meetings.

During the three or four technical rehearsals, the cast rehearses as usual, and the cues are adjusted from the base established by the designer or technicians and the director in consultation. If the director has communicated his ideas clearly, the lighting director can often lay out the base cues himself with minimal consultation with the director. Adjustments can be made during regular rehearsals. It is vital, however, that the lighting board crew have a full cue sheet before the first technical rehearsal. This method cannot work if the board crew and the stage manager are expected to write in the cues during the rehearsal.

If especially difficult problems develop, they can be worked on during intermissions or after regular rehearsals so that the actors need not be interrupted. However, the director must make himself available to the technical staff during rehearsals.

The actors should be developing their roles on their own under the watchful but unintrusive eye of the assistant director. He can take notes on the acting and give them to the director, who will decide whether to pass them on to the actors. At this late stage, it is important that the director maintain control over what is said to the actors. Suggestions by the assistant director, however, can be helpful in maintaining the directing staff's responsibility to be an "audience" for the actors, so they can have assistance in knowing how their work is coming out to the audience. The main value of this method is that the director can devote the major portion of his attention to technical considerations without diminishing the actor's work, which continues with little or no interruption by the technicians.

Some designers and technicians may prefer not to work in this manner. They may want the so-called traditional technical rehearsal. Their wishes may have to be granted, but the director must do all he can to prevent the actors' rehearsal time from being continually interrupted. Also, the cast can be released during an all-tech rehearsal, and stand-ins can be used while cues are set and effects tried. The director should require that the technicians show compelling reasons for taking a rehearsal away from the actors at this time.

In truth, however, most technicians appreciate the integrated technical rehearsal, because it allows for preplanning that diminishes the chaos at dress rehearsal time and it requires a director who has done his homework about the technical requirements.

Dress
The first **dress rehearsal** usually occurs during technical rehearsals. If the cast comes early to allow the costumer a brief dress parade

before the rehearsal begins, there need be no interruption of or undue pressure on the actors' rehearsal.

The actors should use the costumes for at least four rehearsals: two technical-dress rehearsals and two rehearsal "performances." Ideally they should be used longer, but if the actor has been using an appropriate rehearsal costume, the transition problems will be minimal.

Rehearsal "Performances"

The difference between rehearsal and performance has been discussed in Chapter 4. Rehearsal is the time when the actor discovers his character's motive, moves beyond to the premotive, and experiments with the means of expressing his discoveries. He works in the space between to develop the role in breadth as well as depth. Performance, on the other hand, is adapting the role to the changing conditions of each particular encounter with the other actors and the audience. Rehearsals, therefore, should be a time of experimenting with the possibilities of a role, while performance adapts the discoveries to the conditions of playing before an audience.

Because this shift in purpose presents special problems, the cast should have some experience with performances before opening night. For this reason the director should schedule at least two **rehearsal performances**. A small audience (friends, students, teachers of drama, nonperforming staff members, or a paying preview audience) is invited to attend. They usually have not been permitted at rehearsals until then. In these rehearsals the cast can test the breadth of their roles to see if characterization is wide enough to allow the audience to participate without strain. Often important adjustments will be made as a result of rehearsal performances.

These rehearsal performances ought to be in performance mode. The theatre should be cleaned and made ready for the audience. The set should be finished—painted and otherwise made ready. The technicians' table should be removed from the house. Ushering and house management can train their personnel and make final preparations.

If these rehearsal performances are clearly indicated in the rehearsal schedule and planned for from the beginning of the production process, there is no reason why everything should not be ready two days before opening night. Many theatres do not have the luxury of several preview performances or an out-of-town tryout. The rehearsal performances are most useful in these cases to help ensure a strong professional performance for the opening night audience and critics.

PERFORMANCE

For performance the last member, the audience, is added to the cast. Rehearsals should have made the actors flexible enough so that they can comfortably accept this new cast member. They should react to this new "person" without distorting the motive of their roles.

Just as actors must respond to a different audience each night, so they must respond to different coactors. If members of the company respond to the subtle changes in each other's performances, while remaining within the discovered boundaries of their characters, they will be fresh and alive no matter how many times they perform.

The cast must realize that a performance can never be repeated. The cast may hope to do a successful performance again, but it cannot be done in exactly the same way. If they think it can, they will anticipate reactions and then lose confidence if the audience reactions are different. They may begin to compare performances while they are performing. This monitoring becomes a distraction and will lead to disasters, which can overtake inexperienced casts even when they have a fundamentally good production. The director may detect patterns or tendencies over several performances, but the actors should not look for them.

A good performance—one praised by critics and the actor's friends—has in it the seeds of its own destruction. The more the actor hears how good he is, the more he will be tempted to watch his own performance. When this happens, he loses concentration and his performance begins to disintegrate. He begins to play the patterns in an effort to keep the "perfect" performance, instead of playing essences. In consequence, the soul drops out of the role because the actor is no longer responding directly to the conflict in the action. Acting is a humbling profession. The actor must give himself to the role. The minute he tries to gratify his ego on the stage, the role begins to die. The actor can get his ego gratification off the stage.

The director should stay with the cast during early performances of the run, giving oral or written notes as necessary. If it is a long run, he should attend from time to time to watch for symptoms of developing problems.

The director should prepare a cast, especially an inexperienced one, for the reviews that usually follow an opening night. He should suggest that the cast pay little attention to praise or blame. If they believe the good comments, then they may have to believe the bad.

By opening night the cast ought to be convinced that their interpretation of the play and their individual roles are the best they are capable of at this time. If anyone in the cast suffers under the stress of a bad review, the director should go over the motives and purposes of the role with the actor. To be effective, the actor should feel confident that his performance is appropriate to the total production concept.

Things can be learned from a review or the comments of others, but the cast should not make changes that go beyond the boundaries of their already created role. If the director decides changes are called for, the whole company should go back into rehearsal.

POSTPERFORMANCE EVALUATION

The director has an obligation, especially to student actors (there should be no other kind), to evaluate the rehearsals and performance after the show closes. A frank discussion of the experience, good points and bad, should be helpful to all. It is wise to wait for a few weeks after the closing before attempting an evaluation. By then everyone can be more objective about the show. It is probably best to meet individually with each actor.

Although actors ought to be open to a discussion of their work, they should not depend on the opinion of others for an evaluation. The ultimate evaluator of an actor's work is the actor himself. The opinion of others can tell actors how one person reacts and can help actors modify and improve their craft, but if actors place too much importance on the judgments of others, they place their craft—and art—in the hands of others. In the world of the professional theatre it leaves them too vulnerable. Most successful actors can tell stories about being told they were "no good" or "had no talent." Directors can help young actors arm themselves against judgments that will be leveled against them, often for reasons that have little to do with their acting ability.

The director also has an obligation to do a self-evaluation. Although the comments of others should be solicited and considered, the best criticism for a director comes from honest self-evaluation. In the final analysis the experienced director must depend on himself as the arbiter of his work. A director may go on reviewing his productions for years, finding new ideas from continuing evaluations and trying to understand why something failed or succeeded.

Failures—as well as successes—must be faced as squarely as possible. The director ever remains a student of his art. If his self-analysis reveals mistakes, his gloom at facing these mistakes can be offset by his joy at learning something new. Most learning comes from acknowledging mistakes. Success is hard to analyze and harder to learn from. Those who are unable to acknowledge or examine their own failures are unable to learn from them. Their egos arrest their development as artists and cause the gap between expectations and performance to widen. The self-evaluation should lead to a determination to start preparing for the next show. The director's major question is, What specifically can I do to learn more about my art and to enhance my skill as a director?

EXERCISES

1. We suggest that directors give themselves certain tasks on each read-through of the script. Why? Can you suggest tasks other than those mentioned in the text?

2. What is the creative state of "I don't know"? Why should a director or actor be in that state?

3. Which of the following statements should the director make to a designer? Which should he not?
   a. "I want a door right here."
   b. "I see the couch as brown, the walls beige."
   c. "I'd like to set the show in the Victorian era."
   d. "This sketch is my idea of what the costume should look like."
   e. "I really don't know what this show is about. We're going to play it by ear."
   There may properly be disagreement in responding. Defend your answers in terms of the ideal designer–director relationship.

4. Why should preblocking floor plans be in precise scale?

5. What is the "totem" problem? How can a director deal with it?

6. What is the difference between pattern rehearsals, action rehearsals, and rehearsal performances?

GROUP ACTIVITY

The group should attend auditions (if they are open) for a local production and prepare without consultation a cast list with two actors in each role, taking into consideration all the factors discussed in the chapter. (One copy should be turned in to the leader before the casting is discussed by the entire class.)

DIRECTING WORKSHOP

An effective way to learn the concepts developed in this text is to prepare scenes for class so that the concepts can be illustrated with "hands-on" experience. A scene should be no more than ten minutes long, which will allow ample time to work with it in a fifty-minute session. The directors should be aware that the emphasis is on learning and testing concepts, not on a finished product. Directors should not choose a scene that has special personal significance for them, in order to minimize any defensiveness. The scene should be rehearsed to the point that it is at least at the end of the pattern stage (lines and blocking learned). Two working sessions are recommended, if time and class size allow it. When discussing the scenes, the group should make an effort to use the terminology from the text. It is useful to schedule a final viewing of all the scenes at one meeting. These performances can then be analyzed by the group in a special session.

NOTES

1. First mentioned in a letter by John Keats to his brothers George and Tom, December 21–27, 1817, *English Romantic Writers*, ed. David Perkins (New York: Harcourt, Brace and World, 1967), p. 1209.
2. Jerzy Grotowski, "Towards the Poor Theatre," trans. T. K. Wiewiorowski, ed. Kelly Morris, *Tulane Drama Review*, 11, No. 3 (T35) (Spring 1967), 60–65.
3. Norman Marshall, *The Producer and the Play* (London: Macdonald, 1962), p. 285.
4. Clive Godwin and Tom Milne, "Working with Joan," in *Directors on Directing*, ed. Toby Cole and Helen Chinoy (Indianapolis, Ind.: Bobbs-Merrill, 1963), pp. 390–401.

A Final Word

We have stressed throughout the necessity for a director to know the nature of drama. Learning how to discover the structure and dynamics of a play's form is the principal requirement of a director.

We have also stressed that a director must be well versed in the technical aspects of stagecraft. Attending a specialized, professional school can give the prospective director adequate technical training. However, such training can sometimes be rather narrow, too vocational.

Great directors possess more than analytical skill and more than craft. By some means they have become well educated. In many respects the best preparation for a directing career is to attend a university where one can study the theatre in the context of the other arts and sciences, where one can become steeped in the humanistic tradition of our culture.

A director whose knowledge extends beyond the narrow confines of the craft is always fascinated by the effort to "hold as 'twere the mirror up to nature." And though she knows that art is not life, she explores the relationship of one to the other and brings understanding to the playwright's endeavor to imitate the actions of people in the metaphor of the play.

Finally, a director, like all artists, must ultimately be a believer rather than a knower. The director-artist cultivates the creative state of "I don't know." The artist senses that "knowing" limits options. If one "knows," she has only one option open to her: what she knows. But if one can learn to live with the uncertainty of "I don't know," the possibilities are limitless. The artist "believes" where she does not know. She trusts herself and her knowledge of craft, but ultimately she needs faith to take that leap in the dark in pursuit of truth and art. Only if she takes that leap can she be truly creative and reap the full measure of joy from her life in art.

Hello Out There

by William Saroyan

For George Bernard Shaw

CHARACTERS

A YOUNG MAN   A GIRL

A MAN   TWO OTHER MEN

A WOMAN

Reprinted by permission of Samuel French, Inc. from
Razzle-Dazzle by William Saroyan. Copyright 1942 by
Harcourt, Brace and Company, Inc., and in England by
Faber and Faber. For amateur and stock production of this
play, application should be made to Samuel French, Inc.,
45 West 25 Street, New York, NY 10010.

Scene: There is a fellow in a small-town prison
cell, tapping slowly on the floor with a spoon.
After tapping half a minute, as if he were trying
to telegraph words, he gets up and begins
walking around the cell. At last he stops, stands
at the center of the cell, and doesn't move for
a long time. He feels his head, as if it were
wounded. Then he looks around. Then he
calls out dramatically, kidding the world.

YOUNG MAN: Hello—out there! (*Pause.*) Hello—out there!
Hello—out there! (*Long pause.*) Nobody out there. (*Still more*
dramatically, but more comically, too.) Hello—out there! Hello—
out there!

A GIRL'S VOICE *is heard, very sweet and soft.*

THE VOICE: Hello.

YOUNG MAN: Hello—out there.

THE VOICE: Hello.

YOUNG MAN: Is that you, Katey?

THE VOICE: No—this here is Emily.

YOUNG MAN: Who? (*Swiftly.*) Hello out there.

THE VOICE: Emily.

YOUNG MAN: Emily who? I don't know anybody named Emily.
Are you that girl I met at Sam's in Salinas about three years ago?

THE VOICE: No—I'm the girl who cooks here. I'm the cook. I've
never been in Salinas. I don't even know where it is.

YOUNG MAN: Hello out there. You say you cook here?

THE VOICE: Yes.

YOUNG MAN: Well, why don't you study up and learn to cook?
How come I don't get no jello or anything good?

THE VOICE: I just cook what they tell me to. (*Pause.*) You
lonesome?

YOUNG MAN: Lonesome as a coyote. Hear me hollering? Hello
out there!

THE VOICE: Who you hollering to?

YOUNG MAN: Well—nobody, I guess. I been trying to think of
somebody to write a letter to, but I can't think of anybody.

THE VOICE: What about Katey?

YOUNG MAN: I don't know anybody named Katey.

THE VOICE: Then why did you say, Is that you, Katey?

YOUNG MAN: Katey's a good name. I always did like a name like Katey. I never *knew* anybody named Katey, though.

THE VOICE: *I* did.

YOUNG MAN: Yeah? What was she like? Tall girl, or little one?

THE VOICE: Kind of medium.

YOUNG MAN: Hello out there. What sort of a looking girl are *you?*

THE VOICE: Oh, I don't know.

YOUNG MAN: Didn't anybody ever tell you? Didn't anybody ever talk to you that way?

THE VOICE: What way?

YOUNG MAN: You know. Didn't they?

THE VOICE: No, they didn't.

YOUNG MAN: Ah, the fools—they should have. I can tell from your voice you're O.K.

THE VOICE: Maybe I am and maybe I ain't.

YOUNG MAN: I never missed yet.

THE VOICE: Yeah, I know. That's why you're in jail.

YOUNG MAN: The whole thing was a mistake.

THE VOICE: They claim it was rape.

YOUNG MAN: No—it wasn't.

THE VOICE: That's what they claim it was.

YOUNG MAN: They're a lot of fools.

THE VOICE: Well, you sure are in trouble. Are you scared?

YOUNG MAN: Scared to death. (*Suddenly.*) Hello out there!

THE VOICE: What do you keep saying that for all the time?

YOUNG MAN: I'm lonesome. I'm as lonesome as a coyote. (*A long one.*) Hello—out there!

THE GIRL *appears, over to one side. She is a plain girl in plain clothes.*

THE GIRL: I'm kind of lonesome, too.

YOUNG MAN (*turning and looking at her*):   Hey—No fooling? Are you?

THE GIRL: Yeah—I'm almost as lonesome as a coyote myself.

YOUNG MAN: Who *you* lonesome for?

THE GIRL: I don't know.

YOUNG MAN: It's the same with me. The minute they put you in a place like this you remember all the girls you ever knew, and all the girls you didn't get to know, and it sure gets lonesome.

THE GIRL: I bet it does.

YOUNG MAN: Ah, it's awful. (*Pause.*) You're a pretty kid, you know that?

THE GIRL: You're just talking.

YOUNG MAN: No, I'm not just talking—you *are* pretty. Any fool could see that. You're just about the prettiest kid in the whole world.

THE GIRL: I'm not—and you know it.

YOUNG MAN: No—you are. I never saw anyone prettier in all my born days, in all my travels. I knew Texas would bring me luck.

THE GIRL: Luck? You're in jail, aren't you? You've got a whole gang of people all worked up, haven't you?

YOUNG MAN: Ah, that's nothing. I'll get out of this.

THE GIRL: Maybe.

YOUNG MAN: No, I'll be all right—*now.*

THE GIRL: What do you mean—now?

YOUNG MAN: I mean after seeing you. I got something now. You know for a while there I didn't care one way or another. Tired. (*Pause.*) Tired of trying for the best all the time and never getting it. (*Suddenly.*) Hello out there!

THE GIRL: Who you calling now?

YOUNG MAN: You.

THE GIRL: Why, I'm right here.

YOUNG MAN: I know. (*Calling.*) Hello out there!

THE GIRL: Hello.

YOUNG MAN: Ah, you're sweet. (*Pause.*) I'm going to marry *you.* I'm going away with *you.* I'm going to take you to San Francisco or some place like that. I *am,* now. I'm going to win myself some real money, too. I'm going to study 'em real careful and pick myself some winners, and we're going to have a lot of money.

THE GIRL: Yeah?

YOUNG MAN: Yeah. Tell me your name and all that stuff.

THE GIRL: Emily.

YOUNG MAN: I know that. What's the rest of it? Where were you born? Come on, tell me the whole thing.

THE GIRL: Emily Smith.

YOUNG MAN: Honest to God?

THE GIRL: Honest. That's my name—Emily Smith.

YOUNG MAN: Ah, you're the sweetest girl in the whole world.

THE GIRL: Why?

YOUNG MAN: I don't know why, but you are, that's all. Where were you born?

THE GIRL: Matador, Texas.

YOUNG MAN: Where's that?

THE GIRL: Right here.

YOUNG MAN: Is this Matador, Texas?

THE GIRL: Yeah, it's Matador. They brought you here from Wheeling.

YOUNG MAN: Is that where I was—Wheeling?

THE GIRL: Didn't you even know what town you were in?

YOUNG MAN: All towns are alike. You don't go up and ask somebody what town you're in. It doesn't make any difference. How far away is Wheeling?

THE GIRL: Sixteen or seventeen miles. Didn't you know they moved you?

YOUNG MAN: How could I know, when I was out—cold? Somebody hit me over the head with a lead pipe or something. What'd they hit me for?

THE GIRL: Rape—that's what they *said*.

YOUNG MAN: Ah, that's a lie. (*Amazed, almost to himself.*) She wanted me to give her money.

THE GIRL: Money?

YOUNG MAN: Yeah, if I'd have known she was a woman like that—well, by God, I'd have gone on down the street and stretched out in a park somewhere and gone to sleep.

THE GIRL: Is that what she wanted—money?

YOUNG MAN: Yeah. A fellow like me hopping freights all over the country, trying to break his bad luck, going from one poor little town to another, trying to get in on something good somewhere, and she asks for money. I thought she was lonesome. She *said* she was.

THE GIRL: Maybe she was.

YOUNG MAN: She was *something*.

THE GIRL: I guess I'd never see you, if it didn't happen, though.

YOUNG MAN: Oh, I don't know—maybe I'd just mosey along this way and see you in this town somewhere. I'd recognize you, too.

THE GIRL: Recognize me?

YOUNG MAN: Sure, I'd recognize you the minute I laid eyes on you.

THE GIRL: Well, who would I be?

YOUNG MAN: Mine, that's who.

THE GIRL: Honest?

YOUNG MAN: Honest to God.

THE GIRL: You just say that because you're in jail.

YOUNG MAN: No, I mean it. You just pack up and wait for me. We'll high-roll the hell out of here to Frisco.

THE GIRL: You're just lonesome.

YOUNG MAN: I been lonesome all my life—there's no cure for that—but you and me—we can have a lot of fun hanging around together. You'll bring me luck. I know it.

THE GIRL: What are you looking for luck for all the time?

YOUNG MAN: I'm a gambler. I don't work. I've got to have luck, or I'm a bum. I haven't had any decent luck in years. Two whole years now—one place to another. Bad luck all the time. That's why I got in trouble back there in Wheeling, too. That was no accident. That was my bad luck following me around. So here I am, with my head half busted. I guess it was her old man that did it.

THE GIRL: You mean her father?

YOUNG MAN: No, her husband. If I had an old lady like that, I'd throw her out.

THE GIRL: Do you think you'll have better luck, if I go with you?

YOUNG MAN: It's a cinch. I'm a good handicapper. All I need is somebody good like you with me. It's no good always walking around in the streets for anything that might be there at the time. You got to have somebody staying with you all the time—through winters when it's cold, and springtime when it's pretty, and

summertime when it's nice and hot and you can go swimming—
through *all* the times—rain and snow and all the different kinds of
weather a man's got to go through before he dies. You got to have
somebody who's right. Somebody who knows you, from away back.
You got to have somebody who even knows you're wrong but likes
you just the same. I know I'm wrong, but I just don't want anything
the hard way, working like a dog, or the *easy* way, working like a
dog—working's the hard way and the easy way both. All I got to
do is beat the price, always—and then I don't feel lousy and don't
hate anybody. If you go along with me, I'll be the finest guy
anybody ever saw. I won't be wrong any more. You know when
you get enough of that money, you *can't* be wrong any more—
you're right because the money says so. I'll have a lot of money
and you'll be just about the prettiest, most wonderful kid in the
whole world. I'll be proud walking around Frisco with you on
my arm and people turning around to look at us.

THE GIRL: Do you think they will?

YOUNG MAN: Sure they will. When I get back in some decent clothes,
and you're on my arm—well, Katey, they'll turn around and look,
and they'll see something, too.

THE GIRL: Katey?

YOUNG MAN: Yeah—that's your name from now on. You're the
first girl I ever called Katey. I've been saving it for you. O.K.?

THE GIRL: O.K.

YOUNG MAN: How long have I been here?

THE GIRL: Since last night. You didn't wake up until late this
morning, though.

YOUNG MAN: What time is it now? About nine?

THE GIRL: About ten.

YOUNG MAN: Have you got the key to this lousy cell?

THE GIRL: No. They don't let me fool with any keys.

YOUNG MAN: Well, can you get it?

THE GIRL: No.

YOUNG MAN: Can you *try?*

THE GIRL: They wouldn't let me get near the keys. I cook for this
jail, when they've got somebody in it. I clean up and things like
that.

YOUNG MAN: Well, I want to get out of here. Don't you know the guy that runs this joint?

THE GIRL: I know him, but he wouldn't let you out. They were talking of taking you to another jail in another town.

YOUNG MAN: Yeah? Why?

THE GIRL: Because they're afraid.

YOUNG MAN: What are they afraid of?

THE GIRL: They're afraid these people from Wheeling will come over in the middle of the night and break in.

YOUNG MAN: Yeah? What do they want to do that for?

THE GIRL: Don't *you* know what they want to do it for?

YOUNG MAN: Yeah, I know all right.

THE GIRL: Are you scared?

YOUNG MAN: Sure I'm scared. Nothing scares a man more than ignorance. You can argue with people who ain't fools, but you can't argue with fools—they just go to work and do what they're set on doing. Get me out of here.

THE GIRL: How?

YOUNG MAN: Well, go get the guy with the key, and let me talk to him.

THE GIRL: He's gone home. Everybody's gone home.

YOUNG MAN: You mean I'm in this little jail all alone?

THE GIRL: Well—yeah—except me.

YOUNG MAN: Well, what's the big idea—doesn't anybody stay here all the time?

THE GIRL: No, they go home every night. I clean up and then I go, too. I hung around tonight.

YOUNG MAN: What made you do that?

THE GIRL: I wanted to talk to you.

YOUNG MAN: Honest? What did you want to talk about?

THE GIRL: Oh, I don't know. I took care of you last night. You were talking in your sleep. You liked me, too. I didn't think you'd like me when you woke up, though.

YOUNG MAN: Yeah? Why not?

THE GIRL: I don't know.

YOUNG MAN: Yeah? Well, you're wonderful, see?

THE GIRL: Nobody ever talked to me that way. All the fellows in town—(*Pause.*)

YOUNG MAN: What about 'em? (*Pause.*) Well, what about 'em? Come on—tell me.

THE GIRL: They laugh at me.

YOUNG MAN: Laugh at *you*? They're fools. What do they know about anything? You go get your things and come back here. I'll take you with me to Frisco. How old are you?

THE GIRL: Oh, I'm of age.

YOUNG MAN: How old are you?—Don't lie to me! Sixteen?

THE GIRL: I'm seventeen.

YOUNG MAN: Well, bring your father and mother. We'll get married before we go.

THE GIRL: They wouldn't let me go.

YOUNG MAN: Why not?

THE GIRL: I don't know, but they wouldn't. I know they wouldn't.

YOUNG MAN: You go tell your father not to be a fool, see? What is he, a farmer?

THE GIRL: No—nothing. He gets a little relief from the government because he's supposed to be hurt or something—his side hurts, he says. I don't know what it is.

YOUNG MAN: Ah, he's a liar. Well, I'm taking you with me, see?

THE GIRL: He takes the money I earn, too.

YOUNG MAN: He's got no right to do that.

THE GIRL: I know it, but he does it.

YOUNG MAN (*almost to himself*): This world stinks. You shouldn't have been born in this town, anyway, and you shouldn't have had a man like that for a father, either.

THE GIRL: Sometimes I feel sorry for him.

YOUNG MAN: Never mind feeling sorry for him. (*Pointing a finger.*) I'm going to talk to your father some day. I've got a few things to tell that guy.

THE GIRL: I know you have.

YOUNG MAN (*suddenly*): Hello—out there! See if you can get that fellow with the keys to come down and let me out.

THE GIRL: Oh, I couldn't.

YOUNG MAN: Why not?

THE GIRL: I'm nobody here—they give me fifty cents every day I work.

YOUNG MAN: How much?

THE GIRL: Fifty cents.

YOUNG MAN (*to the world*):   You see? They ought to pay money to *look* at you. To breathe the *air* you breathe. I don't know. Sometimes I figure it never is going to make sense. Hello—out there! I'm scared. You try to get me out of here. I'm scared them fools are going to come here from Wheeling and go crazy, thinking they're heroes. Get me out of here, Katey.

THE GIRL: I don't know what to do. Maybe I could break the door down.

YOUNG MAN: No, you couldn't do that. Is there a hammer out there or anything?

THE GIRL: Only a broom. Maybe they've locked the broom up, too.

YOUNG MAN: Go see if you can find anything.

THE GIRL: All right. (*She goes.*)

YOUNG MAN: Hello—out there! Hello—out there! (*Pause.*) Hello—out there! Hello—out there! (*Pause.*) Putting me in jail. (*With contempt.*) Rape! Rape? *They* rape everything good that was ever born. His side hurts. They laugh at her. Fifty cents a day. Little punk people. Hurting the only good thing that ever came their way. (*Suddenly.*) Hello—out there!

THE GIRL (*returning*):   There isn't a thing out there. They've locked everything up for the night.

YOUNG MAN: Any cigarettes?

THE GIRL: Everything's locked up—all the drawers of the desk, all the closet doors—everything.

YOUNG MAN: I ought to have a cigarette.

THE GIRL: I could get you a package maybe, somewhere. I guess the drug store's open. It's about a mile.

YOUNG MAN: A mile? I don't want to be alone that long.

THE GIRL: I could run all the way, and all the way back.

YOUNG MAN: You're the sweetest girl that ever lived.

THE GIRL: What kind do you want?

YOUNG MAN: Oh, any kind—Chesterfields or Camels or Lucky Strikes—any kind at all.

THE GIRL: I'll go get a package. (*She turns to go.*)

YOUNG MAN: What about the money?

THE GIRL: I've got some money. I've got a quarter I been saving. I'll run all the way. (*She is about to go.*)

YOUNG MAN: Come here.

THE GIRL (*going to him*):   What?

YOUNG MAN: Give me your hand. (*He takes her hand and looks at it, smiling. He lifts it and kisses it.*) I'm scared to death.

THE GIRL: I am, too.

YOUNG MAN: I'm not lying—I don't care what happens to me, but I'm scared nobody will ever come out here to this Godforsaken broken-down town and find you. I'm scared you'll get used to it and not mind. I'm scared you'll never get to Frisco and have 'em all turning around to look at you. Listen—go get me a gun, because if they come, I'll kill 'em! They don't understand. Get me a gun!

THE GIRL: I could get my father's gun. I know where he hides it.

YOUNG MAN: Go get it. Never mind the cigarettes. Run all the way. (*Pause, smiling but seriously.*) Hello, Katey.

THE GIRL: Hello. What's *your* name?

YOUNG MAN: Photo-Finish is what they *call* me. My races are always photo-finish races. You don't know what that means, but it means they're very close. So close the only way they can tell which horse wins is to look at a photograph after the race is over. Well, every race I bet turns out to be a photo-finish race, and my horse never wins. It's my bad luck, all the time. That's why they call me Photo-Finish. Say it before you go.

THE GIRL: Photo-Finish.

YOUNG MAN: Come here. (THE GIRL *moves close and he kisses her.*) Now, hurry. Run all the way.

THE GIRL: I'll run. (THE GIRL *turns and runs. The* YOUNG MAN *stands at the center of the cell a long time.* THE GIRL *comes running back in. Almost crying.*) I'm afraid. I'm afraid I won't see you again. If I come back and you're not here, I—

YOUNG MAN: Hello—out there!

THE GIRL: It's so lonely in this town. Nothing here but the lonesome wind all the time, lifting the dirt and blowing out to the prairie. I'll stay *here*. I won't *let* them take you away.

YOUNG MAN: Listen, Katey. Do what I tell you. Go get that gun and come back. Maybe they won't come tonight. Maybe they won't come at all. I'll hide the gun and when they let me out you can take it back and put it where you found it. And then we'll go away. But if they come, I'll kill 'em! Now, hurry—

THE GIRL: All right. (*Pause.*) I want to tell you something.

YOUNG MAN: O.K.

THE GIRL (*very softly*): If you're not here when I come back, well, I'll have the gun and I'll know what to do with it.

YOUNG MAN: You know how to handle a gun?

THE GIRL: I know how.

YOUNG MAN: Don't be a fool. (*Takes off his shoe, brings out some currency.*) Don't be a fool, see? Here's some money. Eighty dollars. Take it and go to Frisco. Look around and find somebody. Find somebody alive and halfway human, see? Promise me—if I'm not here when you come back, just throw the gun away and get the hell to Frisco. Look around and find somebody.

THE GIRL: I don't *want* to find anybody.

YOUNG MAN (*swiftly, desperately*): Listen, if I'm not here when you come back, how do you know I haven't gotten away? Now, do what I tell you. I'll meet you in Frisco. I've got a couple of dollars in my other shoe. I'll see you in San Francisco.

THE GIRL (*with wonder*): San Francisco?

YOUNG MAN: That's right—San Francisco. That's where you and me belong.

THE GIRL: I've always wanted to go to *some* place like San Francisco—but how could I go alone?

YOUNG MAN: Well, you're not alone any more, see?

THE GIRL: Tell me a little what it's like.

YOUNG MAN (*very swiftly, almost impatiently at first, but gradually slower and with remembrance, smiling, and* THE GIRL *moving closer to him as he speaks*): Well, it's on the Pacific to begin with—ocean water all around. Cool fog and seagulls. Ships from all over the world. It's got seven hills. The little streets go up and down, around and all over. Every night the fog-horns bawl. But they won't be bawling for you and me.

THE GIRL: What else?

YOUNG MAN: That's about all, I guess.

THE GIRL: Are people different in San Francisco?

YOUNG MAN: People are the same everywhere. They're different only when they love somebody. That's the only thing that makes 'em different. More people in Frisco love somebody, that's all.

THE GIRL: Nobody anywhere loves anybody as much as I love you.

YOUNG MAN (shouting, as if to the world): You see? Hearing you say that, a man could die and still be ahead of the game. Now, hurry. And don't forget, if I'm not here when you come back, get the hell to San Francisco where you'll have a chance. Do you hear me?

THE GIRL stands a moment looking at him, then backs away, turns and runs. The YOUNG MAN stares after her, troubled and smiling. Then he turns away from the image of her and walks about like a lion in a cage. After a while he sits down suddenly and buries his head in his hands. From a distance the sound of several automobiles approaching is heard. He listens a moment, then ignores the implications of the sound, whatever they may be. Several automobile doors are slammed. He ignores this also. A wooden door is opened with a key and closed, and footsteps are heard in a hall. Walking easily, almost casually and yet arrogantly, a MAN comes in.

YOUNG MAN (jumps up suddenly and shouts at THE MAN, almost scaring him): What the hell kind of a jailkeeper are you, anyway? Why don't you attend to your business? You get paid for it, don't you? Now, get me out of here.

THE MAN: But I'm not the jailkeeper.

YOUNG MAN: Yeah? Well, who are you, then?

THE MAN: I'm the husband.

YOUNG MAN: What husband you talking about?

THE MAN: You know what husband.

YOUNG MAN: Hey! (*Pause, looking at* THE MAN.) Are you the guy
that hit me over the head last night?

THE MAN: I am.

YOUNG MAN (*with righteous indignation*):   What do you mean
going around hitting people over the head?

THE MAN: Oh, I don't know. What do you *mean* going around—
the way you do?

YOUNG MAN (*rubbing his head*):   You hurt my head. You got no
right to hit anybody over the head.

THE MAN (*suddenly angry, shouting*):   Answer my question! What
do you mean?

YOUNG MAN: Listen, you—don't be hollering at me just because
I'm locked up.

THE MAN (*with contempt, slowly*):   You're a dog!

YOUNG MAN: Yeah, well, let me tell you something. You *think*
you're the husband. You're the husband of nothing. (*Slowly.*)
What's more, your wife—if you want to call her that—is a tramp.
Why don't you throw her out in the street where she belongs?

THE MAN (*draws a pistol*):   Shut up!

YOUNG MAN: Yeah? Go ahead, shoot—(*Softly.*) and spoil the
fun. What'll your pals think? They'll be disappointed, won't they.
What's the fun hanging a man who's already dead? (THE MAN *puts
the gun away*). That's right, because now you can have some fun
yourself, telling me what you're going to do. That's what you came
here for, isn't it? Well, you don't need to tell me. I *know* what
you're going to do. I've read the papers and I know. They have fun.
A mob of 'em fall on one man and beat him, don't they? They tear
off his clothes and kick him, don't they? And women and little children stand around watching, don't they? Well, before you go on
this picnic, I'm going to tell you a few things. Not that that's going
to send you home with your pals—the other heroes. No. You've
been outraged. A stranger has come to town and violated your women.
Your pure, innocent, virtuous women. You fellows have got to set
this thing right. You're men, not mice. You're home-makers, and
you beat your children. (*Suddenly.*) Listen, you—I didn't know she
was your wife. I didn't know she was anybody's wife.

THE MAN: You're a liar!

YOUNG MAN: Sometimes—when it'll do somebody some good—
but not this time. Do you want to hear about it? (THE MAN *doesn't*

answer.) All right, I'll tell you. I met her at a lunch counter. She came in and sat next to me. There was plenty of room, but she sat next to me. Somebody had put a nickel in the phonograph and a fellow was singing *New San Antonio Rose.* Well, she got to talking about the song. I thought she was talking to the waiter, but *he* didn't answer her, so after a while *I* answered her. That's how I met her. I didn't think anything of it. We left the place together and started walking. The first thing I knew she said, This is where I live.

THE MAN: You're a dirty liar!

YOUNG MAN: Do you want to hear it? Or not? (THE MAN *does not answer.*) O.K. She asked me to come in. Maybe she had something in mind, maybe she didn't. Didn't make any difference to me, one way or the other. If she was lonely, all right. If not, all right.

THE MAN: You're telling a lot of dirty lies!

YOUNG MAN: I'm telling the truth. Maybe your wife's out there with your pals. Well, call her in. I got nothing against her, or you—or any of you. Call her in, and ask her a few questions. Are you in love with her? (THE MAN *doesn't answer.*) Well, that's too bad.

THE MAN: What do you mean, too bad?

YOUNG MAN: I mean this may not be the first time something like this has happened.

THE MAN (*swiftly*):   Shut up!

YOUNG MAN: Oh, you know it. You've always known it. You're afraid of your pals, that's all. She asked me for money. That's all she wanted. I wouldn't be here now if I had given her the money.

THE MAN (*slowly*):   How much did she ask for?

YOUNG MAN: I didn't ask her how much. I told her I'd made a mistake. She said she would make trouble if I didn't give her money. Well, I don't like bargaining, and I don't like being threatened, either. I told her to get the hell away from me. The next thing I knew she'd run out of the house and was hollering. (*Pause.*) Now, why don't you go out there and tell 'em they took me to another jail—go home and pack up and leave her. You're a pretty good guy, you're just afraid of your pals.

THE MAN *draws his gun again. He is very frightened. He moves a step toward the* YOUNG

MAN, *then fires three times. The* YOUNG MAN
falls to his knees. THE MAN *turns and runs,*
horrified.

YOUNG MAN: Hello—out there! (*He is bent forward.*)

THE GIRL *comes running in, and halts suddenly,*
looking at him.

THE GIRL: There were some people in the street, men and women
and kids—so I came in through the back, through a window. I
couldn't find the gun. I looked all over but I couldn't find it.
What's the matter?

YOUNG MAN: Nothing—nothing. Everything's all right. Listen.
Listen, kid. Get the hell out of here. Go out the same way you
came in and run—run like hell—run all night. Get to another
town and get on a train. Do you hear me.

THE GIRL: What's happened?

YOUNG MAN: Get away—just get away from here. Take any train
that's going—you can get to Frisco later.

THE GIRL (*almost sobbing*):   I don't want to go any place without
you.

YOUNG MAN: I can't go. Something's happened. (*He looks at her.*)
But I'll be with you always—God damn it. Always!

He falls forward. THE GIRL *stands near him,*
then begins to sob softly, walking away. She
stands over to one side, stops sobbing, and
stares out. The excitement of the mob outside
increases. THE MAN, *with two of his pals, comes*
running in. THE GIRL *watches, unseen.*

THE MAN: Here's the son of a bitch!

ANOTHER MAN: O.K. Open the cell, Harry.

The THIRD MAN *goes to the cell door, unlocks it,*
and swings it open.

A WOMAN *comes running in.*

THE WOMAN: Where is he? I want to see him. Is he dead? (*Looking down at him, as the* MEN *pick him up.*) There he is. (*Pause.*) Yeah, that's him.

Her husband looks at her with contempt, then at the dead man.

THE MAN (*trying to laugh*):   All right—let's get it over with.

THIRD MAN: Right you are, George. Give me a hand, Harry.

They lift the body.

THE GIRL (*suddenly, fiercely*):   Put him down!

THE MAN: What's this?

SECOND MAN: What are you doing here? Why aren't you out in the street?

THE GIRL: Put him down and go away.

She turns toward the MEN.

THE WOMAN *grabs her.*

THE WOMAN: Here—where do you think *you're* going?

THE GIRL: Let me go. You've no right to take him away.

THE WOMAN: Well, listen to her, will you? (*She slaps* THE GIRL *and pushes her to the floor.*) Listen to the little slut, will you?

They all go, carrying the YOUNG MAN'S *body.*
THE GIRL *gets up slowly, no longer sobbing. She looks around at everything, then looks straight out, and whispers.*

THE GIRL: Hello—out—there! Hello—out there!

CURTAIN

Suggested Readings

Albright, Hardie. *Stage Direction in Transition.* Encino, California: Dickenson Publishing Company, 1972. An eclectic text bringing together many contemporary ideas of directing practice. Written by an ex-actor, the text emphasizes the work of the actor and the actor–director collaboration.

Brook, Peter. *The Empty Space.* London: MacGibbon and Kee, 1968. One of the most popular and influential books by perhaps the most popular and influential contemporary director. Brook delineates forms of theatre (for example, "deadly," "rough," "holy") under which he identifies what is "good" and "bad" theatre. Influenced by Artaud and Brecht, Brook proposes iconoclastic approaches to theatre that rise from the rubble of destroyed theatre traditions and conventions.

Canfield, Curtis. *The Craft of Play Directing.* New York: Holt, Rinehart, and Winston, 1963. Beginning with emphasis on the importance of analysis, this text moves to the practical application of directing techniques. The appendix has a section devoted to "The Collegiate Theatre."

Clurman, Harold. *The Fervent Years.* New York: Alfred Knopf Publishing, 1945. A retrospective on the Group Theatre by one of its founders. Though not a directing text, it is a valuable resource book on modern American theatre history. It does offer some interesting material on the director's role in the collaborative process of producing a play.

_____. *On Directing.* New York: Macmillan Publishing Company, 1972. A look at Clurman's perspective on directing from his over forty years of experience. The book is addressed not only to directors but also to interested playgoers who may wish to expand their theatre knowledge.

Cohen, Robert and John Harrop. *Creative Play Direction.* Englewood Cliffs, New Jersey: Prentice-Hall, 1974. This text stresses interpretation, composition, and style. Eclectic in approach, the text presents many points of view encouraging prospective directors to select what appeals to them and to "try their wings."

Cole, Toby and Helen Krich Chinoy. *Directors on Directing.* Indianapolis: Bobbs-Merrill Publishing, 1963. A source book of articles and notes by the world's leading directors.

Dean, Alexander and Lawrence Carra. *Fundamentals of Play Directing.* Fourth Edition. New York: Holt, Rinehart and Winston, 1980. The original Dean text (1941), a pioneer in the field of directing texts, has been revised by Carra, but the major principles remain the same.

Dietrich, John E. and Ralph W. Duckwall. *Play Direction.* Second Edition. Englewood Cliffs, New Jersey: Prentice-Hall, 1983. A revision of the popular 1953 edition in which the concept of the "motivational unit" was introduced. A handbook approach makes the material easily accessible to the student.

Gallaway, Marian. *The Director in the Theatre.* New York: Macmillan Company, 1963. Using four classic plays as examples, Gallaway guides the reader through a method of play production based primarily on an intelligent application of Stanislavsky's methods. Emphasizes the practical aspects of play production, with lesser attention to directing theory.

Glenn, Stanley. *A Director Prepares.* Encino, California: Dickenson Publishing Company, 1973. A basic approach to directing for the beginning director. Emphasizes the work of the director prior to rehearsal.

Gorchakov, Nikolai. *Stanislavsky Directs.* Minerva Press, 1968. Using the student-teacher mode employed in *An Actor Prepares*, this book examines Gorchakov's development from a new student to a full director under the tutelage of Stanislavsky.

Grotowski, Jerzy. *Towards a Poor Theatre.* New York: Simon and Schuster, 1968. A series of articles and interviews that illuminate the methods of Grotowski. Important because of Grotowski's influence on contemporary avant-garde theatre.

Hodge, Francis. *Play Directing: Analysis, Communication and Style.* Second Edition. Englewood Cliffs, New Jersey: Prentice-Hall, 1982. A very detailed approach for a two-year course in directing. Based on the ideas of Alexander Dean, the text also applies concepts of Stanislavksy; emphasizes the director as communicator.

Lawson, John Howard. *The Theory and Technique of Playwriting.* New York: Hill and Wang, 1949. A stimulating examination of drama form from Aristotelian and Hegelian perspectives. Although the text is ostensibly for playwrights, it advances provocative ideas for all areas of theatre. Also provides a personal view of theatre history from Lawson's point of view.

Lewis, Robert. *Method or Madness.* New York: Samuel French, 1958. Transcripts of eight lectures in which Lewis attempts to describe the "method," the Actors' Studio version of Stanislavsky's teachings. The definitive book on the American version of the Stanislavsky system.

McGaw, Charles M. *Acting is Believing.* New York: Holt, Rinehart, and Winston, 1975. A popular acting text since its first publication in 1955. It provides a clear and workable approach to using Stanislavsky techniques in actor training.

Morrison, Hugh. *Directing in the Theatre.* London: Pitman Publishing, 1973. A widely used British text, it takes examples from various scripts to teach concepts. Considerable treatment of directing different styles of plays as well as experimental productions.

Ommanney, Katharine Anne and Harry H. Schanker. *The Stage and the School.* Fourth Edition. St. Louis: McGraw-Hill, 1972. This text has been the definitive high school theatre text for over fifty years. It attempts to cover a great deal of material under one cover. Although it has gone through many revisions, it still retains much of the prescriptive approach of the original.

Roose-Evans, James. *Directing a Play.* New York: Theatre Arts Books, 1968. Roose-Evans's thoughts on directing, contained in short essays on each aspect of play production. The section entitled "Reflections" provides interesting commentary on various directing problems and controversies.

Stanislavsky, Constantin. *An Actor Prepares.* Translated by Elizabeth Reynolds Hapgood. New York: Theatre Arts Books, 1936. The basic book of the Stanislavsky method. A warm, readable chronicle of some student actors' struggle to learn their craft from their teacher.

_____. *My Life in Art.* Translated by J. J. Robbins. New York: Theatre Arts Books, 1952. Personal memoirs, including discussions of Stanislavsky's approach to acting and directing.

Staub, August. *Creating Theatre: The Art of Theatrical Directing.* New York: Harper and Row, 1973. Emphasis on getting results in the theatre. Valuable discussion of auditory, kinetic, and visual aspects of theatre.

Wills, J. Robert, Editor. *The Director in a Changing Theatre: Essays on Theory and Practice, with New Plays for Performance.* Palo Alto, California: Mayfield, 1976. A collection of essays, interviews, and articles about contemporary theatre people and practices. A stimulating look at a cross section of contemporary theories of production.

Biographical Notes

Aristotle (384–322 B.C.)   Greek philosopher. Studied under Plato. His *Poetics* deals mainly with an analysis of tragedy, probably written to counteract Plato's condemnation of the form. Sophocles' *Oedipus* served as the principal model for his theories. Since the sixteenth century, the *Poetics* has been one of the most influential critical studies on the nature of tragedy as well as other forms of drama.

Beckett, Samuel (1906–   )   Irish-born dramatist and novelist. Educated in Ireland, Beckett became a resident of France in the 1930s. Influenced by the work of the Irish writer James Joyce, he wrote in French and English. An existential playwright, he writes in what has been called the "absurdist" tradition. His *Waiting for Godot*, first produced in Paris in 1953, deals with the search for meaning in contemporary life. Received the Nobel Prize in 1969. Other major plays: *Endgame, Krapp's Last Tape.*

Burke, Kenneth (1897–   )   American philosopher and critic. A precocious student, Burke entered Columbia University at seventeen, but remained there only one semester, forsaking the classroom for the New York Public Library, where he spent the next seven years educating himself. Brilliant and iconoclastic, Burke wrote criticism for *The Dial* and engaged in other literary "odd jobs" while he wrote books about the nature of form. His range of subjects and the depth of his perceptions have made his work seminal in many areas of contemporary thought, including philosophy, sociology, history, and literature. He has written a novel and has published an anthology of poetry, but he will be best remembered for his works of critical inquiry. Major works: *The Philosophy of Literary Form: Studies in Symbolic Action; A Grammar of Motives; A Rhetoric of Motives; The Rhetoric of Religion: Studies in Logology; Language as Symbolic Action: Essays on Life, Literature, and Method.*

Chekhov, Anton (1860–1904)   Russian dramatist. Chekhov's first literary recognition came as a short story writer. After several of his early plays failed, *The Seagull* won acclaim when directed by Constantin Stanislavsky at the Moscow Art Theatre. Chekhov has been hailed as a social realist who documented the passing of the old order in Russia. His strength, however, is not in depicting social themes but in imbuing characters with a strong sense of individuality—characters who, full of grace, are unable to cope successfully with a world grown graceless. Other major plays: *Uncle Vanya, The Three Sisters, The Cherry Orchard.*

Grotowski, Jerzy (1933–   )   Polish director and acting teacher. Founder and director of the Polish Laboratory Theatre. Influenced by Antonin Artaud, the French actor and writer, Grotowski proposed to strip the theatre to its essential element: acting. He emphasized a physical approach in seeking the "via negativa," which strives to remove everything between the stimulus and the actor's response. The actor moves from physical impulse to contiguous physical impulse without intervening metaphysical steps. In recent years Grotowski has moved away from traditional performance of any kind. Major work: *Towards a Poor Theatre.*

Ibsen, Henrik (1828–1906)   Norwegian dramatist. Exerted a major influence on the development of modern drama. Associated with Norwegian theatres, but spent many years in Italy and Germany. His themes—exploring the inhibiting effect on an individual of the conventional ideas of society—were treated with a frankness new to the theatre. Some critics, preoccupied with thematic social statements, fail to see the intensely human conflicts in the plays. Major plays: *A Doll's House, Ghosts, An Enemy of the People, The Wild Duck, Hedda Gabler, John Gabriel Bjorkmann.*

Inge, William (1913–1973)   American dramatist. In his most successful plays, Inge depicts the inner lives of ordinary people in small-town settings. Structurally sound, his plays are in the realistic tradition of the American theatre. Major plays: *Come Back, Little Sheba; Picnic; Bus Stop; Dark at the Top of the Stairs.*

Ionesco, Eugène (1912–   )   Rumanian-born dramatist. Lives in France and writes in French. First came to the attention of the theatre-going public with *The Chairs* in 1952. Rejecting conventional stagecraft, Ionesco has been labeled an exponent of "anti-theatre." Everything in the theatre, Ionesco says, must be pushed "to paroxysm." Ionesco writes about a world in which surface conventions obscure contrasting inner values. He is deeply concerned about the irony of the human condition in which we are given life only to realize we must die. Other major plays: *The Bald Soprano, The Lesson, Victims of Duty, The Killer, Exit the King, Rhinoceros.*

Klee, Paul (1879–1940)   Swiss painter. Klee (pronounced *Clay*) joined the faculty of the Bauhaus School, Germany, in 1921. There, in association with other artists, Klee experimented with techniques, media, and surfaces. Klee was particularly interested in the dynamics of line, space, and structure, and is considered a precursor of surrealism. Major works: *Creative Credo; Pedagogical Sketch Book; The Thinking Eye: The Notebooks of Paul Klee;* "The Twittering Machine"; "Fish Magic"; "Ad Parnassum."

Miller, Arthur (1915–)   American dramatist. In 1944 Miller's first Broadway play, *The Man Who Had All the Luck*, failed. In 1947 his *All My Sons* received the Drama Critics Circle Award. Both developed a theme of guilt, as do most of his later plays. In 1949 *Death of a Salesman*, his most successful play, won the Drama Critics Circle Award and the Pulitzer Prize. Other major plays: *The Crucible, A View from the Bridge, After the Fall.*

Molière (1622–1673)   French dramatist. At first an actor, then manager and playwright of a troupe that failed in Paris before touring the provinces for twelve years. Eventually the company gained royal patronage and took up permanent quarters in Paris. His tenure there was constantly threatened by the controversial nature of his plays, whose penetrating satire exposed the follies and vices of society. He is regarded as one of the world's greatest comic dramatists. Major plays: *Tartuffe, The Misanthrope, The Miser, The Bourgeois Gentleman, The Imaginary Invalid.*

Pinter, Harold (1930–)   British dramatist and director. Pinter has also written for radio, television, and screen. Influenced by Franz Kafka and Samuel Beckett, Pinter gained recognition as a major playwright with *The Caretaker* in 1960. His plays combine elements of farce and tragedy. Placing absolute emphasis on dramatic action, Pinter often ignores conventional plot elements and provides little or no verifiable exposition. His characters struggle to survive in a world they cannot understand. Pinter's specific idiomatic dialogue provides sharp character delineation. Other major plays: *The Room, The Dumb Waiter, The Birthday Party, The Homecoming, Old Times, No Man's Land.*

Saroyan, William (1908–1981)   American dramatist, short story writer, novelist. Recognition as a writer came in 1934 when he won an O. Henry award for his short story, "The Daring Young Man on the Flying Trapeze." In 1939 *The Time of Your Life* won a Pulitzer Prize, but Saroyan rejected it. Most of his plays exhibit a youthful romanticism and vitality set against the evils of an oppressive society.

Often they verge on sentimentality. Other major plays: *The Man with His Heart in the Highlands; Hello, Out There; The Cave Dwellers; My Name is Aram.*

Shakespeare, William (1564–1616)   English dramatist. Recognized as the world's greatest playwright, Shakespeare began his career in London about 1586. Although details of his life are sketchy, we do know that in the 1590s he was not only an actor, but a playwright turning out plays at a steady rate. His canon consists of about thirty-seven plays, with outstanding examples in the genres of comedy, history, and tragedy. Major plays: *A Midsummer Night's Dream, Romeo and Juliet, Henry IV, Julius Caesar, Hamlet, All's Well That Ends Well, Othello, King Lear, Macbeth, Antony and Cleopatra.*

Shaw, George Bernard (1856–1950)   Anglo-Irish dramatist. A novelist and journalist-critic before becoming a dramatist, Shaw became an advocate of the "new" drama. His plays were vehicles for his iconoclastic social and political views. After facing early opposition, Shaw was established as a leading modern dramatist. Major plays: *Mrs. Warren's Profession, Arms and the Man, Caesar and Cleopatra, Man and Superman, Major Barbara, Pygmalion, Saint Joan.*

Sophocles (496?–406 B.C.)   Greek dramatist. Along with Aeschylus and Euripides, he is regarded as one of the world's great tragedians and a major figure in the development of Greek tragedy. He excelled in depicting profoundly human characters. Of his 120 or so plays, only seven survive. Major plays: *Antigone, Oedipus the King, Oedipus at Colonus.*

Stanislavsky, Constantin (1863–1938)   Russian actor and director. One of the founders in 1888 of the Society of Literature and Art. Stanislavsky first gained public recognition as an actor, then director, in the Society. In 1898 he helped found the Moscow Art Theatre. He rejected extravagant and artificial styles of acting and indeed in all aspects of production. Stanislavsky's internal psychological approach had a significant effect on twentieth century acting theory. Major works: *My Life in Art, An Actor Prepares, Building a Character, Creating a Role.*

Synge, John Millington (1871–1909)   Irish dramatist. Summers on the Aran Islands, off the west coast of Ireland, provided Synge with inspiration and themes. The dialogue of his plays reveals the richly poetic language of the Irish people. As a member of the Irish National Theatre Society, Synge joined with others in establishing the Abbey Theatre. Major plays: *Riders to the Sea, The Playboy of the Western World.*

Wilder, Thornton (1897–1975)   American novelist and dramatist. Wilder's novel, *The Bridge of San Luis Rey,* won the Pulitzer Prize in 1927. In 1938 he won his second Pulitzer Prize, this one for the play *Our Town.* His third Pulitzer Prize came in 1942 for *The Skin of Our Teeth.* While realistically depicting the shortcomings of human nature, Wilder nonetheless urges a fuller awareness of the broadest dimensions of human experience. His themes reaffirm the value of the human spirit. His experimental staging techniques make the audience aware that they are in a theatre while experiencing the play. Other major play: *The Matchmaker* (the basis for the musical, *Hello, Dolly!*).

Williams, Tennessee (1914–1983)   American dramatist. Williams's unhappy early life undoubtedly influenced the tone and themes of his plays. His apprentice work deals with broad social themes, but in his mature plays he focuses sharply on lonely, sensitive individuals who find it difficult to function in the harsh world. *The Glass Menagerie* was his first Broadway success. He won Pulitzer Prizes for *A Streetcar Named Desire* and *Cat on a Hot Tin Roof.* Other major plays: *Summer and Smoke, The Rose Tattoo, The Night of the Iguana.*

Glossary

Action: Purposeful activity. Dramatic action is the play's struggle to resolve its root conflict.

Action Rehearsal: Designed to get actors to respond to the conflict each moment they are onstage. It focuses on interaction rather than on psychological introspection.

Actor–Human Being: An actor's human self reacting honestly to each moment. Contrasts with the actor–puppet.

Actor-Puppet: An actor's overlay of stock responses and cliché stage postures that mask the genuine human response. Contrasts with the actor–human being.

Antagonist: Character who opposes the protagonist, or the character who responds to the protagonist's initiative.

Arena Staging: Occurs in the center area of a square or circle with the audience surrounding the acting area.

Beat: A character's personal goal in each moment of a scene. A beat carries from the initial impulse until the want is accomplished, thwarted, or postponed by the interaction with others. A clash of opposing beats creates a cycle of action, which is a minor conflict–resolution process within the root conflict of the play.

Blocking: The process of creating the patterns of movement used by the actors to support the action of the play. These patterns are often recorded in the prompt book for use in rehearsal.

Catastrophe: The event that immediately precipitates the climax. It may occur simultaneously with the crisis (as in many melodramas), or it may be separated from the crisis by much of the play (as in most tragedies). This event tells us that the climax, which has been promised by the crisis, will come now.

Character: An individual locus (or center) of motives.

Characteristics: Surface physical traits that help to set one character apart from another.

Climax: The moment of resolution of the root conflict, the culminating moment of the root action. The climax must be narrowed to a single moment, after which there is no more conflict in the play.

Conflict: The essence of dramatic action. The clash of opposing forces is the power source of the play, which gives rise to everything else in the play.

Continuity Rehearsal: The cycles of action of the play rehearsed in sequence from beginning to end so that actors can experience the continuity of the action.

Counter: A movement by a character when another character passes downstage of him. The upstage character moves a few steps in the opposite direction.

Cover: When one actor or object onstage is between the audience and another actor or object so that the audience's view is obstructed. (Sometimes called a "block.")

Crisis: The event that makes the resolution of the conflict inevitable. The crisis turns the two forces toward each other in a way that demands a culminating confrontation that will end the conflict.

Cycles of Action: Minor conflicts that contribute to the root action and lead to the resolution of the root conflict. Each cycle of action is structured like a play in miniature with an inciting incident and a climax. Sometimes a cycle is interrupted or truncated without an immediate resolution.

Denouement: Occurrences after the climax that may illuminate the climax but that contain no conflict. Many plays do not have a denouement.

Depth Space: The space that downstage actors or objects command in the upstage planes. An actor or object in another's depth space is blocked from some part of the audience.

Dominance: The sense of strength or power a character or actor receives from his position on stage in relation to other characters or actors.

Dramatic Question: The question the play exists to answer. Formulating the question helps the analysis process because it provides another way to discover the root action.

Dramaturge: A person providing consultation and advice about literary or historical matters pertaining to a production. A dramaturge is often an historian or literary scholar.

Dress Rehearsal: The actors wear their performance costumes under performance conditions. Adjustments are made for fit, and the actors practice using the costume properly.

Ensemble Playing: Each actor is fully open to the point of contact between himself and all the other actors or characters in the production. Nothing is fully anticipated because the performer responds to the immediate possibilities of the moment, which are constantly changing.

Floor Plan: A scale plan indicating all the walls and objects that occupy the floor space on stage. A director must be able to read floor plans so he can design the movement patterns accurately.

Flow Theory: Refers to the dynamics of time—the fourth dimension—as it affects our perception of events on stage. All elements of a production are part of the continuous flow of the action.

Focus: The point of attention of an audience.

Force Field: The psychic dimensions of the relationships between characters while on stage.

French Scene: A method of defining scenes based on the entrance and/or exit of a character.

Hostile Counter: Occurs when the countering character cuts the downstage character's trailing line.

Improvisation: A spontaneous performance of an action; the dialogue and movements are not predetermined.

Inciting Incident: The event that starts the conflicting forces moving, thereby beginning the root action. It is not necessarily the first event in the play, although it should be near the opening curtain. In the rarest of instances, it may occur before the opening curtain.

Line: "Force with directionality." It has a psychic dimension onstage as a line that precedes or trails a moving character.

Motion: Activity without purpose. It is distinguished from action, which is activity with purpose.

Motive: The basic want, or the driving force, of a character. It corresponds to "spine," a term used by some Stanislavsky disciples. It is distinguished from purpose, which is a minor desire that fuels a character's beats.

Pace: Maintaining the flow of action during a production. Poor pacing allows breaks in the flow or superimposes a flow that is not related to the demands of the action.

Pattern Rehearsal: An early rehearsal devoted to learning the dialogue and movement patterns.

Pentad: Consists of five terms (act, scene, agent, agency, purpose), which, when used as ratios in analysis, can help clarify a particular point in the action. *Act* stands for what a character actually does and says. *Scene* is the context in which a character acts. *Agent* refers to all the personal characteristics of a character. *Agency* is anything the character uses to accomplish his purpose. *Purpose* applies to the conscious goals of a character: what he professes to want or believes he wants.

Pentadic Ratios: Pentadic terms combine into ten ratios (act–scene, act–agent, and so on), which measure the interaction of the terms as they modify one another.

Phenomenology: An approach to critical analysis, holding that "everything necessary for understanding or describing a phenomenon is contained within it."

Plane: "The tension between two lines." It provides a way of understanding the physical and psychic dimensions of stage space by considering the power of planes in depth, height, and width.

Plot: The series of events that constitute the play. The root action lies beneath the plot and determines its nature and function.

Point: (1) A "cosmic moment," a potential source of power that is made kinetic by line. It is a moment of promise about to explode into some kind of directionality. (2) To point is to separate a moment from all that surrounds it so that it is given emphasis.

Point of Clash: The point at which the desires of one character encounter those of another character or motive source. The actor's task is to find the specific point of clash in each moment of his performance.

Preblocking: The blocking done and recorded in the prompt book before rehearsals begin.

Premotive: The profound awareness of the absence of what is desired. The actor should search in each point of clash for the premotive. The premotive begins with the question "What do I want to get from or to do to this person at this moment?" and proceeds beyond the rational to the deep feeling of absence that powers great acting.

Projected Line: The psychic line an actor projects before him when he moves or indicates the intention to move.

Prompt Book: The director's version of the script. Also called prompt script or director's book, it contains blocking plans; notes about character, sound, and lights; and other plans for the production.

Proscenium Staging: Staging on a framed stage with the audience located on one side of the playing space.

Protagonist: Character who initiates the action and is usually the prime mover of the action. The play is usually about the protagonist.

Purposes: The several ancillary "wants" of a character. The purposes together add up to the character's motive. A character may determine his purposes, but his motive controls him. A character has only one motive that accounts for everything he does in a play.

Rehearsal Performance: Devoted to testing rehearsal discoveries under performance conditions before an audience just prior to opening night.

Resolution: The climax of the play, where the root conflict and, therefore, the action end.

Rhythm: Regular or irregular recurrence of something in the flow of a scene or performance.

Root Action: The process that resolves the root conflict. A root action statement identifies the protagonist, the protagonist's motive, the protagonist's act, the antagonist, the antagonist's motive, the antagonist's act, and the resolution. A root action statement distills a play into a sentence (or two) that isolates and clarifies its power source.

Root Conflict: The basic conflict that creates the main action. It identifies the principal competing forces, which almost always center in characters.

Space Between: The place where the desires of a character clash with other characters or objects. It is here, at the point of contact, where the actor discovers his character at each specific moment of his life onstage.

Spine: (1) The term used by disciples of Stanislavsky to identify the basic motive that accounts for everything a character does. (2) The through-line of action in a scene or play.

Style: A characteristic way of doing. Whenever there are enough instances of an occurrence so that one can discern a characteristic way of doing, it is possible to identify a style.

Super-objective: Stanislavsky's term for the through-line or main line of action. It corresponds to root action.

Technical Rehearsal: Rehearsal late in the rehearsal period allowing the designer or the technicians to incorporate the scenic and technical elements into the production.

Tempo: The rate of speed at which things happen on stage.

Theme: The central argument or social statement of the play. Theme concerns the "rhetoric," while action concerns the "poetic" of a play.

Totem: The name applied to the idea that actors siphon off creative energy into a specific part of the body, which becomes tense and somewhat disfunctional as a result. If the totem is released, the energies become available to the actor in his performance and the body part becomes functional again.

Trailing Line: The psychic line a character trails as he passes through space. It indicates space still "possessed" by the character.

Index

Act, as defined in Pentadic analysis, 121, 229
Acting Is Believing (McGaw), 216
Action, 2–16
  character and, 14–15, 116–120
  climax and, 12
  conflict as, 10–11
  cycles of, 34–35, 39, 177, 227
  defined, 225
  motion vs., 4
  motive and, 10–11
  in new drama, 15–16
  plot vs., 13–14
  root, 25–29, 45–47, 231
  structure and, 11–12
  time and, 12–13
  in the universe, 2–3
Action-centered character, 14–15, 120–125
Action rehearsals, 126–130, 182, 225
Action schedule, 39–40, 177, 178
Actor Prepares, An (Stanislavsky), 216
Actor–human being, 120, 171, 225

Actor-puppet, 120, 171, 225
Actors, 108–141
  in action rehearsals, 126–130
  blocking and, 102–104
  casting of, 169–175
  director's relationship with, 108–110, 119–120, 132–134, 137–138, 159–160
  experimentation by, 137
  improvisation by, 130–132
  intuition of, 137
  line and, 78–80, 81, 91
  in performance, 187–188
  performance evaluation of, 188–189
  plane and, 80–85
  preblocking and, 66–68, 139–141
  production planning and, 65–68
  psychic center of, 91
  self-surrender of, 118
  space between and, 117–120
  totems, 171–172
Aeschylus, 146
Aesthetics. *See* Visual aesthetics
After the Fall (Miller), 148

233

Agency, as defined in Pentadic analysis, 122, 229
Agent, as defined in Pentadic analysis, 121–122, 229
Albee, Edward, 150
Albright, Hardie, 213
Analysis, 19–63, 146–148
  case for, 21–24
  cycles of action, 34–35
  example of, 39–56, 57
  form for, 63
  group, 62
  Pentadic, 58–61, 120–125
  point of clash, 35–36
  structural elements, 24–34
  word-bound, 57
  See also Character analysis
Antagonist, 25, 225
Arena, 84
Arena staging, 99–102, 225
Aristotle, 2, 5, 110, 219
Arsenic and Old Lace (Kesselring), 86
Assistant director, 158–160, 185
Audience, 135, 136–137, 187
Auditions, 169–173
  augmenting, 172–173
  conducting of, 170–172
  direction during, 171
  preparing for, 169–170
  releasing totems during, 171–172

Balance, and flow, 88, 89
Beat, 34–35, 226
Beckett, Samuel, 6, 16, 219
  Waiting for Godot, 2, 7
Birth, and character, 112–113, 114
Block, 226
Blocking, 92–104
  actor and, 102–104
  arena staging and, 99–102
  conflict and, 96–99
  defined, 226
  floor plan for, 92–96
  planning and, 66–68 (see also Preblocking)
  in prompt book, 157, 161, 162, 166
  in rehearsals, 181–182
  set design and, 153

  See also Movement; Visual aesthetics
Blocking diagram, 161, 166
Brook, Peter, 213
Browne, E. Martin, 151
Brunetière, Ferdinand, 5
Burke, Kenneth, 4, 11, 71, 219–220
  Pentadic analysis, 58–61, 120–125
Bus Stop (Inge)
  blocking diagram for, 161, 166
  floor plan for, 93–96
  movement in, 90

Cain (Byron), 176
Callback session, 173
Canfield, Curtis, 213–214
Caretaker, The (Pinter), 16
Carra, Lawrence, 214
Cast. See Actors
Casting, 169–175
  actors in performance, 173
  auditions, 169–173
  callback sessions, 173
  dangers in, 173–175
  interviews, 169–173
Catastrophe, 32–33, 52, 226
Character, 108–141
  action and, 116–120
  action-centered, 14–15, 120–125
  defined, 14, 111–116, 226
  motive and, 36–39, 41
  Pentadic analysis of, 120–125
  power source of, 116, 117–120
Character analysis, 36–39, 52–56
Character briefs, 126
Character-centered productions, 111
Character description handouts, 169–170
Character study
  in action rehearsals, 126–130
  director's role in, 125–126
  improvisation in, 130–132
Characteristics, 116, 226
Chekhov, Anton, 220
  Cherry Orchard, The, 98–99
  Seagull, The, 128–129, 176
Cherry Orchard, The (Chekhov), 98–99
Chinoy, Helen Krich, 214

Climax, 12, 29–30, 47–49, 226
Clurman, Harold, 214
Cobb, Lee J., 174
Cocktail Party, The (Eliot), 152
Cohen, Robert, 214
Cole, Toby, 214
Comedy, conflict in, 7
Confidential Clerk, The (Eliot), 152
Conflict, 5–10
    blocking and, 96–99
    character and, 111
    defined, 226
    effects of, 10
    necessity of, 5–7
    point of clash in, 6, 11
    root, 24–25, 40–45, 231
    source of, 8–10
    visual aesthetics and, 69–71,
        74–75
Construction drawings, 155–156
Contemporary drama, action in,
    15–16
Continuity rehearsals, 182–183, 226
Contrast, 74–75, 76
Costume design, 156
Costume parade, 156, 185–186
Counter, 78–80, 81, 226
Counterflow, 86
Cover, 94–95, 226–227
Craft of Play Directing, The (Can-
    field), 213–214
*Creating Theatre: The Art of Theat-
    rical Directing* (Staub), 216–217
Creative atmosphere, 133–134
Creative Play Direction (Cohen and
    Harrop), 214
Crisis, 31–32, 51–52, 227
Criticism, 132, 133–134
    literary, 148
    reviews, 188
Crucible, The (Miller), 131
Cue sheet, 156, 184
Cycles of action, 34–35, 40, 177, 227

Dean, Alexander, 69, 214
Death
    artist and, 114, 115, 146
    character and, 112–113, 115
Death of a Salesman (Miller)

action schedule for, 178
conflict in, 75
Lee J. Cobb in, 174
rehearsal schedule for, 179
root conflict in, 40–41
sample prompt book for, 162–165
Denouement, 29, 227
Depth space, 94–95, 227
Design, 153–157
    costumes, 156
    lighting, 156
    planning and, 65–68
    set, 153–157
Dialogue, 139–140
Dietrich, John E., 214
Directing a Play (Roose-Evans), 216
Directing in the Theatre (Morrison),
    216
Directing workshop, 191
Director
    auditions and, 170–172
    as collaborator with playwright,
        151–153
    criticism by, 132, 133–134
    prompt book of, 92, 139, 157–166
    relationship with actors, 108–110,
        119–120, 132–134, 137–138,
        140, 159–160
    "result," 139
    role in character study, 125–126
    script analysis by, 146–148 (*see
        also* Analysis)
    script readings by, 145–146
    self-evaluation by, 189
    set design and, 154–155
    style of, 148–149
    See also Assistant director
Director in a Changing Theatre
    (Wills), 217
Director in the Theatre, The (Gal-
    laway), 215
Director Prepares, A (Glenn), 215
Directors on Directing (Cole and
    Chinoy), 167, 214
Dominance, 70, 72–73, 78, 227
Drama
    conflict in, 7
    contemporary, 15–16
Dramatic question, 34, 227

Dramatism, 58
Dramaturge, 148, 227
Dress rehearsals, 156, 180, 185–186, 227
Duckwall, Ralph W., 214

Eisenstein, Sergei, 89–90
Eliot, T. S., 151–152
Empty Space, The (Brook), 213
Ensemble playing, 138, 227–228
Entropy, 3
Euripides, 146
Everett, Edward, 20
Evocation exercises, 142
Exercises
    evocation, 142
    mirror, 141–142
Exposition, 30, 150

"Facing off," 83
Fallacy of intent, 21
Family Reunion, The (Eliot), 152
Fergusson, Francis, 2
Fervent Years, The (Clurman), 214
"First Law of the Theatre, The" (Brunetière), 5
Floor plan, 92–96
    for arena staging, 100, 101
    defined, 228
    in prompt book, 161, 162, 164, 166
    set design and, 154, 155
Flow theory, 85–86
    counterflow and, 86
    defined, 228
    imbalance and, 87–88, 89
    movement and, 88–92
Focus, 70, 73, 80, 81, 228
Force field, 71, 78, 228
French scenes, 34, 228
Freytag, Gustav, 12
Frontal plane, 82–83
Fry, Christopher, 151
Functional exposition, 30
Fundamentals of Play Directing (Dean and Carra), 214

Gallaway, Marian, 215
Gettysburg Address (Lincoln), 20

Glass Menagerie, The (Williams), 37
Glenn, Stanley, 215
Gogol, Nikolai, 7
Gorchakov, Nikolai, 215
Grotowski, Jerzy, 147, 215, 220
Group analysis, 63

Hamlet
    action in 2, 40
    conflict in, 8–9, 43
    flow in, 90–91
    Pentadic ratios in, 59–61
    script of, 150
Harrop, John, 214
Hedda Gabler (Ibsen), 98
Hello Out There (Saroyan)
    action schedule for, 39–40
    analysis of, 23–24, 39–57
    catastrophe in, 52
    character in, 53–56
    climax in, 48–49
    crisis in, 51–52
    cycles of action in, 40
    inciting incident in, 50–51
    Pentadic ratios in, 59, 121, 123–124
    play analysis form for, 57
    root action in, 46–47
    root conflict in, 41–45
    text of, 195–211
Hesse, Hermann, 85
Hodge, Francis, 215
Hostile counter, 78–80, 228
Huxley, Aldous, 13

Ibsen, Henrik, 21–22, 221
    Hedda Gabler, 98
    John Gabriel Bjorkmann, 22
    When We Dead Awaken, 103–104
Idea of a Theatre, The (Fergusson), 2
Imbalance, and flow, 87–88, 89
Improvisation, 130–132, 228
Inciting incident, 30–31, 49–51, 228
Inge, William, 221
    Bus Stop, 90, 93–96, 161, 166
Inspector General, The (Gogol), 7
Intermissions, 151
Interviews, 172–173
Ionesco, Eugène, 16, 221

J. B. (Macleish), 152
John Gabriel Bjorkmann (Ibsen), 22
Jones, Margo, 85

Kazan, Elia, 126, 152, 174
Keats, John, 146
Kesselring, Joseph, 86
Klee, Paul, 77, 78, 80, 221
Lady of Larkspur Lotion, The
    (Williams), 49
Lawson, John Howard, 215
Lewis, Robert, 215–216
Lighting design, 156
Lighting rehearsals, 184–185
Lincoln, Abraham, 20
Line, 78–80, 91, 228
Literary criticism, 148
Littlewood, Joan, 167

Macbeth, 118–119
McGaw, Charles M., 216
MacLeish, Archibald, 152
Makeup charts, 156
Marshall, Norman, 151
Maugham, Somerset, 66
Method or Madness (Lewis),
    215–216
Miller, Arthur, 222
    After the Fall, 148
    Crucible, 131
    Death of a Salesman, 40–41, 75,
      162–165, 174
Mirror exercise, 141–142
Mode, 103
Models, in set design, 155
Molière, 144, 151, 222
    Tartuffe, 28–29, 149
Morrison, Hugh, 216
Mortimer, John, 77
Motion
    vs. action, 4
    defined, 228
Motivational units. *See* Cycles of
    action
Motive
    action and, 10–11
    character analysis and, 36–39, 41,
      53–56, 111
    defined, 229

    in improvisation, 131
    Pentadic analysis and, 123–125
    purpose vs., 38–39
    void and, 113–116
    See also Character; Premotive
Movement, and flow, 88–92
    See also Blocking; Visual aesthetics
Murder in the Cathedral (Eliot), 151
My Life in Art (Stanislavsky), 216

Nicholas Nickleby, 151

Oedipus Rex
    catastrophe in, 33
    climax of, 29–30
    crisis in, 31–32
    dramatic question in, 34
    inciting incident in, 31
    motive in, 38
    root action in, 26–28
    root conflict in, 25
    source of conflict in, 10
Ommanney, Katherine Anne, 216
On Directing, 214
Othello, 59
Our Town (Wilder), 9

Pace, 182–183, 229
Painter's elevations, 156
Pattern rehearsals, 140, 141,
    181–182, 229
Pentad, 58, 229
Pentadic analysis
    of character, 120–125
    of play, 58–61
Performance, 187–188
    as audition, 173
    evaluation of, 188–189
Phenomenology, 147, 229
Philosophy of Literary Form, The
    (Burke), 11
Pinter, Harold, 6, 222
    Caretaker, The, 16
Plane, 80–85, 229
Play. *See* Analysis; Scripts
Play analysis form, 57, 63
Play Directing: Analysis, Com-
    munication and Style (Hodge),
    215

Play Direction (Dietrich and
   Duckwall), 214
"Playing on the corners," 83–84, 99,
   102
Playwrights
   collaboration with director,
      151–153
   script revisions and, 150
Plot
   action vs., 13–14
   defined, 13, 229
Poetic, 20
Poetics (Aristotle), 2, 110
Point, 77–78, 229–230
Point of clash, 6, 11, 15, 35–36, 117,
   230
Preblocking, 66–68, 139–141,
   167–168, 230
Premotive
   character and, 114–115
   defined, 114, 230
   See also Motive
Previews, 135
Primary structural elements, 24–30
   climax, 29–30, 47–49, 226
   root action, 25–29, 45–47, 231
   root conflict, 24–25, 40–45, 231
Production design
   arena, 99–102
   director and, 65–68
   planning and, 65–68
   See also Set design; Visual aesthetics
Profile, 82
Projected line, 78, 79, 230
Prompt book, 157–166
   assistant director and, 158–160
   blocking in, 139, 157, 161, 162,
      166
   defined, 92, 230
   example of, 162–165
   format of, 160–166
   stage manager and, 158–160
Properties, 156
Proscenium, 84
Proscenium staging, 99, 230
   See also Visual aesthetics
Protagonist, 25, 230
Purpose
   analysis of, 55

defined, 38, 230
motive vs., 38–39
in Pentadic character analysis, 122,
   229

Readings
   actors', 173–174
   director's, 145–146
Rehearsal performances, 156–157,
   186–187, 230
Rehearsal schedule, 135, 177–181
Rehearsals, 125–141, 175–187
   action, 126–130, 182, 225
   character study in, 125–132
   continuity, 182–183, 226
   dress, 156, 180, 185–186, 227
   improvisation in, 130–132
   number of, 176–177
   pattern, 140, 141, 181–182, 229
   production planning and, 65–68
   purpose of, 176
   role of assistant director in,
      158–159
   technical, 176, 183–185, 231
   types of, 181–187
Renderings, 155
Resolution, 12, 231
Reviews, 188
Rhetoric, 20–21
Rhythm, 183, 231
Riders to the Sea (Synge), 23, 57
Romeo and Juliet, 97–98
Roose-Evans, James, 216
Root action, 25–29, 45–47, 231
Root action statement, 26, 27, 28, 47
Root conflict, 24–25, 40–45, 231
Royal Hunt of the Sun, The (Shaffer),
   122

Saroyan, William, 23–24, 222–223
   See also Hello Out There
Scene, as defined in Pentadic analysis,
   121, 229
Schanker, Harry H., 216
Scripts, 144–153
   analysis of, 146–148
   cutting of, 149–151
   length of, 150–151
   new, 151–153

Scripts (*continued*)
  readings of, 145–146
  revision of, 149–151
Seagull, The (Chekhov), 128–129,
  176
Secondary structural elements, 30–33
  catastrophe, 32–33, 52, 226
  crisis, 31–32, 51–52, 227
  inciting incident, 30–31, 49–51,
    228
Set design, 153–157
  director and, 154–155
  floor plan and, 92–96, 154, 155
  steps in, 155–157
Shaffer, Peter, 122
Shakespeare, William, 144, 151, 223
  Hamlet, 2, 8–9, 40, 43, 59–61,
    90–91, 150
  Macbeth, 118–119
  Othello, 59
  Romeo and Juliet, 97–98
Shaw, George Bernard, 21, 223
Shepard, Sam, 6, 16
Siddhartha (Hesse), 85
Sketches, preliminary, 155
Soap operas, 87–88
Sophocles, 146
Sound effects, 156
Space between, 15, 38, 117–120, 231
Spatial relationships. *See* Visual
  aesthetics
Spine, 15, 38, 231
  See also Motive
Stage and the School, The (Omman-
  ney and Schanker), 216
Stage Direction in Transition (Al-
  bright), 213
Stage manager, 158–160
Staging. *See* Floor plan; Production
  design; Visual aesthetics
Stanislavsky, Constantin, 130,
  223–224
  acting theories of, 15, 111, 115,
    116, 130
  books by, 216, 224
  rehearsals, 176
  on role of directors, 138
  on "super-objectives," 11
  visual aesthetics and, 69

Stanislavsky Directs (Gorchakov),
  215
Static exposition, 30
Static grouping, 70
Staub, August, 216–217
Streetcar Named Desire, A (Williams), 49–50, 91, 126
Structural elements, 24–34
  catastrophe, 32–33, 52
  climax, 29–30, 47–49
  crisis, 31–32, 51–52
  inciting incident, 30–31, 49–51
  interdependence of, 33–34
  primary, 24–30
  root action, 25–29, 45–47, 231
  root conflict, 24–25, 40–45, 231
  secondary, 30–33
Structure, and action, 3, 11–12
Style, 148–149, 231
"Super-objective," of action, 15, 231
Synge, John Millington, 224
  Riders to the Sea, 23, 57

Tartuffe (Molière), 28–29, 149
Technical rehearsals, 176, 183–185,
  231
Tempo, 182, 231
Theatre in the Round (Jones), 85
Theme, 147, 232
*Theory and Technique of Playwriting,
  The* (Lawson), 215
Time, 3, 12–13, 69
  flow theory and, 85–92
Totems, 171–172, 232
Towards a Poor Theatre (Grotowski),
  215
Tragedy, conflict in, 7
Trailing line, 78, 79, 80, 91, 232
Tryouts. *See* Auditions
Tsar Alexandre, 89–90

Unsatisfactory Supper, The (Williams), 57

Vacuums, 86
Visual aesthetics, 68–85
  basic dimensions of, 69–74
  conflict and, 69–71, 74–75
  contrast, 74–75, 76

Visual aesthetics (*continued*)
  depth space, 94–95
  dominance, 70, 72–73
  focus, 70, 73, 80
  line, 78–80
  plane, 80–85
  point, 77–78
  See also Blocking
Void, and character, 112–116
Voyage Round My Father, A (Mortimer), 77

Waiting for Godot (Beckett), 2, 7

When We Dead Awaken (Ibsen),
  103–104
Wilbur, Richard, 144
Wilder, Thornton, 9, 224
Williams, Tennessee, 224
  Glass Menagerie, The, 37
  Lady of Larkspur Lotion, The,
  49–50
  Streetcar Named Desire, A, 49, 91,
  126
  Unsatisfactory Supper, The, 57
Wills, J. Robert, 216